T0332004

Political Settlements and Development

Political Settlements and Development

Theory, Evidence, Implications

TIM KELSALL
NICOLAI SCHULZ
WILLIAM D. FERGUSON
MATTHIAS VOM HAU
SAM HICKEY
BRIAN LEVY

OXFORD
UNIVERSITY PRESS

OXFORD
UNIVERSITY PRESS

Great Clarendon Street, Oxford, OX2 6DP,
United Kingdom

Oxford University Press is a department of the University of Oxford.
It furthers the University's objective of excellence in research, scholarship,
and education by publishing worldwide. Oxford is a registered trade mark of
Oxford University Press in the UK and in certain other countries

Published in the United States of America by Oxford University Press
198 Madison Avenue, New York, NY 10016, United States of America

British Library Cataloguing in Publication Data
Data available

Library of Congress Control Number: 2021952589

ISBN 978–0–19–284893–2

DOI: 10.1093/oso/9780192848932.001.0001

Printed and bound by
CPI Group (UK) Ltd, Croydon, CR0 4YY
Cover image: Tim Kelsall

Acknowledgements

This book is a collective effort of the Effective States and Inclusive Development Research Centre (ESID) at the University of Manchester, 2011–2017 (Phase 1) and 2017–2020 (Phase 2). Funded by the UK Foreign, Commonwealth and Development Office (FCDO), ESID's research covered twenty-six countries, and worked with research partners in Bangladesh, Ghana, India, Malawi, Rwanda, South Africa, Uganda, and the United States. Led from the Global Development Institute (GDI), Europe's largest global poverty and inequality institute, ESID worked to deepen the understanding of governance in the developing world in ways that impact on policy and practice so that people's lives and livelihoods are improved.

The idea for the book began in the run up to ESID's second phase, when, having grappled with some of the ambiguities in ESID's Phase 1 material, Tim Kelsall began arguing with colleagues for the importance of providing clearer measurement criteria for political settlements analysis—a point Nicolai Schulz, not yet associated with ESID, had also made in an unpublished conference paper with Jörn Grävingholt around the same time. Kelsall and Schulz's belief that a rethink of the conceptual basis of political settlements analysis was needed was also inspired by David Booth, who, in an earlier paper, had argued that Khanian variants of political settlements analysis were insufficiently tied to the idea of conflict-ending agreements, even though the nature of the agreement impacted on the type of elite commitment to development that subsequently emerged. Other members of the ESID consortium, including research directors Kunal Sen and Sam Hickey, and executive director David Hulme, were sympathetic, and early ideas for a new approach to conceptualizing and measuring political settlements were discussed at an ESID Workshop at Dunford House, Sussex, in November 2015. David Booth, Heather Marquette, Hazel Gray, and Nic van de Walle were among the participants who attended that workshop and provided useful comments. The idea was revisited at a workshop in Manchester, in November 2016.

Tim Kelsall subsequently wrote a long conceptual paper on political settlements analysis, discussed at a workshop in London in May 2017, with Nicolai Schulz engaged to provide an exhaustive review of existing databases and ascertain whether any of them could assist us. Several members of the ESID collective, including David Booth and Kunal Sen, provided written comments prior to the workshop, while various ESID colleagues, including Sam Hickey, Tom Lavers, Kunal Sen, and

Sohela Nazneen discussed the implications of the new paper for their own work within the canon. Steve Kosack also discussed approaches to coding large surveys.

Later that year, the paper's hypotheses and relationship to the wider comparative politics literature were deepened in a paper with Matthias vom Hau, discussed at a workshop in Manchester in the autumn of 2017. Maya Tudor, Amy Poteete, and Bill Ferguson provided extensive comments. We also benefited from a presentation by Valeriya Mechkova of V-Dem. The initiative thus developed into ESID's Defining and Measuring Political Settlements workstream, led by Tim Kelsall and Nicolai Schulz, who had innumerable enjoyable and occasionally exhausting conversations around how to operationalize the approach. We continued to develop our ideas and create a plan for a book, further discussed at a workshop in Cape Town where, in addition to the authorial team, Musa Nxele and Alecia Ndlovu provided helpful contributions. The theory was also given an early workout in a presentation at the University of Cape Town's Institute for Democracy, Citizenship and Public Policy in Africa, chaired by Jeremy Seekings, as well as at two UK Development Studies Association conferences in 2019 and 2020, at which we received probing comments from Mushtaq Khan, among others, and at ESID's own flagship conference in 2019. We thank all the aforementioned people who have helped us on our journey.

Other friends helped Kelsall and Schulz with survey design and data collection. Tom Lavers, Pritish Behuria, Matt Tyce, David Jackman, and Ben Page, as well as the joint authors of this book, helped pilot and refine the survey. When it came to running the survey, our research assistants, Whitney Banyai-Becker and Anthony Bladen provided invaluable support in helping us correspond with coders and check the results. We are extremely grateful to them, and to our 129 expert country coders, who filled in a long and demanding survey, and tolerated our sometimes-numerous queries about their codings. We are also grateful to Claire Cummings, who collected additional data on Guinea, and contributed to an early draft of the Guinea study in Chapter 6. Julie Rafferty helped handle the myriad financial transactions, while Julia Brunt, assisted by Kat Bethell, provided excellent, ongoing support with contracts, managing research assistants and organizing conferences and workshops. Massive thanks again to Kat Bethell and Lisa Lucas for help with editing the final stages of the manuscript.

A draft of the manuscript was completed in the summer of 2020—we thank Adam Swallow at Oxford University Press (OUP) and three anonymous referees for comments—and the final version in early 2021. As we have stated, the book is a collective effort, the product of the ideas and contributions of numerous people associated with the ESID project. But when it comes to the actual writing of the manuscript, it may be useful to break things down. As such, Tim Kelsall was the lead author on Chapters 1 and 2, with a significant contribution from Matthias vom Hau; Bill Ferguson was the lead author on Chapter 3, with some contribution from Tim Kelsall (note that this chapter draws heavily on the earlier paper by

Kelsall and vom Hau (2020), as well as Ferguson's 2020 book); Nicolai Schulz was the lead author on Chapter 4, with a significant contribution from Tim Kelsall; Brian Levy was the lead author on Chapter 5, which benefited from a conversation with Jeremy Seekings and Alan Hirsch about the South African political settlement and their respective expert codings of its evolution; Tim Kelsall was the lead author on Chapter 6, with a significant contribution from Sam Hickey and Claire Cummings. The chapter is largely a synthesis of material generated by other ESID research projects and we acknowledge the contribution of ESID researchers Abdul-Gafaru Abdulai, Charles Ackah, Edward Ampratwu, Mohammed Awal, Pritish Behuria, Chuong Chantha, Benjamin Chemouni, Michael Danquah, Robert Darko Osei, George Domfe, Fred Golooba Mutebi, Tom Goodfellow, Yvonne Habiyonizeye, Seiha Heng, Sothy Khieng, Tieng Tek Muy, Franklin Oduro, Tim Williams, and Pablo Yanguas; Chapter 7 is mainly the work of Nicolai Schulz, who led on the quantitative data assembly and analysis throughout the project; and Tim Kelsall was the lead author on Chapter 8. Various iterations of the draft were commented on by the entire authorial team.

We would also like to thank the FCDO for their financial support, and Max Everest-Phillips, David Pedley, and Peter Evans, among other members of its Research and Evidence Division, for ongoing encouragement. The views expressed in the book remain our own.

Table of Contents

List of Figures

List of Acronyms

ANC	African National Congress
ASEAN	Association of Southeast Asian Nations
AusAID	Australian Agency for International Development
BBC	British Broadcasting Corporation
CAMFEBA	Cambodian Federation of Employers and Business Associations
CCM	Chama Cha Mapinduzi
CDRI	Cambodia Development Resource Institute
CEIC	Census Economic Information Center
CHPS	Community Health-Based Planning Services
CLB	contingently loyal bloc
COSATU	Congress of South African Trade Unions
CNRP	Cambodia National Rescue Party
CPM	Communist Party of India (Marxist)
CPP	Cambodian People's Party
CSOs	civil-society organizations
CSSR, UCT	Centre for Social Science Research, University of Cape Town
DCE	District Chief Executive
DED	District Education Directorate/director
DFID	Department for International Development
DIIS	Danish Institute for International Studies
DLP	Developmental Leadership Program
DRC	Democratic Republic of the Congo
ECI	economic complexity index
EFF	Economic Freedom Front
EMI	ESID multiplicative index
EMIS	Educational Management Information System
ESID	Effective States and Inclusive Development Research Centre
EU	European Union
FARC	Fuerzas Armadas Revolucionarias de Colombia
FCDO	Foreign, Commonwealth and Development Office
FDI	foreign direct investment
FUNCINPEC	Front Uni National pour un Cambodge Indépendant, Neutre, Pacifique Et Coopératif
GDP	gross domestic product
GMAC	Garment Manufacturers' Association of Cambodia
GNI	gross national income
G-PSF	Government–Private Sector Forum
HEFs	Health Equity Funds

IBRD	International Bank for Reconstruction and Development
ICC	International Criminal Court
IDS	Institute of Development Studies
IFIs	international financial institutions
IFP	Inkatha Freedom Party
ILO	International Labour Organization
IMF	International Monetary Fund
IMR	infant mortality rate
KANU	Kenya African National Union
KPRP	Kampuchea People's Revolutionary Party
LAO	limited access order
LB	leader's bloc
MAF	MDG Acceleration Framework
MDGs	millennium development goals
MEPV	major episodes of political violence
MICs	middle-income countries
MMR	maternal mortality ratio
MoEYS	Ministry of Education, Youth, and Sport
MOH	Ministry of Health
MP	member of parliament
NARC	National Rainbow Coalition
NBER	National Bureau of Economic Research
NDC	National Democratic Congress
NGO	non-governmental organization
NIE	new institutional economics
NPP	New Patriotic Party
OAO	open access order
OB	opposition bloc
ODA	official development assistance
OEC	Observatory of Economic Complexity
OECD	Organisation of Economic Cooperation and Development
OLS	ordinary least squares
PAS	Parti Islam Se-Malaysia
PC	power concentration
PCA	principal component analysis
PCI	power concentration index
PDCI	Parti Démocratique de la Côte d'Ivoire
PEA	political economy analysis
PS	political settlement
PSA	political settlements analysis
PSD	Political Settlements (PolSett) dataset
RDR	Rassemblement des Républicains
RPA	Rwandan Patriotic Army
RPF	Rwandan Patriotic Front
SF	social foundation

SFI	social foundation index
SFS	social foundation size
SOAs	Special Operating Agencies
TANU	Tanganyika African National Union
TPAP	Teacher Policy Action Plan
TPPS	total powerful population share
UCDP	Uppsala Conflict Data Program
UDF	United Democratic Front
UK	United Kingdom
UMNO	United Malays National Organisation
UN	United Nations
UNDP	United Nations Development Programme
UNESCO	United Nations Educational, Scientific and Cultural Organization
US	United States
USAID	United States Agency for International Development
USD	US dollars
V-Dem	Varieties of Democracy
WBGI	World Bank Governance Indicators
WGIs	Worldwide Governance Indicators
WHO	World Health Organization

The Authors

Tim Kelsall is a senior research fellow at ODI in London, a former co-director of Research for the Effective States and Inclusive Development (ESID) research centre, and currently political settlements research director for the African Cities Research Consortium at the University of Manchester. He specializes in political anthropology and political economy analysis and has interests in governance, democracy, transitional justice, economic growth, education, and health.

Nicolai Schulz is a postdoctoral researcher at the Humboldt-Universität zu Berlin. Prior to that, he worked as a research associate at the University of Manchester and received his PhD from the London School of Economics (LSE) Department of International Development. His research triangulates quantitative with qualitative methods to study the political economy of sustainable development.

William D. Ferguson is the Gertrude B. Austin professor of economics at Grinnell College, where he teaches classes in political economy, applied game theory, labour economics, and policy analysis. He is the author of *The Political Economy of Collective Action, Inequality, and Development* (Stanford University Press, 2020) and *Collective Action and Exchange: A Game-Theoretic Approach to Contemporary Political Economy* (Stanford University Press, 2013).

Matthias vom Hau is an associate professor at the Institut Barcelona d'Estudis Internacionals (IBEI). A sociologist by training, he has a PhD from Brown University and previously held a postdoctoral fellowship at the University of Manchester. Matthias has published widely on the intersection between ethnic politics and development. He has recently received a Consolidator Grant from the European Research Council (ERC) to study the supposedly negative relationship between ethnic diversity and public goods provision.

Sam Hickey is professor of politics and development at the Global Development Institute, University of Manchester. As research director of the Effective States and Inclusive Development (ESID) research centre, he worked collaboratively on the links between politics and development, with particular reference to state capacity, natural resource governance, social protection, education, and gender equity. ESID's multiple books and papers on these topics are available at https://www.effective-states.org.

Brian Levy teaches at the School of Advanced International Studies, Johns Hopkins University and was the founding academic director of the Nelson Mandela School of Public Governance, University of Cape Town. He worked at the World Bank from 1989 to 2012. He has published widely on governance and development, including *Working with the Grain* (Oxford University Press, 2014).

PART I
CONCEPTS AND THEORY

In Part One we introduce the idea of a political settlement and seek to put it on a firmer conceptual and theoretical footing.

1

The Promise of Political Settlements Analysis (PSA)

Few concepts have captured the imagination of the conflict and development community in recent years as powerfully as the idea of a 'political settlement'. At its
most ambitious, 'political settlements analysis' (PSA) promises to explain why
conflicts occur and states collapse, the conditions for their successful rehabilitation, different developmental pathways, and how to better fit development policy
to country context. As such, it provides an analytical framework for development agencies increasingly tasked with working in fragile and conflict-affected
states, and frustrated by frequently disappointing 'good governance' results in
more stable ones (Ingram 2014). As of 2018, the Department for International Development (DFID), the World Bank, Australia's Department of Foreign Affairs and
Trade, the Organisation of Economic Cooperation and Development (OECD), the
European Union (EU) and others were all using PSA. Jointly, they had poured
many millions of pounds into political settlements research, funding at least five
major research centres, several flagship reports, hundreds of published working
papers and articles, three journal special issues, and at least eight books, not to
mention numerous colloquia and workshops dedicated to or inspired by the idea.[1]
For some donor agencies, notably the United Kingdom's DFID,[2] PSA was a required component of the diagnostic work used to inform country office strategies
and programming, shaping, at least to some extent, the deployment of billions of
pounds worth of aid.

---

[1] Research Centres include, the Crisis States Research Centre; the Elites, Production and Poverty
research programme; the Effective States and Inclusive Development Research Centre; the Political
Settlements Research Programme, and the Anti-Corruption Evidence Programme. Flagship reports
include World Bank (2011); DFID (2010); OECD (2011). Journal special issues include: *Journal of
International Development* (2017)Volume 29, Issue 5. *African Affairs* (2017). Virtual Issue: Political
Settlements Research in Africa. *Conflict, Security and Development* (2017) Volume 17, 3. Special Issue:
Political settlements, rupture and violence. Books include Whitfield et al. (2015); Levy (2014); Gray
(2018); Hickey and Hossain (2019); Nazneen, Hickey, and Sifaki (2019); Pritchett, Sen, and Werker
(2018); Ferguson (2020); Bebbington et al. (2018); Levy et al. (2017).

[2] Note that in June 2020 it was announced that DFID would merge with the Foreign and Commonwealth Office to create the Foreign, Commonwealth and Development Office (FCDO).

Political Settlements and Development. Tim Kelsall et al., Oxford University Press.
© Tim Kelsall et al., (2022). DOI: 10.1093/oso/9780192848932.003.0001

Yet despite the meteoric rise of the term and its tremendous promise, not all is well in the world of PSA. Rival definitions of the concept abound; there are disagreements about its scope and the way it should be used; a growing schism between conflict specialists and economists; basic concepts are ambiguous; and little progress has been made on measurement. Given these problems, it is no surprise that the approach has made little headway in the mainstream social science community and is regarded by some as little more than a fashionable and mildly obfuscatory 'fuzzword' (Tadros and Allouche 2017). If PSA cannot overcome these problems, it risks, despite all this investment, being consigned to the 'dustbin of ideas'.

This book, which grows out of the Effective States and Inclusive Development Research Centre at the University of Manchester (ESID), consequently has three main aims. The first is to argue for a revised definition of a political settlement, capable of unifying its diverse strands, and opening new opportunities for the analysis of conflict and development. The second is to put the concept on a more solid theoretical and scientific footing, providing a method for measuring and categorizing political settlements, and using new data to provide a four-country comparative analysis of different types of political settlements and their political and developmental consequences, and a large-*n* forty-two-country study. The third is to examine the implications of the findings for mainstream social science analysis and for policymakers.

A genealogy of PSA

According to Sue Ingram (Ingram 2014), PSA has its origins in several literatures and fields of practice and the concept of political settlements has acquired three distinct, yet overlapping meanings: 'A negotiated settlement to end interstate or intrastate conflict', 'A new and transformed political order born of crisis and achieved through elite cooperation', and 'The interdependent arrangement of political power and institutions on which a regime is based' (Ingram 2014).

The first and arguably best known of these meanings is based in international law and peacekeeping. Here, a political settlement typically refers either to the *process* of settling a conflict by political means, or the political *outcome* of a negotiated settlement. As early as 1919, for example, the Covenant of the League of Nations provided for 'adjudicated settlements' to prevent disputatious states going to war, while Article 6 of the United Nations is entitled, 'Pacific Settlement of Disputes'. The idea of a political settlement as an outcome came more into its own as the Cold War drew to a close and the field of international peacekeeping expanded. In 1989, the United Nations (UN) General Assembly requested 'The UN Secretary General to encourage and facilitate the early realization of a *comprehensive political settlement* in Afghanistan' and later passed a series of resolutions supporting 'a *comprehensive political settlement*' of the Cambodia conflict (Ingram 2014: 3, our italics). Such settlements typically spell out in some detail 'the provisions for the organization and exercise of political power', and often involve recourse to democratic elections or formal power sharing (4).

The second meaning, that is, 'a new and transformed political order' (Ingram 2014) emerges from a fairly niche field of comparative politics. Notably, Michael Burton and John Higley use the term 'elite settlements' to refer to, 'relatively rare events in which warring national elite factions suddenly and deliberately reorganize their relations by negotiating compromises on their most basic disagreements' (1987: 295). Such compromises often follow a period of inconclusive internecine conflict and/or are triggered by some sort of crisis or threat to elite survival. Examples include England's 'Glorious Revolution' in 1688, Sweden in 1809, Columbia in 1957, and Venezuela in 1958. Burton and Higley argued that such compromises, which imply a norm of mutual forebearance in the resolution of disputes, are one of the preconditions for a stable democracy.[3]

The third meaning or approach originally appeared in a handful of works in historical sociology and political economy in the 1990s. In Joseph Melling's writing, for example, the idea of a political settlement is used to explain the rise of welfare state policy in late nineteenth- and early twentieth-century Britain (Melling 1991) where a new form of welfare politics, based on changing patterns of class power and the ideological threat of socialism, reflected a new, 'shared discourse on the scope and limits of social citizenship' (237). In 1994, John Zysman (Zysman 1994) used the term to describe the way in which different societies solved the political problems generated by economic growth. The political settlement 'allocates' the costs of industrial change (257), with some settlements compensating losers, some repressing them, and others ignoring them, each solution implying distinct institutional arrangements that shape the subsequent character of growth.

A similar conception made its debut in development studies in 1995, via Mushtaq Khan's critique of New Institutional Economics (NIE) (Khan 1995). The argument was a response to 'New Institutional' approaches which criticized state interventionist development policies on grounds of their presumed inferiority to hypothetically free and 'efficient' markets. Khan's work addressed two puzzles: one was that institutions such as free markets which worked well in one context, for example the United Kingdom, functioned less well in much of the developing world; the other was that some institutions for addressing market failure, such as industrial policy, worked well in some developing countries, for example South Korea, but not in others, such as Pakistan (Khan 2018a). Khan consequently argued that the growth-enhancing efficiency of a given institution, such as a market, should not be determined by reference to a contextless hypothetical alternative,

---

[3] As we shall see, this idea is echoed in later work on 'protection pacts' (Slater 2010), albeit for authoritarian contexts.

but rather to how the institution would function given the prevailing 'political settlement', which he defined as 'an inherited balance of power' (Khan 1995) or 'the balance of power between the classes and groups affected by that institution' (81). The nub of his argument was that where new institutions threatened the interests of powerful groups they would be resisted, with the transition costs sometimes so great as to offset the hypothesized benefit of the new institution.[4]

It is only in the past decade or so, however, that the term has begun to get increasing traction in donor circles. In 2007, a DFID-funded paper by Verena Fritz and Alina Rocha-Menocal described political settlements as one of the 'constitutive domains of the state', defining them as, 'the expression of a negotiated agreement (at least in principle) binding together state and society and providing the necessary legitimacy for those who govern over those who are ruled' (Fritz and Rocha-Menocal 2007). Shortly thereafter, in a 2008 paper on state-building and the role of the state in development (Whaites 2008), Alan Whaites claimed that, 'The structures of the state are determined by an underlying political settlement; the forging of a common understanding, usually among elites, that their interests or beliefs are best served by a particular way of organizing political power' (4) elaborating that, 'Political settlements are not the same as peace agreements (although the latter may be part of establishing the former). Political settlements are the deeper, often unarticulated, understandings between elites that bring about the conditions to end conflict, but which also in most states prevent violent conflict from occurring' (7). Similar definitions appeared in major policy reports by the OECD (OECD 2011) and DFID (DFID 2010), while in the Australian Agency for International Development's (AusAID) 2011 Guidance for Staff (AusAID 2011), political settlements were referred to forty-seven times![5]

At around the same time, Jonathan Di John and James Putzel were defining political settlements as 'bargaining outcomes among contending elites' which 'manifest themselves in the structure of property rights and entitlements ... and in the regulatory structures of the state' (Di John and Putzel 2009), claiming that, 'The political settlement and the elite bargains from which it emerges are central to patterns of state fragility and resilience' (18). Invoking Khan, the political settlement was, 'the balance or distribution of power between contending groups and social classes, on which any state is based' (4). Di John and Putzel's definition went on to inform the work of DFID's Crisis States Research Programme Consortium, a major finding of which was that politically durable states were underpinned by

---

[4] The term appears again at several places in Khan and Jomo (2000), including in Khan's chapter, 'Rent-seeking as process', where Malaysia's success in attracting multinational investment is partly attributed to the credible commitments provided by its 'centralized political settlement' (Khan 2000, 100).

[5] For the United States Agency for International Development (USAID), the term has been less central, though it does get a couple of mentions in its 2016 guide to applied political economy analysis (PEA) (USAID 2016), as it does in the EU's (Anonymous 2012) and in the European Parliament's background paper on fragile states (Policy Department 2013).

'inclusive' elite bargains and political settlements (Putzel and Di John 2012). In 2011, the World Bank Development Report also invoked Di John and Putzel's political settlement definition, arguing that sustainable peace demanded the creation of 'inclusive enough' coalitions (World Bank 2011).

In 2010 Khan produced a major restatement of his position (Khan 2010).[6] In this reworking, a political settlement was now to be understood as a relatively stable combination of power and institutions, in which institutions delivered to powerful groups rents or benefits that were in line with their expectations. Khan produced a highly influential typology of 'clientelist' political settlements based on their organization of 'holding power', with each type having distinct implications for the sort of institutions that could be expected to enhance economic growth. We discuss Khan at greater length throughout the book, and in particular in Appendix A. Put briefly, however, Khan argued that where a 'ruling coalition' was weak vis-à-vis 'external [oppositional] factions' it would likely have a short time-horizon, and thus few incentives to plan for long-term industrial development. Conversely, where it was weak vis-à-vis 'internal factions', it might have an incentive to pursue long-horizon industrial policy but would struggle to implement it effectively in the face of lower-level rent-seeking contests. Only where a ruling coalition was strong vis-à-vis both internal and external factions, would it have the incentive and ability to successfully implement long-term industrial policy of the kind found in developmental South Korea. Inspired by Khan, the Elites, Power and Production Program at the Danish Institute of Strategic Studies, went on to produce several important studies in comparative industrial policy (Whitfield 2011, Whitfield and Therkilsden 2011, Whitfield et al. 2015).

In 2011, DFID began funding the Effective States and Inclusive Development Research Centre at the University of Manchester (ESID). Drawing on Khan and the partly Khan-inspired approach of Brian Levy (Levy 2010, Levy and Walton 2013), it placed PSA at the heart of its analytical approach, while trying to make it more sensitive to questions of ideology, transnationalism, and gender (Hickey 2013). Also making occasional use of political settlements was the Developmental Leadership Program at the University of Birmingham. Ed Laws and Adrian Leftwich described political settlements as: 'informal and formal processes, agreements, and practices that help consolidate politics, rather than violence, as a means for dealing with disagreements about interests, ideas and the distribution and use of power' (Laws and Leftwich 2014: 1). In another, significant conceptual study, Laws argued that political settlements were 'two-level games, involving horizontal negotiations between elites and vertical relations between elites and their followers' (2012: 36). Another influential paper, introducing the term, 'sub-national political

---

[6] The paper appeared to have been influenced by the work of Douglass North et al. (see below), who maintained that for most states in human history, peace was the product of an elite, rent-sharing bargain, or 'limited access order' (North, Wallis, Webb, and Weingast 2006, North et al. 2007, North, Wallis, and Weingast 2009). See also Khan (2009).

settlements' to refer to areas of a country which seemed to be governed by different rules to the centre, or in which there was persistent conflict, came out of The Asia Foundation (Parks and Cole 2010). In a further DFID-backed initiative Bruce Jones et al. studied the political settlement in several countries transitioning from conflict (Jones, Elgin-Cossart, and Esberg 2012).

The Political Settlements Research Programme at Edinburgh University, also DFID-funded, started work in 2015 and took PSA back to its roots in peace studies. For the most part the programme has analysed peace processes and peace agreements, but it has occasionally engaged with approaches and debates in the wider political economy literature, in particular the issue of inclusivity, with special reference to gender (O'Rourke 2017, Bell 2015, Bell and Pospisil 2017). The concept has also been used by Downing Street's Stabilisation Unit to analyse the conditions for securing and sustaining conflict-ending elite bargains (Cheng, Goodhand, and Meehan 2018). Khan, since 2015, has taken forward his approach with the DFID-funded Anti-Corruption Evidence Research Centre.[7] In 2020, the United Kingdom's newly minted Foreign, Commonwealth and Development Office began funding the £32 million African Cities Research Consortium, which will also have PSA at its heart.

Political settlements and the 'post-institutionalist' turn in development studies

It is helpful to view the rise of PSA, or at least its political economic variants, against the background of a wider 'post-institutionalist turn' in development studies. In the 1980s and 1990s, New Institutional Economic approaches, epitomized in the work of Nobel Prize Winner Douglass North (North 1981, 1990), explained major differences in country development by reference to the nature of their institutions, with the economic rise of the United Kingdom as the first industrial power in particular, explained by features such as its adoption of secure property rights, the rule of law, and functioning markets. This type of thinking helped legitimize the shift towards neo-liberalism in development circles, with most of the main aid agencies urging developing country governments to roll back the state so as to unleash market forces.

One of the attractions of the institutionalist approach was that it appeared to offer a more fundamental explanation of why countries adopted innovation, economies of scale, education, and other proximate determinants of growth than conventional approaches. Later work claimed that institutions were also a better explanation of long-term differences in country growth than two other popular explanations: geography and culture (Acemoglu et al. 2004). These advances

---

[7] https://ace.soas.ac.uk/what-is-ace/.

notwithstanding, institutionalist approaches themselves were less good at explaining why some countries have good economic institutions and others do not. If good institutions are the key to growth, why don't all countries adopt them? In response, a diverse disciplinary, epistemological, and methodological scholarship has started to unpack the politics that shape the choice and workings, and ultimately, the developmental consequences of institutions.

In economics, Acemoglu et al. (Acemoglu, Johnson, and Robinson 2004) attempted to rectify this by employing an approach very similar to PSA. In their perspective, economic institutions are created and maintained by those groups with political power based on two sources: *de facto* power, that is, the ability to engage in strikes, demonstrations, violent conflict etc., and *de jure* power—that is, political institutions as formal rules of the game. De facto power is largely based on the distribution of resources in society, which is shaped by economic institutions, together with groups' ability to solve collective-action problems, which fluctuates over time.[8] Political institutions are typically more durable than de facto power and are often created by groups with de facto power to try, as far as possible, to lock in their privileges. Consequently, those groups favoured by economic institutions will have the de facto power to create political institutions, which will be used to support economic institutions that reproduce a particular distribution of resources, which in turn will permit de facto power and political institutions to be maintained. Typically, powerful groups will block the emergence of economic institutions which could lead to growing de facto power for rival groups, since that might allow them to change political and economic institutions, eroding the former group's privileges. As with PSA, power and institutions combine to produce relative stability, with equilibrium only punctuated when technological or other forms of economic change alter the balance of de facto political power, generating struggles to create new economic and political institutions.

Acemoglu et al. provide two main illustrations of their theory in action. In early modern England, Atlantic trade created opportunities for new economic groups, in particular merchants and the gentry. These groups subsequently began to regard monarchical power as a threat to their continued prosperity. As a result, these new enriched economic classes tended to side with Parliament in the English Civil War. After the Restoration, they again sided against the Stuart monarchy, inviting William of Orange to take the throne in the Glorious Revolution of 1688. William's accession was accompanied by new political institutions that locked in the political power of the new classes, distributing economic rights more broadly through society, and providing the foundations for subsequent growth. However, as industrialization proceeded, the urban and working classes acquired increasing amounts of de facto power. They used this to push for reforms to political institutions, in particular the extension of the franchise. Facing the threat of serious

---

[8] A concept they do not develop, but which we address in Chapter 3.

political unrest or even revolution, the ruling class made several concessions to these new economic classes, progressively widening the franchise throughout the nineteenth and early twentieth century. As these new classes gained political representation, they triggered changes in economic institutions, not least rights for trades unions and the creation of a modern welfare state, that significantly altered the distribution of resources in society (cf. Melling 1991).

The argument developed by Acemoglu et al. at least implicitly draws inspiration from a larger scholarship in political science and sociology that emphasizes the centrality of (the threat of) political violence in determining the choice, workings, and consequences of institutions. According to this literature, conflicts and (the threat of) political violence shape institutional change through the channel of elite political survival considerations. In one variant of this argument, the extent of intra-elite conflict is pivotal: Struggles between different elite factions and their followers shape what kinds of institutions emerge, and when and how those institutions function in ways that transform the economy and contribute to public service provision. Following this line of reasoning, elite cohesion among incumbent leaders and powerful economic actors facilitates the promotion of industrialization and public goods provision, whereas elite disunity and factionalism makes it more likely that broad cross-class coalitions form, with ultimately negative implications for the construction of developmental states (Kohli 2004, Waldner 1999). Other scholars are more concerned with clashes between the ruling elite and subordinate sectors. Contentious events such as the convergence of ethnic tensions and urban mass protest (Slater 2010) or sustained ethnoracial mobilization (Marx 1998), bring elites together in encompassing 'protection pacts', which in turn facilitate revenue extraction and enable states to more effectively intervene in the economy, provide public services, and/or redistribute resources. Conversely, in cases where elites perceive subordinate pressures as manageable and episodic, flimsy 'provision pacts', focused on rent-sharing emerge, and flimsy institutions are the consequence (Slater 2010).

Another important contributor to the post-institutional turn is Douglass North himself. North, Wallis, and Weingast's 2009 book, *Violence and Social Orders*, starts from the premise that 'social science has not come to grips with how economic and political development are connected either in history or in the modern world' a problem that stems, they think, from the 'lack of systematic thinking about the central problem of violence in human societies'. 'How societies solve the ubiquitous threat of violence' they claim, 'shapes and constrains the forms that human interaction can take, including the form of political and economic systems' (North, Wallis, and Weingast 2009: xi).

Claiming that until they have solved the problem of violence societies cannot progress economically, North et al. posit that most countries do this by creating what they call a 'natural state' or Limited Access Order (LAO); that is, a personalized bargain in which powerful elites agree to divide economic rents from sources such as trade, monopolies, taxation and aid among themselves, giving each a stake in the system and thereby providing an incentive to refrain from using violence (2). LAOs emerged around ten thousand years ago from what they call 'The first social revolution' and remain the modal form of government in the world today. 'The natural state has lasted so long' they argue, 'because it aligns the interests of powerful individuals to forge a dominant coalition in such a way that limits violence and makes sustained social interaction possible on a larger scale' (13).

By creating the conditions for peace, LAOs provide for some economic growth. However, by selectively allocating rights and entitlements to participants in the elite bargain, they also limit competition, which stifles efficiency, innovation, and change. This is to be contrasted with an 'Open Access Order' (OAO), characteristic of advanced industrial societies, in which rights are generalized. In an OAO, both the political and economic arena are open for competition: 'access to organizations becomes defined as an impersonal right that all citizens possess' (6). Rents come not from limiting access to competition, but from innovation and technological change.

Both LAOs and OAOs tend to be self-reinforcing. In an LAO, only a select few people hold economic and political power, and they consequently use that power to prevent others from growing in strength. In OAOs, the supposed openness of the political arena means that groups which seek to create rents by limiting competition in the economic sphere tend to be opposed in the political sphere, maintaining the openness of the system. Power and institutions provide, as it were, a double bind.[9] But if power and institutions bind each other, how do some countries transition from LAO to OAO status? North et al. chart out a stylized process of evolutionary change, in which some LAOs consolidate internally, moving from 'fragile' to 'basic' to 'mature' LAOs, via a virtuous, mutually reinforcing spiral of increasingly capable public and private organizations, and increasingly complex institutional rules of the game. Then, building on a platform of 'mature' LAOs, elites first secure rule of law for themselves, create impersonal organizations and secure political control of the military, before extending impersonal rights to non-elites: these put societies 'on the doorstep' of Open Access Orders (23–7).[10]

---

[9] The degree to which Western democracies are genuinely politically open as opposed to being captured by certain elite or sectional interests is of course the subject of some critique. See for example, Fukuyama (2014).

[10] In more detail: The introduction and concluding synthesis chapters of North et al. (2013) focus centrally on the 'spectrum of LAOs' (10–14); 'development within LAOs' (14–16); and 'dynamics of LAOs' (331–3), including the following as the first on their list of most promising areas for future research: 'a deeper understanding that the principal development problem is making improvements within the LAO framework ... The first development problem focuses on the movement of LAOs from fragile to basic, from basic to mature, and from mature into the doorstep conditions. Attempting to skip these steps and focus instead on the transition from an LAO to an OAO is more likely to fail than succeed' (346). PSA, especially in Brian Levy's (2014) approach, can be seen as an attempt to say more about the different pathways LAOs can take.

Yet another body of work in sociology and political science that associates variants of political violence with distinct institutional outcomes is the so-called bellicist approach that is epitomized by Charles Tilly (Tilly 1975, 1992). This scholarship seeks to explain changes in the form and workings of institutions, and in particular state institutions by focusing on large-scale interstate war. According to this approach, international security concerns ultimately spurred the move towards OAOs in early modern Europe (Downing 1992, Ertman 1997). War (or the threat of war) motivated ruling elites to create a skilled bureaucracy capable of coordinating the deployment of armies and the acquisition of military technology. Similarly, war pushed rulers to search for public revenues, most importantly by expanding the extractive capacities of the state, but also by adopting 'growth-oriented' policies to enhance (taxable) economic activity. Other scholars emphasize that with the imposition of conscription ruling elites became more responsive to the demands of citizen-soldiers for the expansion of social provision (Hobsbawm 1990, Skocpol 1992). Taken together, this body of scholarship suggests that contrasting patterns of international conflict lead to different coalitional strategies, which in turn shape the kinds of state institutions that emerge. In the cut-throat environment of the 'total wars' confronted by early modern European states, broad political coalitions formed that included economic elites and at least part of the subordinate sectors, and led ruling elites to construct strong states that were capable of waging war, but also implementing growth-oriented and welfare-enhancing public policies. By contrast, in the context of 'limited wars' that characterized much of the rest of the world, ruling elites did not confront a comparable level of threat, and therefore built weak states unable to pursue economic transformation and extensive social service provision (Centeno 2002).

The bellicist approach has its critics. Research has shown that different kinds of international conflicts had very different consequences for the performance of state institutions. A certain level of institutional capacity is required for international threats to render states developmental: wars do not make states if there is no state machinery to begin with (Kohli 2004, Centeno 2002). Moreover, comparative historical work on state-building in China, Latin America, and Southeast Asia shows how states industrialized and expanded social provision even in the relative absence of major geopolitical threats or international wars (Hui 2005, Soifer 2015). But recently, a number of studies have come to the rescue, maintaining that—when used in a more qualified and nuanced manner—the bellicist approach still yields important insights into variations in institutional strength. Most prominently, some have shown that victory or defeat in international war matters for differences in state strength (Schenoni 2021), while others argue that the way interstate wars are financed shape subsequent institutional developments (Queralt 2019).

PSA builds on but arguably also goes beyond the insights provided by these existing post-institutionalist approaches in certain important respects. In sync with

Acemoglu et al. and other works that focus on elite threat perceptions, PSA rests on the interdependence of institutions and power and views the threat of social and economic disorder as a driver of institutional change. And similar to Douglass North and his coauthors, PSA emphasizes the self-reinforcing nature of political and institutional systems.

Yet, in contrast to existing approaches, and as we will show in later chapters, PSA provides a clearer conceptualization of the *specific kinds of power* that are associated with institutional persistence and change: the organizational capabilities of groups to either instigate or survive violent conflict (see Khan 2010). For example, while Acemoglu and Robinson recognize the importance of de facto power relationships for political and economic institutions, de facto power is scarcely theorized in their work. This has led some interpreters to the glib conclusion that getting the right economic institutions is simply a matter of getting the right political institutions, a position supportive of conventional good governance policies (Cameron 2012).

PSA, as seen, for example, in the work of Khan, implores us not to take formal institutions at face value. Making formal political institutions more inclusive will only result in more inclusive economic institutions if the de facto organizational capability to demand such institutions already exists. But in many developing countries, organized economic interests do not want a level playing field while the poor, for various reasons may be unable, collectively, to take advantage of inclusive political institutions (Khan 2018a). Moreover, PSA moves beyond North et al. in pointing towards different, either dominant or competitive, pathways of institutional change from LAO to developed OAO (Levy 2014).

Similarly, PSA draws inspiration but also critically engages with the bellicist approach. The two perspectives share an analytical focus on conflict when seeking to explain the workings of institutions. Both maintain that violent conflict (or the threat thereof) is pivotal in influencing the interests and coalitional networks of ruling elites, whose choices ultimately shape the structure and workings of political institutions. At the same time, the bellicist approach—even in its more nuanced form—privileges variants of interstate war in its explanations of institutional change. PSA, by contrast, incorporates a broader perspective. It treats the threat of any kind of conflict aimed at overthrowing the existing political order, whether international war, intra-elite struggles or subordinate mobilization, as a potential force for realigning political coalitions, and thus for subsequent institutional and developmental changes.

It finally bears emphasis that PSA does not assume a linear relationship between political settlements and institutional strength. As we have argued in this section, a major contribution of PSA is that it injects politics into the study of development by drawing attention to how political settlements shape the structure and workings of institutions. But there are obviously important feedback loops. Most prominently, greater state strength facilitates the subsequent co-optation of outsider groups into the political settlement (Wimmer 2018), while it also enables states to target benefits and/or repression to specific groups, thereby facilitating the successive exclusion of former insider groups (Holland 2017). Seen in this light, PSA is attuned to bringing in a temporal dimension and tracing interactions between institutional antecedents, political settlements, and subsequent institutional outcomes over time.

Highlights of PSA

Over the past decade, PSA has provided the theoretical frame for a slew of empirical studies that have enhanced our understanding of the conditions in which countries transition from conflict to sustainable peace, why economic development is more rapid in some countries than others, why some states make good progress in some areas of development but not others, and how development partners should work in different political contexts. For example, the Crisis States Research Centre conducted several empirically fertile streams of research, encompassing urban politics, decentralization, drug economies, warlordism, peacebuilding, state-military relations, access to justice, and others in Africa, Asia, and Latin America, which used the political settlements frame to varying degrees. In one of its more influential outputs, Stefan Lindemann's study of Zambia, the author argued that a deliberate policy of ethno-linguistic balancing in the composition of cabinet, civil service, and armed forces provided the foundation for national unity and political stability, at the cost of bureaucratic meritocracy and economic dynamism. The Zambian case could be contrasted with that of Uganda, characterized by 'exclusionary' elite bargains and repeated civil-war outbreaks (Lindemann 2010). The comparison contributed to the idea of a potential trade-off between 'inclusion' and 'growth', which continues to preoccupy development practitioners today (e.g. Rocha-Menocal 2020).[11]

Mushtaq Khan's (2010) comparison of Thailand, Tanzania, Maharashtra, Bengal, and Pakistan/Bangladesh used the political settlements approach more systematically. It showed how different types of historically constituted political settlement created different 'growth-stability' trade-offs in each case, shaping the type and fate of industrial policy. For instance, in 'vulnerable-authoritarian' Pakistan, rulers had the authority to implement an ambitious industrial policy that concentrated rents on West Pakistan. However, organized groups in East Pakistan opposed this, and the result was civil war and state break-up. In Thailand, the state's ability to create a long-term industrial policy à la South Korea was constrained by the leadership's vulnerability to a military coup or peasant

---

[11] Interestingly, Lindemann leaned more heavily on the idea of an 'elite bargain' than the 'political settlement' per se, believing the former to be easier to operationalize.

uprising, while in Tanzania, the 'weak-dominant' ruling party of Benjamin Mkapa was unable convincingly to implement neo-liberal economic reforms, partly because of competing pressures from factions within his own party. In Maharashtra, the dominant Congress Party initially presided over a relatively successful industrial licensing system that led to long-term industrial growth around Mumbai, but as 'competitive clientelistic' pressures in the system increased, the political certainties required by such a system eroded and economic activities shifted into areas such as construction and services with shorter-term pay-offs.

As noted earlier, the Elites, Production and Poverty programme elaborated on Khan's framework. States successfully promoted economic sectors, it argued, when those sectors were deemed crucial to ruling elites' political survival *and* when elites were cohesive enough to be able to create a pocket of bureaucratic effectiveness linking the state with emerging capitalists, a thesis they illustrated with (mostly negative) case studies from Ghana, Uganda, Tanzania, and Mozambique. Another noteworthy contribution, which combined a 'socialist' ideological variable with Khan's framework, was Hazel Gray's comparison of economic transformation in Tanzania and Vietnam (Gray 2012, 2018).

The largest body of political-settlements-inspired empirical research to date has come out of ESID. The Centre has studied the effects of the political settlement on economic growth, natural resource governance, education and health provision, social protection, gender-based violence legislation, state capacity, and more, focusing on a limited number of cases within a comparative framework. With some important qualifications, it has found Khan's prediction that ruling coalitions which are 'dominant' vis-à-vis internal and external factions will have better enforcement capacity and longer time-horizons than ones that are weaker, sound. For example, its work on economic growth found that growth-accelerating 'ordered' business environments in places like Cambodia, Malaysia, and Rwanda were more likely to be associated with politically 'dominant' settlements than 'competitive' ones (Pritchett, Sen, and Werker et al. 2018). Its work on natural resource governance found Uganda's 'weak dominant' political settlement had afforded the leadership a longer time-horizon in which to build state capacity for better deals with oil companies than in 'competitive clientelist' Ghana, where technocrats were overruled in the interest of quick political wins (Hickey et al. 2015).

ESID's project on maternal health found that the most rapid progress in maternal mortality reduction came via state-based provision in strong, 'dominant' Rwanda, though 'competitive clientelist' Bangladesh had also made strong gains, partly explained by innovative non-governmental organization (NGO) initiatives and a rapid expansion of private health provision. 'Weak dominant' Uganda and 'competitive clientelist' Ghana had fared less well, though good results were found in pockets (Kelsall 2020). Indeed, ESID's Phase 1 work found that there were alternative pathways to good development outcomes under different types of settlement, with elite ideas, election pressures, or donor-backed coalitions sometimes helping to offset short time-horizons and weak enforcement capacity.

Social protection programmes also appeared to be better targeted and less prone to political interference in 'dominant' Rwanda and Ethiopia than in 'weak dominant' Uganda and 'competitive' Kenya (Lavers and Hickey 2015). ESID's study of the creation and implementation of gender-based violence legislation found that dominant settlements, notably Rwanda and South Africa, were much better at enforcing the legislation than more 'competitive' Bangladesh, while 'weak dominant' Uganda had a more equivocal approach to the issue altogether (Nazneen, Hickey, and Sifaki 2019). In education, meanwhile, the results were more nuanced, with both dominant and competitive settlements performing well when it came to accomplishing the relatively simple logistical task of getting children into school, but less so when it came to increasing educational quality, though for different reasons, with the evidence again supporting an interpretation of equifinality (Hickey and Hossain 2019).

Relatedly, Kelsall et al. have explored the relationship between political settlements and progress on universal health coverage (Kelsall, Hart, and Laws 2016) while Wales et al. did something similar with progress on education reforms (Wales, Magee, and Nicolai 2016). In addition to these empirical studies, there have been various attempts to inject PSA with more operational relevance. While Levy and Walton (Levy and Walton 2013, Levy 2014) and Kelsall (Kelsall 2016) have tried to derive generic pointers for development strategy from political settlement type, Khan and his collaborators have focused more on using a political settlements perspective to analyse the reform potential of specific institutional and policy measures.[12]

Problems with PSA and possible solutions

Despite these accomplishments, controversies in and about PSA abound. In the next section we briefly discuss definitional issues, measurement issues, value-neutrality, explanatory and predictive power.

Definitional issues

One of the most basic controversies in the field surrounds the very referent of the term. As Mick Moore asked provocatively in a 2012 blog, 'What on earth is a political settlement?'[13] As we have seen, the origins of PSA in at least three different streams of research and practice make disagreements around the term's extension

[12] See https://ace.soas.ac.uk/resources-2/.
[13] Moore (2012). See also https://www.odi.org/comment/6816-why-political-settlements-matter-response-mick-moore.

unsurprising. Moore recounts a workshop in which one participant was using it to refer to a peace agreement, and another to something like a country political system, with little prospect of clear communication between the two. Although a good deal of useful conceptual work has been done to try and identify what these different conceptions have in common (e.g. Laws 2012), disagreements remain. One of them is whether a political settlement is a *mutually constitutive* and relatively stable combination of power *and* institutions, or whether it is a configuration of power that *underpins* institutional stability; another is whether an agreement is necessary for a political settlement, and if so, what sort of agreement; another is whether a political settlement even entails an end to or reduction in violent conflict (Kelsall 2018a, Khan 2018a and b, Kelsall 2018b). In Chapter 2 of this book we aim to clear up these controversies via an extended conceptual discussion that encompasses the usages of both conflict and development specialists.

Measurement issues

Not unrelated to definitional problems are measurement issues, for how can one measure something without agreeing on what it is? This is compounded by the fact that political settlements, at least in their broader conceptualization, are 'unobservable'. There is no single thing one can point to and say: 'There, that's your political settlement.' While Khan has argued that the process of analysing political settlements is more akin to an art than a science, Levy (2014) has at least attempted to provide objective indicators. However, while he makes a useful conceptual distinction between 'cohesive' and 'incohesive' political settlements, similar to the one we will employ in this book, he then uses the familiar (but misleading) democracy–authoritarianism distinction as an empirical proxy. One of the purported strengths of PSA, however, is its ability to unpack the democracy–authoritarianism distinction and identify states with similar power attributes yet different regime types (Kelsall 2016). As explained later in the book, we improve on existing efforts by constructing a novel and original cross-national dataset of political settlements that covers forty-two countries from the Cold War era onwards. Our scoring of the cases relies on an expert survey administered to multiple specialists for each included country, an approach that has recently gained traction in a variety of fields, most prominently the long-run comparative study of political regimes (the Varieties of Democracy dataset) and the study of ethnic politics (the Ethnic Power Relations dataset).

Value-neutrality

Another controversy surrounds the concept's normative content. The field is split between scholars who use political settlements as a value-neutral analytical approach for understanding and explaining politics and development, separating the political settlement itself from its positive or negative developmental effects, and those who either imbue the concept itself with positive connotations, or else have clear ideas about what a 'good' political settlement looks like. Khan, Parks and Cole, Levy, and the approach we will adopt in this book are examples of the first. These authors tend to focus on how to bring about developmental progress by *working with the grain* of the existing political settlement, although they might occasionally admit that for progress to occur, a political settlement must change. The Political Settlements Research Centre in Edinburgh, by contrast, while sidestepping the issue of what a political settlement *is*, views PSA as '*a project of engagement with the possibilities of transformation* in situations where powerful and violent actors appear to hold all the cards' (our emphasis) (Bell 2015). Perhaps the most normative definition is from Fritz and Rocha-Menocal (2007), who, by tying the very definition of a political settlement to legitimate state–society relations, invest it with a significant ethical load.

These differences are not unrelated to charges that mainstream PSA suffers from an inherent elite-bias. As we have seen in some of the definitions earlier, political settlements have been linked to elite bargains, either as their analogue, antecedent, or outcome. O'Rourke has argued that this elite bias has sometimes led political settlements analysts to be blind to the agency of non-elites, especially women (O'Rourke 2017). In reality, most political settlements theorists realize that political settlements, as in the definition by Laws, are two-level games among elites and their followers. Others prefer to think less in terms of elites and non-elites and more in terms of the social distribution of organizational power (Khan 2018a). Nevertheless, the criticisms about the lack of comparative attention to non-elites have an element of truth and open up questions about the appropriate scope of PSA, to which we will return.

Closely linked to these debates is what is meant by an 'inclusive' or 'inclusive enough' political settlement. Alina Rocha-Menocal usefully distinguishes between settlements that are inclusive on the horizontal plane, accommodating a broad range of ethnic and religious elites, for example, and those that are inclusive on the vertical plane, spanning different social strata or classes (Rocha-Menocal 2015). Another teasing distinction is between settlements that are inclusive in terms of process: for example, they incorporate some form of electoral democracy or other popular consultative governance mechanisms, and those that are inclusive in terms of outcomes, in the sense of delivering broad-based growth and development. As comparisons of places such as Ghana and Kenya with Rwanda and Ethiopia have shown, the first does not necessarily equate to the second. This creates a problem for development agencies, for example DFID, which have stated a commitment to 'inclusive political settlements and processes' (DFID 2010), and a source of consternation for liberal scholars who reject the idea that there may be a trade-off, in some circumstances, between democracy and development (van de Walle 2016).

Explanatory and predictive power

There is a further debate over whether PSA has predictive or merely interpretive power. There are two basic issues to consider here. One is whether any social science, given the complexities of the social world, can be predictive in the way that natural science is. Anyone who responds to this question in the negative is bound to think that PSA is similarly non-predictive. But even if one answers the question in the affirmative, there is still the possibility that political settlements are so ineffable and unobservable that they can never be measured with the kind of precision that would permit adequate prediction. This is the position that seems to be held by Khan, who advocates a form of PSA based on an artful historical and contextual understanding of organizational power in a society and the use of political settlements as an analytical framework for assessing the implications of changing institutions (Khan 2018a). PSA 'provides a way of evaluating the sustainability of the institutions and policies that emerge [in a society], but it does not of course predict the precise institutions and policies that actually emerge' (Khan 2018a: 7). But it is not clear that this position is intellectually defensible, for if changes in policies and institutions are not, as Khan argues, mechanically reflective of the distribution of power (7), why should their sustainability be? Further, any attempt to advise policymakers, which Khan and his collaborators are keen to do, implies that the past and present are some kind of guide to the future, which secretes a belief in prediction. A similar criticism can be levelled at claims that PSA should not be used to make predictions, but can be used to inform mid-range hypotheses (Behuria, Buur, and Gray 2017).

Finally, a problem shared by both the Khan and Levy approaches, as we shall see, is that although they can explain why certain ruling coalitions have the potential to promote development, they provide scant insight into *why* some elites choose to act on this. Khan's approach, based on the relative strength or holding power of the ruling coalition, provides a necessary *but not sufficient condition* for the emergence of a developmental state (2010: 66). Levy's 'dominant discretionary' type decomposes into the different sub-types of 'dominant developmental', 'dominant predatory' and even 'dominant patrimonial' settlements, with little explanation for why one type emerges in one place and one type in another (Levy and Walton 2013, Levy 2014).

A way forward

In response to these concerns we argue that PSA can be enriched by the incorporation of elements from other bodies of work. Our starting point is the following observation: existing PSA scholarship rightly suggests that mounting conflicts, whether elite feuds or subordinate mass protest, can provide a powerful and rather sudden impetus for the realignment of political coalitions, and subsequent changes to institutional arrangements. At the same time, the causal privileging of conflict bears the danger of overlooking the fact that intra-elite struggles and lower-class mass mobilization do not fall from the sky, but are often endogenous to the wider distribution of power in society. In this book, we will therefore draw on the insights of a rich literature in political science and sociology that explores the critical role of social classes and their organizational resources (e.g. trade unions, political parties, business associations) in the transformation of state institutions and their redis-tributive effects (Huber and Stephens 2012, Korpi and Palme 1998, Albertus and Menaldo 2014, Haggard and Kaufman 2008). According to this 'power resources' tradition, differences in how social classes are organized and how their political representatives relate to each other shape the choice and functioning of institutions and, ultimately, developmental outcomes. Thus, in countries where pro-poor civil society associations and political parties are comparatively strong over a sustained period of time, political coalitions are likely to install state institutions with equal-izing distributional effects. Conversely, in countries where subordinate sectors lack organizational resources, distributional coalitions are unlikely to emerge.[14]

A complementary but slightly different perspective is provided by the *power configurational* approach. Rather than social class, it focuses on power differences between ethnic groups and their inclusion among the ruling elite (Cederman, Wimmer, and Min 2010, Wimmer 2002, 2018). According to this perspective, ac-cess to the highest level of government power grants ethnic groups influence over the institutional set-up of society, thereby shaping the distribution of resources (e.g. subsidies for industry-specific human capital and infrastructure) and the al-location of public goods (e.g. health care, basic sanitation). This is largely because of intra-ethnic favouritism (Adida 2015), but also other processes through which politically powerful ethnic groups gain advantages (Franck and Ranier 2012). Thus, in countries where most, if not all major ethnic groups are integrated into the central power structure and form part of the ruling elite,[15] more universalist and equalizing forms of public goods provision are likely to emerge, whereas in countries where many if not most ethnic groups remain excluded, less equalizing institutional arrangements are likely to prevail (Wimmer 2018).

Whatever their differences, the power resources and power configurations approach converge in emphasizing that trajectories of development, whether economic transformation or public service provision, are crucially affected by

---

[14] Barrington Moore's study of the political conditions under which different agrarian societies make the transition to industrialization is arguably an early example of this approach. Moore argued that in countries where the middle class was strong, industrialization proceeded under democratic insti-tutions, but where it was weak, authoritarian transitions were the norm. Thus, political institutions (democracy or authoritarianism) and economic institutions (pre-capitalist and capitalist) are explained by pre-existing social and class structures (Moore 1966).

[15] Another logical possibility implied by a power-configurational approach is that countries with only one (very large) ethnic group have, *ceteris paribus*, more equalizing institutional arrangements.

the distribution of power between different social groups, whether defined by class, ethnicity, or another social category. The overall causality runs from power resources/configurations to institutions to development, with coalitions as the crucial intervening mechanism. Power differences among social groups lead to distinct patterns of political competition and coalition formation, and these coalitions in turn shape the choice and performance of institutions—largely to achieve political stability and ensure that the distribution of state resources is in line with the existing distribution of power (whether analysed in terms of income, collective organization, and/or status) in society.

We believe that injecting some of the ideas from this broader literature on power resources and power configurations into PSA can help enhance the latter's explanatory power and precision, solving some of the puzzles that the approach has so far failed to explain. Why do some politically strong ruling coalitions embark on transformative developmental programmes while others are content with a more predatory approach, and what explains, in many areas, the unevenness of state capacity across different issue areas? As we explain in later chapters, we do this by providing a new definition for a political settlement which invites us to add a new, 'social foundation' dimension to the more configurational approach of existing typologies. Arguably this can help PSA fulfil its promise of explaining how the solutions a society provides to the problem of violence shape subsequent trajectories of development, *and* how development practice can be improved by a proper understanding of these patterns.

An overview of the book

As discussed, this book thus has three main aims: to provide a revised and improved definition of a political settlement capable of uniting a fractured field, to put PSA on a firmer theoretical and scientific footing, and to illustrate some of the advantages for policymaking.

We begin in Chapter 2, where we define a political settlement as *an ongoing agreement among a society's most powerful groups over a set of political and economic institutions expected to generate for them a minimally acceptable level of benefits, which thereby ends or prevents generalized civil war and/or political and economic disorder*. We provide an extended and nuanced defence of this definition, arguing that in contrast to most extant versions, it is both theoretically fertile *and* consistent with commonsense understandings of a political settlement. Universally applicable, the concept is compatible with many different and distinct political settlement theories, frameworks, and hypotheses, yet it directs our attention to what should be PSA's distinctive contribution, that is, an analysis of how the problem of violence shapes ruling elites' commitment to different sorts of development policy, or not as the case may be. The chapter also briefly introduces a new typology of political settlements, based on two, novel dimensions: *the social foundation* and *the power configuration* of the settlement. In Appendix A, we explain in more detail how our approach differs from those of Brian Levy and Mushtaq Khan, two of the authors who have inspired us most.

In Chapter 3, we take a further step towards enhancing PSA's formal rigour, laying out our typological theory in some detail, explaining its dimensions, and in particular their relationship to the phenomenon of collective action. We argue that economic and political development requires resolving two types of collective-action problem. First-order problems involve externalities, common pool resources, human security, public goods, and other market failures. Resolution entails forging agreements about sharing associated costs and benefits. Implementation, however, requires credible coordination and enforcement: a set of second-order problems typically related to creating institutions that can offer incentives, information, and common expectations—though often in a sub-optimal manner. Political settlements underlie institution-building by establishing boundaries for violent conflict. They address the most fundamental collective-action problem of development. Some settlements permit resolving many other development problems, whereas others create self-enforcing sub-optimal equilibria that exclude many parties—especially the poor—damage the environment, and otherwise impede development.

Part Two of the book moves to measurement and testing. As discussed earlier, a problem that has bedevilled PSA and limited its acceptance by the social scientific mainstream is its lack of clear guidelines for measurement. Chapter 4 discusses how to identify evolutions or changes in political settlements, how to code in a rigorous way some of their key dimensions, and how to construct tentative typological variables therefrom. We illustrate this by providing a mapping based on a survey of political settlements in forty-two countries since 1960 or independence. In Chapter 5 we provide an extended illustration of our new approach by applying it to South Africa, showing in some detail how our new measures can be used to describe in quantitative terms and simulateneously supply additional analytical focus to a story that is qualitatively already well known. Then in Chapter 6 we corroborate our typological theory with a study of economic growth, maternal health, and education in four archetypal cases: Ghana, Guinea, Cambodia, and Rwanda, also introducing the concept of the 'policy domain' to explain some of the nuances we find. Then, in Chapter 7, we take PSA to a new level by providing a regression analysis of the relationship between political settlement type, economic and social development in our forty-two countries. The chapter demonstrates, as our theory predicts, a strong relationship between power concentration and economic development, the social foundation and social development.

The promise of PSA is to demonstrate a relationship between the nature or type of political settlement and the commitment, opposition, or indifference of political elites and state officials to creating and implementing policies of one type or another. Understanding the nature of the political settlement, its social foundation and configuration of power, consequently provides development partners and reformers in general a head start when it comes to assessing what kinds of policy reform are likely to get traction, which are likely to be opposed, or where there may be considerable room for manoeuvre and creative coalition building. It also provides pointers as to whether traction is most likely to be found with state or non-state actors and at which levels of the political system.

Chapter 8 concludes, summarizing the argument, the main findings, and considering the implications for policymakers and reformers. It also points to several potential areas for future research. PSA has begun to deliver on its promise of understanding conflict and development, we argue, and there is much it can still achieve.

2

The Idea of a Political Settlement

In his magnum opus of social scientific methods, John Gerring argues that so-cial scientific concepts are 'linguistic containers we use to carve up the empirical world' (Gerring 2011, Loc 3005). They should 'resonate with everyday usage', and not unnecessarily disturb their 'semantic field' (Gerring 2011, Loc 3005). Mean-while Gary Goertz, in his extended treatment of the subject, argues that concepts should also 'identify ontological attributes that play a key role in causal hypotheses, explanations, and mechanisms' (Goertz 2006: 5). Most concepts have a structure that is multilevel and multidimensional. The basic level names the concept, that is the term that is used in high-level theoretical propositions. The secondary level identifies core attributes or constitutive features of the concept, sometimes also referred to as 'dimensions', which are presumed to have causal powers (Goertz 2006).

In this chapter, we provide a more rigorous grounding for the idea of a political settlement than has been provided hitherto: identifying what it is, what it is not, what its constitutive features are, and how these can generate causal hypotheses about the relationship between politics and development. In Chapter 4 we dis-cuss the 'indicator', 'data', or 'operationalization' level, which concerns the actual empirical data that serve to identify the concept, categorize, and/or measure it.

The basic concept

Before digging into the constitutive dimensions of the idea of a political settlement, it is necessary to examine it at a basic level.

Political settlements in ordinary language

'Political settlement' is a compound neologism that you will not find in a dictio-nary. It therefore has a rather tenuous presence in ordinary language. However, insights into its meaning can be gleaned by examining its constituent parts. 'Po-litical' is an adjective derived from the noun 'politics', for which the *Oxford Living Dictionary* provides several definitions that range from, 'The activities associated

Political Settlements and Development. Tim Kelsall et al., Oxford University Press.
© Tim Kelsall et al., (2022). DOI: 10.1093/oso/9780192848932.003.0002

with the governance of a country or area, especially the debate between parties having power' to 'the principles relating to or inherent in a sphere or activity, especially when concerned with power and status'.[1] *Merriam-Webster* also provides several definitions, ranging from 'the art or science of government' through 'competition between competing interest groups or individuals for power and leadership (as in a government)' to 'the total complex of relations between people living in society'.[2]

Naturally, the concept of politics also has a long career in political science. To give three influential examples, David Easton defined politics as 'the authoritative allocation of values' (Easton 1965), Harold Lasswell (1936) associated it with distributional issues, or: 'Who gets what, when and how', while Adrian Leftwich (2004) argued that, 'politics comprises all the activities of cooperation and conflict, within and between societies, whereby the human species goes about organizing the use, production and distribution of human, natural and other resources in the course of the production and reproduction of its biological and social life' (65).

'Settlement', meanwhile, is a noun that derives from the verb 'to settle'. Etymologically, 'settle' derives from the Old English *setlan*—from *setl*, seat. *Merriam-Webster* defines, 'settle', as, among other things, 'to come to rest', 'become fixed, resolved, or established', or 'to become quiet or orderly', with the *Oxford Living Dictionary* defining a 'settlement', in the first instance, as 'an official agreement intended to resolve a dispute or conflict'.[3]

From these sources, we might infer a political settlement to be a settling down, resolution, or aversion of conflict, most likely the result of an agreement, perhaps official, presumably between the parties to conflict, but possibly also the result of a natural sedimentation or tacit acceptance, which creates a degree of fixity in who has political power, the institutions of government or governance, and/or distributional issues.

Political settlements in journalistic and academic usage

Such a reading would be consistent, for example, with the occasions when 'political settlement' does appear as a term in popular discourse. In January 2017, an article on the British Broadcasting Corporation (BBC) website, for example, claimed that the South Sudanese opposition wanted 'a political settlement' to the war in that country.[4] On 4 January 2013, a story appeared in *The Guardian* about Hezbollah calling for a 'political settlement' to the Syria conflict and the prospect of UN

---

[1] https://en.oxforddictionaries.com/definition/politics.
[2] https://www.merriam-webster.com/dictionary/politics.
[3] https://en.oxforddictionaries.com/definition/settlement.
[4] http://www.bbc.co.uk/news/av/world-africa-38575104/south-sudan-opposition-wants-political-settlement.

talks on the matter.[5] *The New York Times* used the term in March 2011, in a leader calling for a 'negotiated political settlement' in Afghanistan. In all these cases a political settlement is presented as an alternative to ongoing war and invokes the meaning most commonly ascribed to political settlements in peacekeeping circles (see Chapter 1). It appears in a similar sense in a 1972 document of the same name, issued by the Ulster Government in response to the troubles in Northern Ireland (Great Britain. Northern Ireland Department 1972).

These attributes resonate to a considerable degree with the academic and development literature on settlements. DFID's (2010) definition, for example, arguably invokes an agreement (a common understanding), parties to the agreement (elites and social classes), governance (how power is organized), and distributional issues (how power is exercised). Khan's invokes power (power), governance (institutions, albeit mainly informal), and, in some instances, distributional issues (rents) (Khan 2010). Levy's invokes governance institutions (institutional relationships) and conflict resolution (restraint of violence) (Levy 2014). Perhaps the most encompassing definition comes from Laws (Laws 2012). It too includes agreements (political settlements are ongoing political processes that include one-off events and agreements), parties to conflict (political settlements are two-level games, involving horizontal negotiations between elites and vertical relations between elites and their followers) and institutions (political settlements shape the form, nature, and performance of institutions. In turn, institutions and their interaction with organizations can consolidate and embed political settlements).[6]

If there is a difference between these academic definitions and everyday or journalistic understandings, it seems to be a focus in the former that goes beyond *official* agreements, which are likely to take place at discrete points in time and be formally recorded, to informal or tacit agreements and ongoing processes. Indeed, this processual dimension to the academic concept is partially responsible for Laws advising that we look beyond political settlements to 'political orders' (Laws 2012: 38). And herein lies the source of some of the confusion, alluded to earlier in the critique by Mick Moore. How can a political settlement be a one-off agreement, like a peace agreement, and at the same time a set of processes that are more akin to what others might call a 'political order' or 'political system'?

The confusion can be partly cleared up by acknowledging the compound nature of the term. The settlement is an agreement among parties *to* something. The 'settlement' part describes the agreement, which helps stabilize by means of a set of mutual expectations what it is they are agreeing to—political and economic

---

[5] https://www.theguardian.com/world/middle-east-live/2013/jan/04/syria-hezbollah-political-settlement-live.

[6] By contrast, the Political Settlements Research Consortium at Edinburgh departs significantly from academic and everyday usages, preferring to use 'political settlements' as shorthand for 'a project of engagement' (Bell 2015: 5).

institutions/a distribution of benefits. Moreover, although the agreement may be marked by a declaration or document, to be sustained it must be remade, more informally, on a daily basis.

Perhaps an analogy will help. Most people would not have any problem in understanding that a 'marriage' can refer to both an event, as in a wedding, solemnized with vows and an official document, and at the same time to an ongoing relationship between two people. And while the vows made during the marriage ceremony might reflect the understanding of the parties at the time as to the duties and obligations of one to the other, thus providing a useful starting point for analysing their ongoing relationship, it will not tell us all we need to know about that relationship, which almost certainly will involve ongoing negotiations, adjustments, and compromises.

We would argue that the idea of a political settlement can be compared to a concept like marriage, in the sense that there is no contradiction in viewing it, on the one hand as a one-off event, and on the other as an ongoing relationship. Some analysts will want to focus on the event and its effects, others will prefer to look at the relationship overall. Moreover, just as in some countries there is the concept of a 'common law marriage' to describe two people living together as partners even though they have not been through an official ceremony, so there are some political settlements that are never enshrined in a one-off event or document.

An improved definition

With this discussion behind us, we are in a position to propose a definition of political settlements which draws on everyday usage, is compatible with the way the term is used in the peace and conflict literature, yet also fit for the kind of institutional and policy analysis for which it has been deployed by Khan and others in development studies.

To wit, a political settlement is *an ongoing agreement among a society's most powerful groups over a set of political and economic institutions expected to generate for them a minimally acceptable level of benefits, and which thereby ends or prevents generalized civil war and/or political and economic disorder.*

Constitutive dimensions

If this is our basic concept, it is time now to look a little more closely at its secondary level, that is, its core attributes or constitutive elements, as depicted in Figure 2.1.

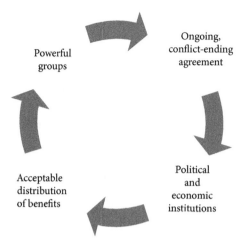

Fig. 2.1 Dynamic relationships within a political settlement
Source: Authors' own

An agreement that ends or prevents generalized war or disorder

As we have already seen, this is one of the most contentious and misunderstood aspects of the idea of a political settlement, and it is contentious in at least two ways.

Let us start with the idea that a political settlement involves an agreement. For some, this involves an explicit agreement, as in a peace agreement, or a constitution that is popularly ratified. But there are good reasons for thinking that agreements need not be explicit, or at least formal, as in the case of a common law marriage, referred to earlier. The parties to such a marriage will have a tacit understanding that they are living together 'as' partners, which could probably be articulated if necessary, but which may not be explicit, let alone written down. Moreover, they will have a set of more or less explicit, more or less tacit understandings about their mutual obligations to one another within the marriage. They 'agree' to their marriage on a daily basis.

To provide another, this time fictional, example of how tacit agreements can underpin a settlement, we can look to the film *The Godfather*. There is a scene in the film in which Sonny Corleone proposes killing a policeman to avenge an attack on his father, mafia boss Don Corleone. His father's advisor tries to dissuade him: 'Now, *nobody* has ever gunned down a New York Police Captain, never. It would be disastrous. All the other Five Families would come after you, Sonny. The Corleone Family would be outcasts! Even the old man's political protection would run for cover!' But Sonny's younger brother, Michael, played by Al Pacino, objects, 'Where does it say that you can't kill a cop?'[7] Eventually, Michael persuades the Family that the rule may be flexible, and the policeman is killed. This proves a miscalculation,

[7] https://www.youtube.com/watch?v=by5YzWJ9W4U.

however. The killing does provoke a war, upending the relatively peaceful division of criminal activities among the city's prominent mafia families, with causalities on all sides. Peace is only restored after the families meet and renegotiate the terms of their relationship. Tacit agreements, then, may be sufficient to ground a settlement, and may be especially important in contexts where formal institutions are weak.

For some commentators, however, not even a tacit agreement is required. Khan, for example, argues that all that is needed for a political settlement is for there to be a balance of power sufficient to produce a 'sustainable' level of violence (Khan 2018a: 641).[8] Khan is not very clear about what he means by 'sustainable' here, but it seems that very intense levels of warfare could, in principle, be sustainable, so long as the conflicting parties remained locked in a stalemate. Although this is arguably consistent with the idea of a settlement as a kind of equilibrium or 'coming to rest', it nevertheless strikes us as intuitively wrong. To our minds it seems to violate ordinary language understandings of what a political settlement is, which are so frequently linked to the ending or prevention of civil war. It also arguably robs the term of some of its distinctiveness, by taking away the idea that powerful groups are at least minimally mutually invested in a set of institutions that bring (relative) peace and stability, and which will therefore be somewhat resistant to change—on which more later.[9] Another objection is that it appears to remove human agency and intention entirely from the equation. Natural ecosystems such as coral reefs or savannah grasslands have a sustainable balance of power, but we would likely not want to describe them as having political settlements.[10]

Another misunderstanding relates to the idea that settlements should be amicable. However, this is not always the case, especially if settlements are entered into by groups of unequal strength or standing. Often, in legal cases, a party 'agrees' to a settlement that is highly unpalatable to them, simply because they fear that by *not settling* they will get much less, or lose much more. In such cases, a settlement is practically 'imposed' on one of the parties. So it can be with political settlements. In some conflicts, one of the parties may 'agree' to stop fighting only to

---

[8] See also the debate between Khan and Kelsall: Kelsall (2018a), Khan (2018b); Kelsall (2018b). In the final piece Kelsall argues that while there is much to admire in Khan's work, 'political settlement' is something of a misnomer: 'power configuration analysis' would be a more appropriate label for his approach.

[9] Ironically, this is an idea to which Khan himself seemed previously to subscribe: 'once a political settlement based on a compatible combination of institutions and power emerges, both the institutions and the distribution of power become supportive of each other. As a result, the operation and introduction of further institutional changes has to take this social distribution of power as given' (2010: 5). 'The political settlement can therefore help to explain the performance of *particular* institutions because of specific costs of enforcement and resistance' (2010: 5).

[10] Khan would probably retort that coral reefs do not have 'political' settlements because they do not have 'political institutions'. But this would be to concede the point. Political institutions are the intended and unintended product of individual and collective human agency and persist at least in part because some people (in a minimal sense) want them to.

protect themselves from almost certain death or incarceration. Such 'agreements' have the character of forced acquiescence. Moreover, the agreement may be maintained only thanks to the ongoing threat or application of violence by the stronger party on the weaker one.

If agreements can be imposed, then agreements among the most powerful groups may be compatible with substantial violence against or repression of other groups; they may also be compatible with considerable levels of 'tolerated' violence, for instance in the domestic or criminal sphere, which brings us to the second source of misunderstanding. Various commentators have pointed out that a settlement does not imply an end to conflict or violence or even necessarily a reduction in it. The level of violence in society per se is not a good indicator for whether or not there is a political settlement. Rather, a political settlement is associated with a reduction or aversion of a particular type of 'competitive' violence, that is, violence which is deliberately aimed at overthrowing the ruling coalition or its political institutions (Cheng, Goodhand, and Meehan 2018).

Complicating matters further, a political settlement may be said to exist even though some groups *are* engaging in competitive violence. For instance, most people would agree that the United Kingdom has a political settlement, despite sporadic acts of violence by Islamic and Irish terrorists. Because these groups do not seriously threaten existing governing arrangements, the settlement prevails. Indeed, an agreement among a country's most powerful groups may be compatible with quite virulent regional insurgencies, as in Northern Ireland in the 1970s, or Mindanao in the contemporary Philippines. It seems, then, that our intuitive understanding of a settlement relates not just to the type of violence, but also its level. If a settlement is being challenged, but is not really in imminent danger of collapse, we would probably want to say that a settlement exists.

Powerful groups

A second constitutive element of our political settlement concept is a set of powerful groups that agree to the settlement. We have already seen that these groups are unlikely to be identical to the groups that sign a peace agreement and may also be broader than the groups that are privy to an 'elite pact'. Rather, these will be groups that encompass both elites and non-elites, which have the power to make or unmake the settlement, yet which 'agree' to it in the sense of taking actions that are consistent with its core institutions and/or refraining from actions designed to overturn them, on a day-to-day basis. That might include groups that possess the constitutional authority to change the rules of the game (either directly, through law-making, or indirectly, as in a democracy, through voting); groups that possess considerable military or other violence capabilities; or groups that could bring about mass disruption or disorder of an economic or political kind. Groups that lack this ability, acting either singly or with others, are not parties to the settlement, even though they will doubtless be affected by it. To be sure, they may have 'agency' in a limited sphere, but they do not affect the struggles that shape the settlement. Insofar as they are appropriate objects for a PSA, they are interesting on account of their marginality.

A key claim of political settlements theory to date has been that the way powerful groups are configured or organized can help us explain why particular institutional reforms succeed in some countries and fail in others; or more ambitiously, why different societies take divergent development pathways. Most of this work has focused on what has been called the 'ruling coalition' and its strength relative to other coalitions, factions, or organized groups in the polity. In Chapter 4 we explain our approach to analysing the configuration of powerful groups, which builds on existing approaches at the same time as improving them.

Political and economic institutions

Third, these powerful groups must agree on something. Abstractly, this might be some kind of vision for society and the direction in which it is heading, even if that is only a very basic conception of sharing the spoils of peace. Some of ESID's work, for instance, has addressed the 'paradigmatic ideas' that are constitutive of settlements, a point we return to later (Lavers 2018). We note in passing that there is some affinity here with Thomas Piketty's definition of ideology, that is, 'a set of a priori plausible ideas and discourses surrounding how society should be structured' (Piketty 2020: 3).

More concretely, the groups must agree on a set of institutions that are likely to realize this vision. The institutions are likely to govern such matters as who gets to make the rules and how; who gets to run the government, how they acquire power, and what, if any, are the limitations on it; who gets to make policy and what is the broad, or sometimes very specific, thrust it will take.[11]

The institutions may be formal, embodied in constitutions, electoral systems, and other relevant pieces of legislation, or informal, as in norms, conventions, and traditions. Likely they will be a combination of both, and frequently, especially in the developing world, where formal institutions have either been bequeathed as a legacy of colonialism, imposed by international treaty, or superficially adopted for reasons of international respectability, the informal institutions will be out of step with the formal ones. Consequently, it is de facto institutions, the rules in actual

---

[11] Again, we note an affinity with Piketty, who argues that ideologies generally provide justifications for inequality, as manifested through the 'political regime', that is, the rules governing the borders of the political community, who can participate in politics in what way; and the 'property regime', that is, the rules describing the different possible forms of ownership (2020: 4).

use, supported by powerful groups on a daily basis, that help define a political settlement.

A minimally acceptable distribution of benefits

In most cases the institutions that are agreed on will not be regarded as an end in themselves—though this cannot be ruled out. Rather, they will be agreed on as a means to an end. Put differently, institutions will be expected to advance or protect the interests of powerful groups, whether those interests lie in the realm of spiritual belief, social status, or material benefit. Seen in this light, PSA closely aligns with the (re)conceptualization of institutions as distributional instruments rather than solely as pure coordination devices (Mahoney 2010; Mahoney and Thelen 2015). It is a mainstay of PSA that institutions that threaten the interests of powerful groups will be rejected, resisted, or overturned. Another key tenet is that where the configuration of power changes, newly empowered groups may mobilize to change institutions that will better serve their interests. In short, a political settlement will be relatively stable so long as its institutions are delivering to powerful groups a level of benefits that is minimally acceptable to them, where minimally acceptable means that they would rather accept the level of benefits on offer than incur the costs of violent mobilization to try and improve them.

The distributional role of institutions also provides insights into how political settlements are sustained over time. Drawing on Charles Tilly's (1998) seminal work on durable inequalities we suggest that one crucial mechanism is *exploitation*. The exploitation mechanism 'operates when powerful, connected people command resources from which they draw significantly increased returns by co-ordinating the effort of outsiders whom they exclude from the full value added by that effort' (10). Powerful groups thus remain invested in a political settlement because its institutions allow them to appropriate the efforts (i.e. labour) of outsiders. Yet, the reproduction of a political settlement is not limited to the benefits accruing from exploitation. As the case of Hutu peasants in post-conflict Rwanda illustrates, social groups might be exploited in economic terms, but still form part of the political settlement because political elites consider them a potential threat to the current political order and therefore cater to them in their policy decisions. In other words, and developed more thoroughly in Chapter 3, PSA casts the net wider than Tilly and puts the *disruptive potential* of groups at centre stage when explaining the reproduction of political settlements over time.

An important implication is that insider groups that theoretically have the capacity to change the settlement do not need to be perfectly happy with it. They may play games within the rules; they may try to break or bend them to their advantage if they think they can get away with it; they may engage in a vigorous attempt to change the rules if the configuration of power changes and they feel they have the upper hand. But so long as the configuration of power remains relatively stable, they will not engage in an all-out assault on the rules.

The situation for powerless groups outside the political settlement—perhaps women or ethnic minorities, or people with disabilities or the very poor—may be very different. While it is possible that they receive some spillover benefits from the settlement, it is quite probable that they will be not even minimally happy with the level they receive. They may be actively or passively trying to change the settlement, or they may be mired in despair. Whatever the case, they will be too organizationally weak, by definition, to seriously disrupt it. The presence of a political settlement, while arguably desirable insofar as it puts an end to cataclysmic violence, certainly does not imply that all the groups subsumed by it will be equitably treated.

The concept's distinctiveness

Now that we have a better idea of a political settlement's core attributes, we can reiterate what makes PSA distinctive, thereby answering the criticism of Moore, among others. The idea of a 'peace agreement' is, as we have seen, one of the key rivals to a political settlement, with which it is frequently confused. However, as we hope to have made clear, peace agreements are not always based on political settlements, in the sense that they can be struck by individuals who do not adequately represent the most powerful groups in society, which is one of the reasons they often come unstuck. More successful peace agreements tend to be based on political settlements, or try to embody political settlements, from which they are conceptually distinct. Moreover, political settlements are not always a product of formal peace agreements: they can be a product of tacit or informal understandings.

Another related concept is the idea of an 'elite pact'. Elite pacts are typically formal or informal deals struck between elites with the aim of averting conflict and institutionalizing a system of power or a transition thereto. The nature of an elite pact can certainly tell us a lot about the resulting political settlement. But as we have seen, political settlements are two-level games: elites must manage conflict among themselves but also manage conflict between themselves and non-elites. In some cases, non-elites or 'intermediate classes' can be very powerful and can shape the behaviour of elites in line with or beyond what they may have agreed with one another. As such, a political settlement is a broader concept than either a peace agreement or an elite pact. Because it encompasses relations between elites *and* broader groups, it seems better suited than either of these concepts to explain why elites might commit to one type of development policy or another, why they might implement those policies to varying degrees of success, and thus why they might preside over divergent development pathways.

A broader concept with some affinities to the idea of a political settlement is a social contract, as indicated in Di John and Putzel's (2009) influential discussion of the intellectual antecedents of PSA. Social contracts are agreements or mutual understandings, normally tacit, between state and society or state and citizens about the rights, entitlement, and mutual obligations of each; typically, they involve some conception of 'consent of the governed'.[12] Social contract theory gained influence within and beyond political philosophy at two distinct historical moments (Lessnoff 1990). Responding to the period of modern state formation within Western Europe during the seventeenth century, key thinkers such as Hobbes, Locke, and Rousseau set out different forms of social contract theory to help identify the legitimating grounds of political authority. The second moment, led by John Rawls during the second half of the twentieth century, also wrestles with the moral basis of rule and the conditions under which 'citizens' would agree to forego certain freedoms in exchange for the protection offered by centralized forms of government. However, Rawls extends social contract theory to include the legitimacy of *all* social and political institutions, arguing that people would only agree to subject themselves to political authority if certain conditions were in place to ensure their basic freedom and equality, including some form of social protection. It is this latter version of social contract theory that has proved attractive in some policy circles (Hickey 2011).[13]

There is, then, a strongly normative dimension to social contract theory and a sense in which it is firmly located within the particular historical experience of state formation in Western Europe and later debates around the welfare state. The normative dimension has attracted considerable critique from critics who perceive a failure within social contract theory to include a proper appreciation of the unequal relations of power that shape any such deals. For both Rousseau (1961) and later generations of Marxist thinkers, the moralizing language of 'contracts' enabled elites to dupe citizens into surrendering their liberties and institutionalizing inequalities through their control over institutions of power and of property rights in particular. Feminist theorists were quick to point out that social contracts are profoundly gendered, reflecting a sexual/social contract in which not only is the contracting individual male, but this is constructed through the active exclusion of women from the pact (Pateman 1988).

From one perspective, it might have been possible to mobilize political settlements analysis (PSA) and social contract theory within the same intellectual

---

[12] See, for example, https://www.britannica.com/topic/social-contract.

[13] See the European Development Report (2010), Human Development Report (2011) and recent work on this by the World Bank, e.g. Bussolo et al. (2018). Some of the intellectual work underpinning this emphasis on social contracts in development policy circles also operates under some of the same assumptions as proponents of PSA, identifying 'a central channel of causation, from underlying social, economic and political processes through social contracts and institutions to human development outcomes' (Walton, 2010: 38).

project, similar to the way in which North and colleagues envision the shift from 'limited' to 'open' access orders. However, there is a strong sense that any credible theory of how political rule *actually* emerges must take the issue of power as its starting point and should not be so clouded by normative assumptions that these become obscured or elided, especially ones which, rooted in Western philosophy, might not travel well to other parts of the globe. For this reason, we argue that PSA can offer a more grounded, realist, and also more broadly applicable theory of how political authority emerges and becomes wielded in practice than social contract theory.

A cognate concept is Thomas Piketty's recent idea of an 'inequality regime', on which we have already touched. An inequality regime is, 'a set of discourses and institutional arrangements intended to justify and structure the economic, social, and political inequalities of a given society' (2020: 2). The overlap with the idea of a political settlement is partial. Institutional arrangements form part of a po- litical settlement, and legitimating discourses may lie behind their 'agreements' around the structuring of power and distribution of benefits; but a political set- tlement is more than this, since it also focuses on the sociological composition and geometric configuration of powerful groups. In Piketty's work, the emphasis is on changing society through changing ideas. And while he is fully aware that inequality regimes actually change in the interplay and struggle of new constella- tions of ideas *and power*, power is not integral to his conceptual apparatus. Political settlements analysis, by tracking how the size, strength, and composition of power- ful groups changes over time, can help us understand how inequality regimes can sometimes be transformed. Yet it is also the case that Piketty's analysis focuses on the longue durée of history. His inequality regimes tend to span decades, centuries, and sometimes millennia. Political settlements analysis, by contrast, focuses on a 'meso-level' of change. It sits somewhere between epochal transformations and the quotidian processes that are the object of the Thinking and Working Politically (Thinking and Working Politically Community of Practice 2013) and Everyday Political Analysis approach (Hudson et al. 2016).

Another related concept is that of a 'political system'. A political system has been defined as a set of both formal and informal institutions, interactions, processes, pressures, and practices in a given unit of analysis by which collective and (theoret- ically) binding decisions are made for that unit (Leftwich 2004). As we have seen, political settlements typically involve agreements about certain institutions, pro- cesses, and practices, but only those that are critical to preventing the outbreak of intense and competitive violence or disorder. Consequently, a political settlement is a narrower concept than that of a political system and it directs our attention to specific features of a political system which it claims to be pivotal to social and eco- nomic outcomes, and, in particular, to the powerful groups that underpin them. Arguably, maintaining the institutions that sustain a modicum of peace is going to be more of a preoccupation for elites in new or fragile states than it is in better

established or more resilient ones. This provides another reason, then, for thinking that PSA is particularly well suited to development studies, since fragile and
conflict-affected states make up a significant proportion of the developing world.

Finally, we have the idea of a 'political order'. A political order can be defined
as a generalized system of political authority that serves to maintain comparative stability.[14] This, as hinted at by Laws and Khan, is perhaps the concept that
resembles most closely that of a political settlement. Indeed, the two terms are virtually synonymous. But political settlements' emphasis on 'agreement' arguably
steers our attention away from the general and towards the specific groups that
have to agree, and on what. A political settlement is, perhaps, the beating heart of
a political order. Table 2.1 summarizes the discussion.

Table 2.1 Related but analytically distinct concepts to political settlement

Concept	Definition	How a political settlement differs
Peace agreement	An official agreement among warring parties to end hostilities.	The institutional aspects of a political settlement can be included in a peace agreement and political settlements typically underpin or sustain successful peace agreements, which they may precede and/or succeed. But not all political settlements include peace agreements and not all peace agreements are based on a political settlement.
An elite bargain or pact	An agreement or understanding among elites, official or otherwise, that prescribes and or/proscribes certain forms of political behaviour, especially over a specific time period, e.g. 'until elections'.	A political settlement inevitably involves an elite bargain or pact but it also encompasses relations between elites and non-elites.

Continued

---

[14] Huntington argues that societies where there is political order are distinguished by the fact that
their governments govern, and that they are broadly legitimate with strong, adaptable and coherent
political institutions (Huntington 1968). Fukuyama, meanwhile, claims that 'the underlying rules by
which societies organize themselves' define a political order, of which there are three main components:
state, law, and mechanisms of accountability (Fukuyama 2014: 423).

Table 2.1 *Continued*

Concept	Definition	How a political settlement differs
A social contract	An agreement, normally tacit, between state and society or state and citizens about the mutual obligations of each.	A political settlement may or may not include a set of understandings about what a state should provide citizens and vice versa, but it is typically forged between a variety of elite and non-elite groups, not between 'state' and 'society'.
An inequality regime	A set of discourses and institutional arrangements intended to justify and structure the economic, social, and political inequalities of a given society.	Political settlements inevitably involve inequality regimes, but the political settlement concept lays more emphasis on the powerful groups that benefit from the inequality regime.
A political system	A set of both formal and informal institutions, interactions, processes, pressures, and practices in a given unit of analysis by which collective and (theoretically) binding decisions are made for that unit.	Again, a closely linked concept, albeit a broader one. Political settlements typically involve an agreement only about those aspects of a political system that are crucial to preventing intense, competitive violence. Further, PSA directs our attention to the groups that do the agreeing.
A political order	A generalized system of political authority that serves to maintain comparative stability.	The two terms are virtually synonymous, but political settlements' emphasis on 'agreement' steers our attention away from the general and towards the specific groups that have to agree and on what.

Source: Authors' own.

The concept's theoretical potential

Stated this way, our definition preserves the intuitive everyday association of a settlement with an agreement around a set of political arrangements with distributional consequences, thus conforming to Gerring's advice on sound concept formation. It is also extremely rich, and, following Goertz, loaded with causal prop-erties, in the sense that any of its dimensions could in principle be disaggregated and linked to hypothesized characteristics or effects. There is no 'right way' of dissecting these dimensions: it all depends on the questions one wants to answer.

For example, it would be perfectly possible to focus on the nature of the agree-ment that is struck between powerful groups. Does it matter if the agreement is formal or informal? Does it make a difference if it is internationally or domesti-cally brokered and/or monitored? Alternatively, one could focus on the nature of the institutions that are agreed to, whether formal or informal, and whether these, independently, have an impact on development outcomes. Similarly, one could ex-amine whether there is any relationship between the distribution of benefits and development outcomes.

More interesting, arguably, and the source of PSA's real potential, is to focus on the relationships among a political settlement's constitutive elements. Does the identity of the groups that agree to a settlement meaningfully affect the dis-tribution of benefits? Do institutions play a significant role in mediating this, and if so, how? How does the distribution of benefits impact political stability? How do all these elements working in tandem influence patterns of develop-ment? Which, if any of the constitutive elements co-vary? To provide an example, if women have the power to disrupt a political settlement, are they more likely to receive an equitable share of benefits? Does it matter to this whether power in the settlement is concentrated or dispersed? Does it matter whether politi-cal institutions are democratic or autocratic, personalized or impersonal? Are polities where women capture a proportionate share of benefits more politically stable?

To date, PSA's most distinctive contribution has been to help explain eco-nomic and social development by means of an analysis of the configuration of powerful groups in society. As mentioned in the previous chapter, Khan's typol-ogy of clientelist political settlements is the original and best-known example of this. Khan envisages the polity as a collection of organized groups or factions, more or less connected to each other through pyramidal patron-client networks. He then distinguishes between those factions that are aligned with the 'ruling coalition' and those that are excluded from it. The relative strength of the ruling coalition vis-à-vis excluded factions and its own internal factions has profound implications for the success or failure of different types of development policy or institutional reform, via the causal mechanisms of said coalition's time-horizon and implementation capability (Khan 2010).

While we have some minor differences with Khan's approach, our definition can accommodate it comfortably. It is merely one, ostensibly fruitful way, of concep-tually dissecting powerful groups. As we explain in more detail in the next chapter, we adopt an approach that draws heavily on Khan, maintaining his initial focus on three basic factional or coalitional blocs, yet which collapses the configuration of power onto a single typological dimension, describing a range of executive power from concentrated to dispersed. We then combine this with a more sociological approach, based on an analysis of those groups which a) have the potential to disrupt the settlement, and b) are co-opted by the ruling coalition. We call these groups the settlement's 'social foundation', and they can range from broad and deep at one demographic extreme to narrow and shallow at the other.

As we argue in more detail in Chapter 3, governing elites in broad settlements must craft policies that cater to broad and deep social constituencies if they are to survive, while elites in narrow settlements do not. Meanwhile, powerful groups in concentrated settlements have solved internal collective-action problems, allowing them to develop and implement policy efficiently, in contrast to groups in dispersed settlements for whom policymaking will incur higher side-payments and/or transaction costs. This has interesting implications for governing elites' desire and ability to produce the types of public goods associated with inclusive development. Other things being equal, broad-concentrated settlements are the most likely to deliver on this front and narrow-dispersed settlements the least, with broad-dispersed and narrow-concentrated settlements also producing characteristic outcomes.

The concept's theoretical limits

We should be clear at this point that we do not believe that the political settlement dimensions we have identified will explain every salient feature of a country's economic and political development.

Clearly, structural factors such as geography, demography, climate, existing factor endowments, and the like will influence a country's developmental trajectory. They are antecedent variables that partially explain why certain sorts of settlement arise in certain places and how they perform once institutionalized. A country's institutional inheritance will do the same. For example, elites in a country that has inherited a strong state tradition of impersonal administration and meritocratic administration might be more likely to agree to a settlement with a broad social foundation, since a country's leadership will feel more confident about incorporating a broader range of social groups if it knows it has a capable state to serve them. Conversely, of two countries with concentrated power and broad social foundations, we might expect one with an inherited tradition of strong statehood to perform better than one in which state capacity has to be built from scratch. The size, technological sophistication, and political independence of a country's domestic capitalist class might also be thought to strongly influence a country's development prospects, irrespective of settlement type (Whitfield et al. 2015, Khan 2010). The presence or absence of systemic threats, for example, of contentious politics from below or foreign invasion, are also likely to shape the level of elite commitment to development (Doner, Ritchie, and Slater 2005). Ideologies or what are sometimes called paradigmatic ideas may also exert an influence independent of the identity and configuration of powerful groups. Indeed, as Tom Lavers has argued, ideology or a set of shared ideas among factions may be a crucial part of the 'agreement' that establishes and sustains a settlement (Lavers 2018), while for Hazel Gray (2018, 9) 'political commitments to particular political ideologies are a potentially significant force that structures institutions but also the distribution of power', primarily by shaping how legitimate the claims of different groups are perceived to be.

We should also not expect a political settlement to strongly determine outcomes across all a country's policy domains.[15] Some policy domains may be relatively autonomous of the macro-level political settlement and be the source of considerable developmental progress or decline.

As we explain in Chapter 4, in addition to asking questions germane to the main political settlement dimensions mapped earlier, we ask a range of supplemental questions that can help us get a handle on antecedent and additional variables. These can be used as control variables in the process of linking political settlement types to development outcomes, as demonstrated in Chapter 7.

Illustrations of political settlements

By way of a conclusion, we sketch in the next few paragraphs some examples of the diverse ways in which political settlements come into being, namely, by 'revolution', 'conquest', 'secession', 'independence', 'coup/repression', 'democratic transition' and 'peace agreement'.

Settlement by revolution

Our first example comes from England, where a new political settlement was established in the years after 1688 thanks to a 'revolution' in which the Stuart King, Charles II, was overthrown by a Dutch invading force that had William of Orange as its figurehead. As touched on in the previous chapter, the social foundation for this revolution was an anti-Catholic coalition, prominent among whom were the new mercantile classes and landed gentry that had gained increasing wealth over the course of a century of Atlantic trade, not to mention a mass of lower-order Protestants fearful of Catholic dominance. Also included were established, yet non-Catholic, landed interests. The 'agreement' such as it existed, was around

---

[15] By a 'policy domain' we mean a meso-level social field of power relations within which actors promote competing agendas (Yanguas and Mitlin 2016).

preventing Catholics from holding the crown, while simultaneously limiting the powers of the monarch. However, there was much that the pro-William coalition, represented by both the Whig and Tory parties, disagreed on, including the precise extent of monarchical power. Over the subsequent decades, however, mercantile interests, associated mainly with the Whigs, gained the upper hand, introducing organizations and institutions that promoted their interests, such as a Bank of England and free trade; the power of the monarch grew ever more tenuous while the strength of Parliament increased concomitantly (Laws 2010, Pincus 2009). England and the United Kingdom have arguably had several more settlements since then, which can be identified by landmark changes in political institutions or economic policy, for example the 1832 Reform Act, suffrage for women in 1918, the 1945 post-war welfare state, or Mrs. Thatcher's post-1979 neo-liberal settlement. All, however, were, in comparison to 1688, relatively peaceful evolutions on an earlier theme.

Settlement by foreign conquest

In 1945 Japan and West Germany, by contrast, new political settlements were imposed on countries defeated in war. Liberal institutions were implanted by the Allied forces and staffed by a combination of more or less willing collaborators, protected by the continued presence of foreign troops. Ambitious programmes of transitional justice, economic aid, and social engineering provided additional legitimacy for liberal institutions, until the point at which they were delivering sufficient benefits to powerful groups, including industrialists and electoral constituencies, that they acquired their own legitimacy.

Settlement by secession

Bangladesh in 1972 provides a different route: settlement by secession. The story starts in 1947 when the territory now known as Bangladesh became East Pakistan after India's Muslim-majority states seceded from India in 1947. However, relations between East and West Pakistan were never smooth, and came under particular strain during the 1960s, when Pakistan's military government was pursuing a policy of rapid industrial development in a manner thought favourable to West Pakistan. Bangladesh declared its independence from Pakistan in 1971 and after a short war of secession, the Awami League's Sheikh Mujib Rahman became prime minister of the newly independent state, backed by a coalition of party cadres, youth and student movements, paramilitaries, and, more contingently, public sector trades unions and the Communist Party of Bangladesh, with a variety of groups on the left of Bangladeshi politics forming the opposition. Providing a tenuous unity to the ruling coalition was agreement over the desire to escape Pakistan, but its political and economic institutions soon came under strain. In response to political agitation from the left, Rahman introduced a one-party socialist state in 1975, but this was to prove short-lived. He was assassinated later that year and martial law was imposed. Ever since then, Bangladeshi political institutions have continued to exhibit considerable flux with periods of military rule, democratic competition, and de facto single-party autocracy. Although generalized civil war has been averted, for several periods the country is best described as 'semi-settled'.

Settlement by independence from a colonial power

Tanganyika is an example of a settlement that was created through independence from a colonial power. Following a period of largely peaceful nationalist protest and limited representative government, the former Trust Territory was granted independence from Britain in 1961. It was led by Julius Nyerere's Tanganyika African National Union (TANU), a coalition of teachers, civil servants, peasants, and workers, weakly opposed by some traditional chiefs and wealthier farmers, while contingently supported by Asian and European business, and the former colonial power. The Westminster Constitution bequeathed by Britain soon proved unsuitable to the new government, however, which had little tolerance for a formal political opposition when it regarded the eradication of poverty as a national emergency. There were rapid moves to create a Republic and then a one-party state. Then in 1964 the ruling coalition pre-empted another potential threat by becoming Tanzania, forming a union with the islands of Zanzibar which had recently undergone a socialist revolution. This was a precursor to a leftward shift in the country's settlement in 1967, a process which saw the ruling coalition's social foundation narrow, as TANU expelled 'kulaks' and loosened its ties to Britain and European and Asian business. Tanzania's ruling party, with the help of significant evolution in the political settlement, has presided over a remarkable degree of social peace, and remains in power to this day.

Settlement by coup/repression

Ghana in 1981 provides an example of a settlement by military coup and subsequent repression. In that year, Flight Lieutenant Jerry Rawlings deposed the democratically elected yet economically ineffectual Hilla Limann government in a military coup. It was the second coup Rawlings had staged: the first, in 1979, had deposed military leader Frederick Akuffo, Limann's predecessor. This time, Rawlings decided to govern himself, establishing a quasi-military, single-party ruling coalition, the social foundation for which comprised junior officers and other ranks of the military, leftist groups, women's groups, local anti-chief youth associations (People's Defence Committees), and his own Ewe ethnic loyalists. These groups, frequently resorting to intimidation and repression, were able to keep Rawlings's opponents: traditional chiefs, black-market traders, corrupt elites, political blocs of the previous era, and more liberal forces, such as the Ghana Bar Association, in check. Nevertheless, continued economic crisis threatened Rawlings's political ascendancy and in 1983–1984 he struck a deal with the International Monetary Fund (IMF), presaging a more liberal economic approach. Many of Rawlings's former leftist supporters abandoned the coalition, yet their departure was compensated for by the growing importance of cocoa farmers, clientelist business elites, and ethno-regional appointees from the Northern and Upper Regions, all of whom benefited from a mixture of more liberal policies and political patronage. Indeed, the comparative economic success of the government helped this configuration of powerful groups, political and economic institutions persist with only minor changes until 1992, whereupon Rawlings chose to civilianize his regime by holding multi-party elections, assisted post-1994 by the Inter-Party Advisory Committee, an informal body that helped broker elite buy-in for the electoral process.

Settlement by democratic transition

In 1948, with the electoral victory of the National Party, South Africa instituted a system of political and economic apartheid in which blacks and people of colour were denied the same rights as whites. Backed by most whites, business, the security services, and a cohort of African collaborators, this settlement persisted, leaning heavily on repression, until the 1980s when it came under severe challenge from a combination of international economic sanctions and uprisings in the townships. South Africa's white leaders began to contemplate a political transition. However, it was not until 1994 that a system of majority rule was instituted, following a protracted process of formal and informal elite bargaining, the background to which was a virtual civil war in parts of the country. Eventually, a settlement was reached under which blacks would be allowed to acquire political power in return for certain safeguards on white political and especially economic power. Nelson Mandela became the country's first black president, ruling under the political umbrella of the African National Congress (ANC) but with the contingent support of elite Afrikaners in the National Party and Zulu nationalists in the Inkatha Freedom Party (IFP) in a government of national unity, plus organized business. Although Afrikaners and the IFP subsequently left the government, the ANC alliance has narrowed, and violent crime persists at high levels, the party continues to govern under a formally democratic constitution, delivering modest levels of economic growth with a degree of black economic empowerment and poverty alleviation.

Despite a growing radical fringe associated with ANC outcast Julius Malema, it is clear that there is little appetite among the country's most powerful groups for a return to competitive violence.

Settlement by peace agreement

In 1979 in Cambodia, the Vietnamese-backed Kampuchea People's Revolutionary Party (KPRP) overthrew the murderous Khmer Rouge regime and took control of the country. However, civil war persisted, with the government subjected to ongoing challenge from remnants of the Khmer Rouge as well as forces loyal to former King Sihanouk. In 1991, however, the international community brokered a peace agreement among the warring parties and in 1992 the United Nations Transitional Authority came into effect, in which international peacekeepers provided security in the run-up to and conduct of elections. The election, held in 1993, saw Prince Ranariddh Sihanouk's Front uni national pour un Cambodge independant, neutre, pacifique et coopératif (FUNCINPEC) party secure a majority. However, through his control of the military and civil service, KPRP (now Cambodian People's Party (CPP)) leader Hun Sen was able to hold out for a power-sharing government. Both sides thus entered an uneasy settlement in which Ranariddh became prime minister and Hun Sen deputy prime minister, with parallel party hierarchies in control of each ministry. Despite this formal agreement, each side tried informally to outmanoeuvre the other, including courting support from the still-armed Khmer Rouge, which had disavowed the elections. As such, this case is probably best described, following Bell and Pospisil, as a 'formal political unsettlement' (Bell and Pospisil 2017). In 1997, CPP forces defeated FUNCINPEC in an armed struggle on the streets of Phnom Penh. Ranariddh was deposed, and although the CPP remained in a coalition with FUNCINPEC until 2008, Hun Sen clearly held the balance of power, presiding over a 'competitive autocratic' political system, with a social foundation of foreign donors, domestic and foreign business, and a sizeable proportion of peasants and workers. Since then Hun Sen's coalition has narrowed, moved closer to China, and become even more authoritarian. Nevertheless, it has delivered economic benefits to a sufficient number of groups, while effectively repressing others, to forestall a return to civil war.

*

These sketches point not only to the diverse routes through which political settlements can come into being, but also their tendency to evolve or change throughout time, as powerful groups join or abandon the ruling coalition, or as institutions adapt to political and economic opportunities and crises. This tendency, as we shall see in later chapters, creates challenges for measurement, as it is not always easy to be certain when one settlement begins and another ends. A related problem is how long must a settlement endure before we call it a settlement. We provide working solutions to these conundrums in Chapter 4.

Before doing so, however, we deepen our theoretical approach in Chapter 3, by linking political settlements to the resolution of collective-action problems that lie at the heart of economic and political development, and developing a typological theory that provides the basis for a number of hypotheses to be empirically tested in Chapters 6 and 7.

3

Collective-action Problems and Development

A Typological Theory of Political Settlements

Collective-action problems and development

As stated in Chapter 2, a political settlement is an ongoing agreement among a society's most powerful groups over a set of political and economic institutions expected to generate for them a minimally acceptable level of benefits, which thereby ends or prevents generalized civil war and/or political and economic disorder.[1] Such agreement may be informal, as in unwritten shared understandings, or formal, as in some sort of pact—usually an evolving mix of both. Either way, a political settlement reflects a mutual conception of broad methods for resolving disputes and allocating basic authority. Equivalently, political settlements reflect shared (tacit) understandings held among powerful groups to use politics rather than all-out warfare to settle their key disputes. Such understandings, operating as two-level games with both between- and within-group dynamics, underlie institutional evolution. The basic notion of a political settlement, reflecting the distribution of power and the composition of included and excluded groups, fundamentally shapes, circumscribes, and conditions—but does not determine—the creation, reform, maintenance, and demise of political and economic institutions that arise within its parameters. Political settlements establish the foundations of social order.

Accordingly, a political settlement signifies a relatively durable combination of power and institutions—informal and formal—that shape and constrain key political and economic outcomes within a society. These myriad interactions exhibit punctuation dynamics. Settlements and corresponding institutional systems typically persist over medium-term time-horizons, yielding path dependence in the sense that initial outcomes influence (but do not determine) subsequent

---

[1] The analysis presented here is an adaptation, with some minor differences, of that contained in Ferguson (2020).

Political Settlements and Development. Tim Kelsall et al., Oxford University Press.
© Tim Kelsall et al., (2022). DOI: 10.1093/oso/9780192848932.003.0003

developments.[2] Indeed, to become a sustainable medium-term equilibrium, a settlement's corresponding institutional system must deliver policies and (net) political and economic benefits in a manner that reflects and reproduces underlying distributions of power and, for given distributions, at least minimally meets important goals of powerful parties, by which we mean the powerful groups whose agreement underpins the settlement. To do this, a political settlement must foster—usually via a far more detailed set of prescriptions and procedures generated by corresponding institutional systems—the organizational and group dynamics that deliver necessary coordination and enforcement.[3]

In this chapter, we examine the developmental implications of political settlements and a set of corresponding collective-action problems for the intricately linked processes of economic and social development, political stability, and developing state capacity.

Generally speaking, development entails the steady enhancement of human capabilities across a society (Sen 1999). More specifically, economic and social development—broadly conceived—not only involves steady increases in per capita gross domestic product (GDP) with some degree of equity; it also involves widespread provision of public goods and services, including education, health care, and infrastructure, as well as the systematic removal of barriers to economic participation that arise from poverty, environmental degradation, and various forms of discrimination and institutional bias. Such provision, as already suggested, requires minimal political stability in the sense of limiting conflict via organized violence. Moreover, effective delivery of public goods, including many social benefits, requires some initial political development, in terms of state capacity, and at least a rudimentary rule of or by law.[4]

Collective-action problems, meanwhile, arise when the pursuit of individual inclinations and interests generates undesirable outcomes for some group. Relevant groups include nations, cities, communities, clubs, companies, non-profit organizations, religious organizations, colleagues, friends, and various combinations or subsets therein. Examples of collective-action problems range from global climate change and international conflict to deciding who makes the coffee at work, who

---

[2] Certain institutions exhibit longevity that far exceeds the duration of political settlements and social orders. Colonial-era British common law still influences American jurisprudence (Greif 2006), and legal code from the Roman Empire still influences legal practice in Spain, France, and other European countries.

[3] Institutions are informal and formal, mutually understood, behavioural prescriptions. Organizations are structured groupings that pursue some set of common goals in a more or less unified fashion, and structure arises from internal rules (mini institutions). In game-theoretic terms, institutions are rules and organizations are a type of player. Institutional systems are complementary combinations of institutions and organizations, for which the latter often provide the actual or potential enforcement that facilitates realization of institutional prescriptions.

[4] Following Fukuyama, *Rule of law*, implies 'a set of rules of behavior, reflecting a broad consensus within the society, that is binding on even the most powerful political actors in the society'. By contrast, in *Rule by law*, 'law represents commands issued by the ruler but is not binding on the ruler himself' (Fukuyama 2014: 24).

will cook or wash dishes; how to reduce crime, pollution, traffic jams or resolve disputes and control epidemics; and how to provide basic public services, such as parks, roads, adequate R&D, adequate education, and adequate health care.

There are two basic types of collective-action problem. *First-order* collective-action problems involve multiple manifestations of free riding and excess conflict related to providing public goods, reducing negative externalities, enhancing positive externalities, and limiting the use of common resources—all broadly defined. Human security and mechanisms for resolving disputes, for example, are public goods. Pollution, crime, and social conflict generate negative externalities. Research and health care generate positive externalities. Public goods and externalities lie at the heart of political and economic development.

Resolving first-order collective-action problems entails forging agreements or arrangements about distributing various associated costs (including effort and risk) and benefits (including status and position). Agreement alone, however, does not suffice. Will the involved parties actually deliver their promised behaviour? Cutting corners—or pure non-adherence, as in the flouting of all manner of agreed regulations—often requires less effort and cost than does honouring commitments. *Second-order* collective-action problems thus involve arranging requisite coordination across involved parties as well as means for enforcing explicit and implicit promises.[5] Absent some assurance of coordination and enforcement, why should affected parties even bother to negotiate resolutions to first-order collective-action problems?

Indeed, the underutilized concept of second-order collective-action problems underlies political economy. Functional economic and political agreements and contracts rely on credible promises, which, in turn, rely on establishing functional coordination and credible enforcement. Enforcement always involves power. Second-order collective-action problems therefore bridge economic and political dynamics, even at the micro-level of specific exchange contracts. Unfortunately, resolving second-order collective-action problems usually entails intricate processes of creating institutions and organizations that can offer incentives, information, and common expectations, which then facilitate and motivate honouring costly commitments.[6] Furthermore, many resolutions generate additional collective-action problems involving subsequent unequal distributions of power.

Consequently, the concept of collective-action problems offers both guidance and focus to PSA and, more broadly, to developmental inquiry. Collective-action

---

[5] A related concept of second-order collective-action problems, as problems of institution building, appears in Ostrom (1990). The present formulation appears in Ferguson (2013).

[6] One could say that second-order collective-action problems offer key microfoundations of political economy. Douglass North (1990), without using this terminology, makes a related statement, claiming that Ronald Coase failed to understand that problems of enforcement are the major source of transactions costs—indeed the major reason that complex development has eluded humanity for most of its history. See also Bowles and Gintis (1992) on contested exchange.

problems, for example, inform both the success and failure of markets as social mechanisms that allocate resources. Markets coordinate activity, discipline pricing behaviour, and pool information—resolving enormous collective-action problems related to achieving coordination and channelling competition. Yet, market processes also create first-order collective-action problems related to climate change, pollution, insufficient infrastructure, inadequate health care, depletion of common resources, resource conflict, and extreme inequality—as well as second-order collective-action problems of honouring myriad potential and actual contracts and agreements. The associated (transaction) costs may entirely preclude exchange (Akerlof 1970) or engender non-clearing markets signified, for example, by involuntary unemployment and unmet demand for credit (Bowles 1985, Stiglitz 1987). Thus, economic and political development requires resolving many such collective-action problems. Moreover, specific resolutions or failures both reflect and emerge from specific types of political settlements.

Indeed, the process of establishing a political settlement itself entails resolving formidable first- and second-order collective-action problems related to limiting organized violence. And, once established, any given political settlement poses a series of collective-action problems related to maintaining the settlement and achieving various forms of economic and political development.

Collective-action problems in the creation of political settlements

Political settlements address the most fundamental collective-action problem for a society—namely, how to restrain widespread, disruptive violence. As we show statistically in Chapter 7, without a political settlement, development either lags or simply does not occur, as exemplified by Syria between 2012 and 2018. Yet, the process of forging any political settlement presents its own set of formidable collective-action problems.

Establishing any type of political settlement involves ending widespread, disruptive violence, such as a civil war. This process requires offering armed, conflicting groups sufficient motivation to put down their arms and resolve disputes through a political process—often following cycles of atrocity and recrimination. Appendix B illustrates such problems with three simple two-player games; the first of which is a two-player prisoners' dilemma. Here is a verbal summary. At the outset, two armed rival groups engage in violent conflict. To establish a political settlement, they must resolve the first-order collective-action problem of negotiating (perhaps implicitly) an agreement, as well as the second-order collective-action problem of making it credible. Regarding the first, each coalition has two possible strategies: *Negotiate* or *Fight*. In the absence of enforceable norms or rules to limit violence, Fight always offers each party higher returns regardless of the other's choice (it is the dominant strategy). Hence, the dilemma. For the second-order collective-action problem, the strategies are *Honour* an agreement or *Cheat*.[7] Without incentives to deter cheating, Cheat offers higher returns: the second-order dilemma. Anticipating this second dilemma, the parties may not even bother to negotiate. Some form of institution building, often informal—as in the example from *The Godfather* in Chapter 2—thus underlies achieving a political settlement.

The relationships between institutions and political settlements merits some elaboration. Institutions are antecedents, components, and outcomes of political settlements.[8] More specifically, three points apply:

1. A political settlement builds on prior historical processes; it emerges from disruptive political contestation and concurrent and subsequent implicit or explicit bargaining among powerful parties (usually elites) from distinct social groups in a society. Acting as antecedents that specify key elements of pertinent social contexts, pre-existing institutions shape these interactions and condition multiple associated understandings. For example, after decades of struggle, when Nelson Mandela became the first president of non-apartheid South Africa, the new regime retained many pre-existing economic institutions, such as contract law and property rights over land.

2. As a common understanding of a broad behavioural prescription (use politics, not warfare), a political settlement constitutes a type of institution. Even when many associated understandings have not been explicitly negotiated and remain contested, a political settlement establishes a type of, often informal, 'constitutional rule' (Ostrom 2005) that specifies members of a community (those included in the political settlement) and at least rough boundaries for political contestation—specifically regarding exercises of violence. Furthermore, a political settlement establishes either the distribution of broad avenues of decision-making authority that affect dispute resolution and rough allocations of political and economic benefits—or at least an implicit understanding concerning how such allocation can be achieved via political contestation rather than violence.

3. The precise configuration of influence between institutions, institutional systems, and a political settlement depends on the level of analysis. As a foundation of social order, an established political settlement operates at a macro level. Its durability, however, depends on the degree to which such arrangements fit the goals of powerful parties on whose support it rests. Hence, at a macro level, political settlements are endogenous to (usually

---

[7] A parallel game that focuses on cognition might name the strategies *Trust* or *Suspect* the other party.

[8] This list and much of this chapter's discussion appears, with more elaboration, in Chapter 8 of Ferguson (2020).

long-term) political developments within the social environment. In contrast, at a micro or policy-domain level, a political settlement—as well as key institutions within a social order—is effectively exogenous: a political settlement establishes (quasi) parameters that set boundaries for interaction, within which less foundational institutions evolve in the process of establishing prescriptions and arenas for dynamic social interactions, a phenomenon we return to in Chapter 6.

Once established, many political settlements facilitate addressing multiple developmental collective-action problems over their duration. Even so, many create self-enforcing sub-optimal equilibria that exclude many parties, especially the poor, damage the environment, and lock in inefficient economic processes and exchanges, such as bribery. Accordingly, the precise configuration of a political settlement influences the prospects for various beneficial or detrimental outcomes, mediated by a set of related collective-action problems.

Towards a typology of political settlements

In this section, we present the new typology of political settlements we prefigured in Chapter 2.

Our theory ties development outcomes to the political imperatives of settlement creation and reproduction. This is based on an assumption that the political leadership of any settlement will be minded to pay special attention to those groups which, acting singly or jointly with others, are powerful in the sense of being able credibly to threaten to change or seriously disrupt the settlement. So, as Figure 3.1 depicts, we begin by distinguishing between those groups that are powerful (the long, horizontal rectangle) and those that are not. Of those that are, some may be repressed by the leadership (the right-hand, smaller rectangle) while others will be co-opted. There will also be groups subject to roughly equal amounts of co-optation and repression, which we call 'liminal'. *These co-opted and liminal 'insider' groups are what we call the settlement's social foundation* (the darker rectangle, bottom left). To reiterate, to be an insider and thus a part of the social foundation, a group must satisfy two criteria: a) it must be powerful in the sense that acting singly or jointly with others, it can credibly threaten to change or seriously disrupt the settlement, with its existing relations between powerful groups, political institutions, and distribution of benefits; and b) the dominant strategy by which the political leadership tries to incorporate it into the settlement must be co-optive.

By contrast, those that lack plausible disruptive potential are effectively powerless and are 'marginal' to the settlement (the vertical rectangle in the top right). They are 'outside' the political settlement, even if they might be politically aligned with insiders and get some spillover benefits from them. Marginal and repressed

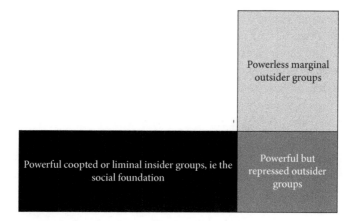

Fig. 3.1 Powerful and powerless, insider and outsider groups in
a settlement
Source: Authors' own

groups (long, vertical rectangle on the right) are both 'outsiders' and not part of
the social foundation. To reiterate, outsider groups must satisfy one or both of two
different criteria: a) they must be powerless, in the sense of not being able credibly
to threaten to change or disrupt the settlement, or b) the dominant strategy by
which the leadership tries to incorporate them under the settlement is repressive.

Depending on context, insider groups can form around party affiliation, ethnicity, race, religion, social class, ideology, labour, and other criteria. In some cases,
foreign diplomats or officials from powerful NGOs or foreign corporations may
also operate as insiders.[9] Groups can be co-opted in a variety of ways, ranging from
ideological overtures to clientelistic side-payments to programmatic economic
and social policies—whatever it takes to ward off active disruption.[10]

Like insider groups, outsider groups can also be based on ethnicity, religion,
gender, etc., but in the case of marginal groups, they are more likely to be organizationally inchoate, 'groups in themselves' rather than 'groups for themselves', to
borrow an old Marxist term. As we explain in Chapter 4, repression can also take
a variety of forms.

Outsider groups may or may not accept a political settlement but (at least initially) they do not successfully disrupt it because they lack the will, resources,
and/or organizational capability for doing so. Three possible relationships en-
sue: (i) during the stable phase of a punctuation cycle, outsiders remain excluded

---

[9] The inclusion of foreign officials/representatives in the social foundation allows PSA to incorporate
international, in addition to domestic, power dynamics.

[10] The substantial organizational collective-action problems that often accompany active disruption
often imply low costs of co-optation. Equivalently, resolving organizational collective-action problems
can create de facto power.

because they fail to attain the resources or resolve pertinent collective-action problems that would generate sufficient de facto power; (ii) an accumulation of power brings them into the political settlement—they become insiders; or (iii) they eventually attain and use sufficient power to undermine the settlement. Fearing the latter, insiders often devote resources to achieving acquiescence among excluded groups via some mix of overt repression, divide-and-conquer technique, and/or symbolic repression and co-optation, but the balance will be repressive.[11]

Our other new concept is the 'power configuration'. This term refers to the way in which power is organized, or its 'geometry'. *Concentrated power* signifies a coherent allocation of decision-making procedures and authority among insiders. This condition reflects some prior resolution of insider collective-action problems related to bridging social cleavages, resolving disputes, delegating broad authority, and achieving certain basic types of coordination. This can be achieved by means of consensus—contending groups sharing a basic vision and a more or less agreed means of resolving any differences—or force—the more powerful faction or factions are simply able to overpower the others, a difference we pick up at greater length in Chapter 4. Conversely, *dispersed power* signifies no such coherence, often reflecting active social cleavages among powerful groups that foment conflicts among insider factions, albeit conflicts that fall short of all-out civil war.[12] Here, scattered and uncoordinated authority ranges across various elites, organizations, coalitions, and other centres of power, such as regional governments, powerful firms, and local patronage networks, often with considerable subnational diversity.

Having established the basic dimensions of our new typological theory, Figure 3.2 represents it in matrix form, and also illustrates, in an admittedly exaggerated and stylized way—how the distribution and organization of powerful groups might look in these settlements. The typology provides a conceptual foundation for systematically analysing relationships between distinct types of political context, associated collective-action problems, and possible developmental outcomes. Each quadrant implies specific sets of developmental collective-action problems.

The vertical dimension, a settlement's social foundation, captures the demographic breadth and depth of the groups that are 'insiders' to the settlement. Where the settlement is broad and deep, a large percentage of the population is powerful and a target for co-optation. Where it is narrow and shallow, a large percentage of the population is either powerless or mainly repressed. For simplicity the ensuing discussion only uses the terms 'broad' and 'narrow'.

---

[11] The latter two reflect exercises of triadic power. See Basu (2000), Oleinik (2016), and Ferguson (2013 and 2020). We are aware that many groups are the target of both co-optation and repression. To be an outsider, the dominant strategy must be repression. For more details see Chapter 4 and Appendix G.
[12] See Easterly, Ritzan, and Woolcock (2006) on social cleavages.

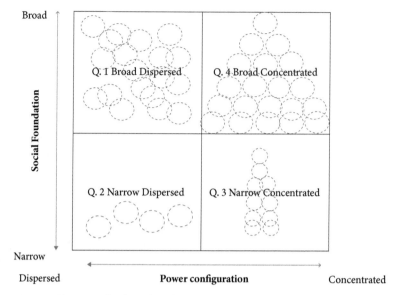

Fig. 3.2 Variants of political settlements
Source: Authors' own

There are four principal reasons for designating the social foundation as one of two underlying dimensions for this typology. First, as the name suggests, the social foundation characterizes a settlement's basis of support. Second, other things equal, exclusion can undermine the long-run viability of a political settlement because excluded groups may attain power in the future. Third, the breadth of a social foundation influences the leadership's incentives to distribute benefits to groups across the general population: the broader the social foundation, the greater the incentive for widespread distribution, primarily because a broad swathe of the population threatens the leadership's political or even physical survival. Fourth, the insider–outsider distinction informs the relationship between a political settlement and the use of violence. A settlement's mutual understanding to avoid violence for politics applies only to insiders. In fact, insiders often utilize violence and credible threats of violence to repress outsiders. Likewise, outsiders may use violence to dismantle political arrangements. If the political settlement holds, however, such violence is not sufficient to disrupt the social order. Thus, in a society like Columbia between the mid-1960s and 2015, one could argue that the nation as a whole had a political settlement, despite violent and unsuccessful efforts of the FARC (Fuerzas Armadas Revolucionarias de Colombia), and other guerilla armies who nominally represented excluded groups, to overthrow the regime.[13]

---

[13] For an insightful discussion of the Colombian civil war, see Steele (2017).

Figure 3.2's horizontal dimension captures the geometry of power. It illustrates the degree to which political settlement insiders have attained organizational coherence—ranging from a dispersed, incoherent configuration to a concentrated, coherent configuration of power, both internally and with respect to outsiders. There are four reasons for designating the configuration of power as a foundation of this typology. First, the extent of concentrated power influences (and reflects) a society's prospects for establishing a rough consensus on broad national purpose or creating or imposing a particular vision of national identity. For example, can members of succeeding ruling coalitions, which may represent different constituencies, roughly agree on the contours of state–market relations or those between the state and religion? Second, concentrated power implies that ruling coalitions can achieve broad policy objectives without resorting to continuous renegotiation among factions. Dispersed power implies the opposite. Accordingly, and third, the extent of power concentration influences prospects for resolving existing and future collective-action problems of policymaking and implementation. Fourth, the prior three points jointly imply that a society's position on this spectrum influences its prospects for building state capacity. Concentrated power facilitates state-building (and often reflects prior state-building).

As illustrated in Table 3.1, which combines data from the Polity 2 dataset with data from our own PolSett Dataset (see Chapter 4) and in Appendix D, concentrated power can exist in vastly different political regimes, ranging from a well-functioning parliamentary system with a rough consensus on national goals—like in Nehru's India or Mbeki's South Africa—to a one-party state, such as Mao's China.[14] Likewise, dispersed power can apply to incoherent democracies as well as disorganized autocracies. Indeed, one of the strengths of political settlements theory is to be able to transcend the democratic–autocratic dichotomy.

Combining both dimensions, Figure 3.2's four quadrants thus designate specific categories of political settlements. Each, moreover, implies a distinct set of collective-action problems that shape and constrain political and economic development.[15] Simply identifying key collective-action problems, even without specifying the likelihood of resolution, facilitates policy analysis because pertinent collective-action problems constitute a core contextual element that influences prospects for developmental success. Indeed, each quadrant implies specific trade-offs between political stability—notably restraining widespread violence—and various forms of economic and political development that—desirability notwithstanding—could undermine such stability. For example, the removal of

---

[14] 1930s Sweden or 1950s Germany would be industrial country examples of broad-concentrated democracies.

[15] The constraints from collective-action problems resemble *binding constraints* from Hausmann, Rodrik, and Velasco (2005) and the concept of collective-action problems can facilitate analysing precisely what is and is not binding.

Table 3.1 Exemplary cases of high power concentration in democracies and low power concentration in autocracies

Country	Leader	Period	Polity 2	Power concentration
High power concentration and democracy				
India	Nehru	1952–1963	9	0.69
South Africa	Mbeki	1997–2008	9	0.77
Ecuador	Febres Cordaro	1985–1988	8.25	0.78
Malaysia	Tunku Abdul Rahman	1964–1965	10	0.86
Sri Lanka	Jayewardene	1978–1983	6	0.88
Low power concentration and autocracy				
China	Chiang Kai-shek	1946–1949	−5.75	0.11
Kenya	Moi	1989–1992	−6	0.13
Rwanda	Habyarimana	1991–1993	−7	0.19
Haiti	Duvalier, Francois	1963–1964	−9	0.19
Syrian Arab Republic	Al-Hafiz	1963–1965	−7	0.24
Ghana	Acheampong	1972–1978	−6	0.24

Note: Autocracy-democracy index (polity2) ranging between −10 (total autocracy) and 10 (total democracy) from the Polity IV dataset; PolSett Power Concentration Index ranging from 0 (low) to 1 (high) (Schulz and Kelsall 2021a).
Source: Marshall et al (2019) and Schulz and Kelsall (2021c)

Libyan dictator Muammar Gaddafi, a development that many considered a step in the direction of democracy, has been followed by considerable political instability and violence. Currently, Libya has, at best, a tenuous political settlement, and developmental prospects appear remote.

Discussion now turns to the four quadrants, with attention to the following: specific implications of each combination of social foundation and configuration of power as well as initially achieved political development in terms of state capacity, a rule of law, and public accountability; inherent tensions; and implied developmental collective-action problems and related implications. Discussion begins with the two dispersed quadrants before proceeding to the two concentrated-power quadrants, which each offer two distinct developmental paths.

Political settlements with dispersed configurations of power

Figure 3.2's Q1 and Q2 exhibit dispersed configurations of power; Q1 with a broad social foundation, and Q2 with a narrow social foundation. In both cases, insiders have not resolved key collective-action problems related to allocating broad decision-making authority and establishing principal tenets of social or national purpose. Factionalized insider groups quarrel over broad policy objectives, such as state–market and state–religion relations. Insider factions thus face the prospect of continuous, often non-productive, negotiation over basic policies; they face high transactions costs to policy decision-making. Accordingly, governing factions often avoid certain topics or enact ambiguous, unenforceable, and/or symbolic measures. A general lack of direction on broad national goals, often with considerable regional and/or sectoral variation, follows. In such environments, tenuous ruling coalitions possess only limited ability to develop state capacity and the impersonal institutions that would foster a rule of law.

A general hypothesis fits the logic of these quadrants: with weak formal institutions and factionalized insider groups, fractious governing parties have limited ability to develop state capacity, but can achieve some coordination within clientelistic coalition or factional networks, with substantial regional variation, but the degree to which governments distribute benefits across groups depends on the breadth of the social foundation.

Furthermore, regimes operating with dispersed configurations of power often encounter somewhat distinct manifestations of what Philip Roessler (2011, 2017) calls the *civil war/coup trap*. The basic idea, detailed later, is that within a factionalized regime, one party may expel and usually repress another because it fears the other will stage a coup, but the act of expulsion creates conditions that could lead to a future civil war.[16] We provide a basic test of this idea in Chapter 7.

Broad social foundation with a dispersed configuration of power (Q1)

Societies operating within broad-dispersed settlements achieve limited political and economic development, we predict. They exhibit relatively weak state capacity and imperfect rule by or of law. Yet, these arrangements achieve some *substantive* public accountability,[17] related to distributing benefits across insider groups. Even the more economically successful variants will tend to encounter a middle-income trap (Eichengreen, Park, and Shin 2013). Here is the logic.

---

[16] For a game-theoretic model of a civil/war coup trap, see Appendix 8A in Ferguson (2020).

[17] Following Fukuyama, '[Substantive] accountability means that the government is responsive to the interests of the whole society' whether or not it is also subject to procedural accountability, i.e. free and fair multi-party elections (Fukuyama 2014: 24).

In this quadrant (Q1), the broad social foundation signifies that a large proportion of salient groups possess sufficient disruptive potential to merit inclusion. Even though the few excluded groups typically cannot threaten political stability, divisions among insider groups could do so. Consequently, maintaining the political settlement requires distributing rents and other benefits across insider-groups, though not necessarily with any degree of equity within or between them.

Note that there may be a preference for social policies that require little sacrifice on the part of the majority and which will be visible in the short term. Examples include expenditures on basic access to education and health care (e.g. via buildings) as opposed to more substantial capability-building investments in these and other areas, which usually require deferred consumption, and suffer from typical collective-action problems of free riding among insiders: Which groups sacrifice how much and who would enforce any agreement on provision? Instead, populist policies with extensive clientelism follow. Governing parties have limited potential to develop either fiscal or legal state capacity; and patron–client relationships condition economic and political exchanges more than impersonal rules can. Public bureaucracies often end up being highly politicized, at least in the upper echelons of the administrative hierarchy. Patron–client networks may selectively enforce property rights among their constituents. Corruption abounds. Responding to demands from powerful clients, governing officials violate formal rules to benefit themselves and their clients, and such behaviour is widely expected. A weak or less than perfect rule of/by law on both political and economic dimensions augments problems of low state capacity. In fact, the deployment of state capacity is often concentrated on public agencies that promise immediate returns or on containing social groups with disruptive potential (e.g. those in charge of coordinating and implementing health care, education, poverty-reduction initiatives).

Archetypal examples include Kofi Busia's Ghana between 1970 and 1971; Manmohan Singh's India between 2004 and 2013; Jakaya Kikwete's Tanzania between 2006 and 2015; and Yingluck Shinawatra's Thailand, 2012–2013. In Chapter 6 we provide a case study of Ghana, 2000–2018.

We mentioned earlier that dispersed political settlements tend to be vulnerable to a coup/civil war trap. The problem arises because coalition partners, all with some access to state and perhaps military power, distrust each other, and therefore experience temptations to mount a coup with a view to acquiring increased power vis-à-vis their rivals. Alternatively, distrusted rivals might be purged from the ruling coalition, narrowing the social foundation and increasing the risk of civil war. However, as we will find in Chapter 7, in the case of broad settlements, the risks appear to be lower. The mechanism is not clear but it might be that a broad social foundation enhances regime legitimacy, making coups riskier.

A general hypothesis, with four components, sums up the broad-dispersed logic. In broad-dispersed settlements, expect to find weak formal institutions, fragile coordination achieved via informal institutions tied to clientelistic distributions of rents across and within coalition and factional networks, with unequal between- and within-group distributions of immediate (short-term) benefits.

In terms of longer-term economic and social development, broad-dispersed political settlements thus face five collective-action problems:

1. Maintaining the broad social foundation, especially in cases with deep social cleavages;
2. Reducing reliance on patron–client relationships without undermining stability by antagonizing one or more potentially disruptive groups;
3. Extending accountability beyond short-term benefits and patronage to longer-term capacity building;
4. Enhancing insider unity by institutionalizing collective-choice rules for allocating authority, yet doing so in a manner that does not exclude current insider groups; and
5. Enhancing state capacity, often via a unified vision of national purpose.

Narrow social foundation with a dispersed configuration of power (Q2)

As in Q1, Q2's dispersed configuration of power yields factionalized insiders who lack clear direction. Because they have not resolved fundamental internal collective-action problems, insider elites must renegotiate even basic policy directives. In the absence of insider procedural and ideological coherence, governing factions possess limited ability to develop state capacity and equally dim prospects for achieving any kind of rule of law. Unlike in broad-dispersed settlements, however, the narrow-dispersed political settlement rests on a narrow social foundation. Any ruling coalition thus also encounters little pressure to distribute benefits broadly, and it operates without accountability to the many outsider groups. The combination of internal division with the prospect that one or more excluded groups could attain de facto power renders a narrow-dispersed political settlement the most fragile of the four quadrants, as we demonstrate in Chapter 7. Moreover, the fear that outsiders could attain de facto power often motivates—often disjointed, faction-specific—repression of excluded groups. Regarding economic and social development, narrow-dispersed societies encounter poverty traps (Bowles, Durlauf, and Hoff 2006).

Maintaining the political settlement involves the following tensions: factional conflict over rents and resources can undermine whatever minimal understandings and agreements exist. In order to gain relative power, factions may competitively recruit (i.e. co-opt) outsiders. Here, they face a prisoners' dilemma scenario:

each faction can benefit from such recruitment, but competitive recruitment enhances overall conflict, exacerbating power dispersion with potentially unstable extension of the social foundation and undermining political settlement stability.

A general hypothesis sums up narrow-dispersed logic: societies with a narrow-dispersed political settlement experience uncoordinated repression of excluded groups, along with patronage networks that operate separately within insider factions. A fragmented ruling coalition with an incoherent authority structure means that immediate political survival considerations dominate interactions between state leaders and the administrative apparatus. Clientelistic appointments of elite allies and the political use of the public bureaucracy for patronage is the order of the day, while administrative reforms tend to be conducted in a short-term and piecemeal fashion. These conditions inhibit economic and social development beyond a narrow provision of goods and services that elites use to maintain their lifestyles and power, often confining the country to a poverty trap.

More generally, societies with narrow-dispersed settlements face the following basic collective-action problems:

1. Achieving a concentrated power configuration among rival factions—a process that requires developing and implementing collective-choice rules;
2. Broadening the social foundation without dramatic contestation so as to evade a civil war/coup trap;
3. Reducing reliance on rents without undermining stability;
4. Creating some substantive accountability, initially via more inclusive and less conditional clientelism—again without undermining stability or further dispersing the configuration of power.

Narrow-dispersed settlements include J Morales's Guatemala, 2016–2018; Norodom Ranariddh's Cambodia, 1994–1997; Al-Bashir's Sudan, 2014–2018; and Ferdinand Marcos's Philippines, 1984–1985. In Chapter 6 we provide a more extended discussion of Guinea, 2000–2018.

Political settlements with concentrated configurations of power

Figure 3.2's Q3 and Q4 exhibit concentrated configurations of power; Q3 with a narrow social foundation, and Q4 with a broad social foundation. In both cases, concentrated power reflects some prior resolution of insider collective-action problems regarding allocations of basic decision-making authority and achieving some sort of basic social or national purpose, usually via prior institutional development and broadly accepted ideology and/or social identities. Consequently, these types of political settlements can achieve levels of state capacity and some-times an impersonal rule by law that eludes societies with dispersed-power configurations, a point we pick up in Chapter 7.

A core question follows: to what end will associated ruling coalitions use their state capacity? Will they direct such capacity towards long-term capability build-ing and institutional development, or towards short-term political gain, patronage, and repression of dissidents and outsiders? Accordingly, broad-concentrated and narrow-concentrated political settlements each possess two distinct developmen-tal paths: one that fosters further institutional construction with some rule by law, and one that does not.

Two general hypotheses fit the broad-concentrated and narrow-concentrated logic. (1) Much long-term developmental potential depends on the presence or absence of two factors that critically affect elite motivation to resolve collective-action problems: (i) a resource constraint (explained later), and (ii) a mutual perception of a compelling external or internal threat to their political survival. (2) The breadth of the social foundation influences the degree to which ruling coalitions distribute benefits, their substantive accountability, and the de-gree to which they address complex collective-action problems of establishing foundations for economic and social transformation.[18]

Discussion begins with the somewhat simpler case of Q3's narrow social foun-dation, before addressing Q4's possibly counterintuitive combination of a broad social foundation with concentrated configuration of power.

Narrow social foundation with a concentrated configuration of power (Q3)

In narrow-concentrated political settlements, ruling coalitions face little pressure to distribute benefits broadly. Rulers create and deploy state capacity primarily with an eye on accommodating their elite allies. Unlike in narrow-dispersed set-tlements, however, the few insider groups have largely resolved internal collective-action problems regarding allocations of basic decision-making authority and forging some sort of basic national purpose. They have some ability to build state capacity and sometimes institute a selective rule by law. Yet, they can also use repression effectively to maintain the exclusion of multiple outside groups. How then will a narrow-concentrated ruling coalition use state capacity?

Two distinct developmental paths follow. On the one hand, a *proto-developmental state* employs its often-limited state capacity to develop specific rule-by-law economic institutions that selectively enforce the property rights of

---

[18] On structural transformation, see Hausmann and Rodrik (2005); McMillan, Rodrik, and Verduzco-Gallo (2014); Sen and Tycee (2018).

certain regime supporters, along with selectively provided public goods (often effectively club goods). This arrangement can achieve some economic development, because such rights and public goods can foster some investment in productive capital. Examples include General Park's South Korea, 1961–1963; Apartheid South Africa, 1961–1975; Meles Zenawi's Ethiopia, 2005–2012; and in Chapter 6 we provide a case study of Hun Sen's post-1998 Cambodia. Narrow-concentrated settlements are also well equipped to impose sometimes disastrous visions of development on society, as in the case of China during the Cultural Revolution (1966–1976) or Pol Pot's Cambodia, 1976–1978. Because of the concentration of power at the top, leadership personality and ideology are likely to make a large difference to outcomes under this type.

Alternatively, a *predatory state* operates without either accountability or rule by law. A narrow ruling coalition uses available resources and capacity for its own benefit and to exclude outsiders. Governing parties use state capacity to seize assets and repress excluded groups. Examples include Mobutu Sese Seko's Zaire, 1979–1989; or Sani Abacha's Nigeria, 1994–1997.

The distinction between these two paths depends largely on the presence of two preconditions:

I. A *resource constraint*, meaning no easily available point-source resources;
II. A mutually understood and shared external or internal threat to the survival of the ruling coalition, and especially to the positions of elites within it.[19]

These preconditions critically influence the motivations of ruling coalitions, especially elites among them, to resolve a series of, often formidable, associated collective-action problems. A ruling coalition that faces a resource constraint must operate with limited sources of finance unless it can develop and utilize state fiscal capacity for relatively efficient taxation, and concurrently foster some economic growth. Precondition II implies a compelling need to generate revenue and bureaucratic and military capacity to ward off an external or internal threat. In combination, preconditions I and II can motivate ruling elites and constituencies to resolve many associated collective-action problems—that is, to make the often-substantial short-term sacrifices that permit building state fiscal and legal capacity and providing public goods, including selective protection of property rights, which can facilitate some economic growth. We observe this pattern in South Korea under General Park.

---

[19] A similar condition appears in Doner et al. (2005): the influence of an external threat on systemic vulnerability.

We note in passing that Mushtaq Khan has identified the political strength and technological sophistication of domestic capitalists as a crucial additional condition in determining the success of industrial development under this route (a condition that would likely also apply to broad-concentrated settlements). In Park's Korea, domestic capitalists were technically capable but politically weak, putting them at the service of the regime's industrial policy (Khan 2010). In Zenawi's Ethiopia, by contrast, domestic capitalists have been domestically weak, but less technologically sophisticated. Irrespective of the fact that the Ethiopian development state appears to have been derailed by a change of settlement post-Meles, the path to industrial development was always likely to be harder there.

In contrast, without a resource constraint, a ruling cabal can fund its own activities and survival—often by repressing excluded groups—with revenue from point-source resources, available commodity exports, and/or sufficient and enduring foreign aid. Absent a compelling and mutually understood external or internal threat, a ruling coalition need not develop state capacity beyond an ability to seize assets, extract resources, or placate foreign providers, and repress external groups.[20] Such cases often lead to a kleptocracy with dim prospects for growth. As mentioned, Mobutu's Zaire and Abacha's Nigeria are archetypal examples.

Their differences notwithstanding, both paths exhibit a set of tensions related to maintaining the narrow social foundation's exclusion, along with sharp trade-offs between often-tenuous political stability and various forms of political and economic development. For example, economic growth in certain areas may distribute resources to initially excluded groups, who might then achieve de facto power and challenge a regime, possibly violently, triggering an even more repressive response. If the leadership chooses to broaden the social foundation, converting repression of excluded groups to co-optation or some other mechanism for addressing deep outsider grievances, an additional challenge may follow. To wit, how to do this without empowering those groups to overthrow and potentially punish insider elites. Even if insiders can pull off such broadening, these variants of narrow-concentrated settlements still face the problem of how to broaden the social foundation without weakening economic discipline and reducing growth.

As we will see in Chapter 6, this is a conundrum that has beset Cambodia over the past decade, as economic growth and education empowered students, garment workers, and parts of the rural population to challenge Hun Sen's autocratic regime in elections in 2013. After successfully quelling the crisis, the government has made some attempts to reform the bureaucracy so as to be able to more effectively supply public goods, especially in education. Yet it has also ramped up repression.

---

[20] For simplicity, discussion here avoids cases where only precondition I or II applies. A proto-developmental state, however, usually requires both. Chapter 9 of Ferguson (2020) develops a game-theoretic model that generates this hypothesis by linking credible economic commitments to preconditions I and II.

Zine Al-Abidine Ben Ali's narrow-concentrated Tunisian regime was less success-ful. It had also overseen considerable economic growth before the government was overthrown in 2011's Arab Spring. On the more predatory side, Bashar al-Assad's narrow-concentrated Syrian regime had experienced a decade of lacklustre growth before reacting forcefully to initially peaceful attempts at regime change, triggering settlement breakdown and protracted civil war.

Two general hypotheses sum up the narrow-concentrated logic:

- Concentrated power facilitates building state capacity and a potential for eco-nomic development with structural transformation, but only in the presence of a resource constraint or a shared perception of a compelling threat to elite power. Otherwise, the state will likely use its resources to repress outsiders.
- In either case, with a narrow social foundation, economic and social benefits will be largely exclusionary, even if positive externalities and trickle down are possible.

Societies with narrow-concentrated political settlements face the following collective-action problem: Broadening the social foundation, that is, convert-ing repression of excluded groups to co-optation or some other mechanism for addressing deep outsider grievances—without fostering a coup or otherwise destroying the settlement.

Broad social foundation with a concentrated configuration of power (Q4)

Finally, societies with broad-concentrated settlements encounter the most promis-ing developmental prospects, in terms of inclusivity—though, again with two possible developmental paths, each of which implies a series of collective-action problems. As in broad-dispersed settlements, the broad social foundation creates pressure for widespread distribution of benefits. Moreover, having resolved a set of internal collective-action problems concerning broad goals and allocations of au-thority, broad-concentrated ruling coalitions can use their ensuing concentrated power to build state capacity and possibly develop substantive formal economic and political institutions, yielding a potentially sophisticated rule by law. It bears emphasis, however, that insider governing coalitions can utilize organizationally competent administrative machinery to either construct inclusive public services that reach beyond the narrow confines of their coalition as they endeavour to engender wider political loyalty across society, or to take on excluded organized groups through outright repression.

Moreover, broad-concentrated societies face a potentially delicate balance related to simultaneously retaining a broad social foundation and concentrated power. Indeed, this combination may seem counterintuitive. Unifying decision-making and national purpose, across insider groups whose perceptions and interests may differ, implies a formidable set of collective-action problems related to bridging social cleavages. The establishment of a broad-concentrated political settlement, therefore, reflects some resolution—a prospect that usually, though not always, arises in the presence of at least one of two conditions:

1. Substantial previous institutional development;
2. A compelling, shared sense of vulnerability held among insider elites, or a strong national identity, that encourages setting aside short-term interests in favour of functional unity.

In Chapter 5, we will discuss how South Africa was able to maintain a broad-concentrated settlement between 1994 and 2009, thanks in part to prior establishment of a strong bureaucracy and rule-of-law institutions. In Chapter 6, meanwhile, we examine post-genocide Rwanda as a case of national elite unity founded on a shared sense of vulnerability.

As in Q3, regimes operating within broad-concentrated settlements encounter two distinct developmental paths, but Q4's broad social foundation motivates greater substantive accountability along both. First, a *potential developmental state* focuses its considerable state capacity on building economic institutions, which can generate growth and broadly distribute benefits. In addition to the Rwandese example, Malaysia between 1964 and 1981, and Deng Xiaoping's China between 1979 and 1988, fit the type. Second, a *patronage state* such as Zambia between 1973 and 1991, utilizes available resources to distribute short-term benefits across its social foundation, in return for political support, but does not engage in substantial institutional development or structural transformation. These different pathways likely reflect differences in the underlying conditions I and II that influence the motivation of ruling elites to undertake the short-term sacrifices needed to resolve the formidable, especially second-order, collective-action problems that typically inhibit the formation of a functional developmental state.

Returning to Q4's overall picture, both paths face two core tensions, but to distinctly different degrees. These are: i) maintaining the unity that facilitates concentrated power, given the diverse interests among the many groups with disruptive potential—more difficult for the relatively unmotivated patronage approach; and ii) maintaining the broad social foundation, given diverse interests and the presence of concentrated power, which an emerging faction might use to exclude rivals—as in cases of a feared coup. The unravelling of resolutions to (especially second-order) insider collective-action problems could, even in broad-concentrated settlements, generate a civil war/coup trap that would move a society towards Q2.

A general hypothesis sums up the broad-concentrated logic: a broad social foundation motivates some substantive accountability with broad distribution of social benefits. The concentrated configuration of power facilitates building state capacity; but whether ruling coalitions utilize such capacity for long-term structural transformation and institution building—along the potential-developmental state path—or for distributing short-term benefits—along the patronage state path—largely depends on the simultaneous presence of a resource constraint and a shared perception among powerful insiders concerning a significant external or internal threat to their political survival.

Societies with broad-concentrated political settlements, especially patronage states, thus face the following collective-action problems:

1. Motivating elites and powerful organizations to sacrifice short-term benefits in order to provide capability-enhancing public goods.
2. Reducing patronage, without undermining functionality or antagonizing potentially disruptive groups.

Meanwhile, given the wide distribution of disruptive power in society, broad-concentrated settlements face a significant threat of political instability if leaders fail, for one reason or another, to deliver sufficient benefits to the population. This problem may be especially acute in those cases where procedural democracy does not provide an outlet for peaceful regime change.

Conclusion

The concept of political settlements offers a foundation for analysing relationships between distributions of power, institutions, collective-action problems, and developmental prospects. Figure 3.2's typology of political settlements, which classifies them in terms of their social foundations and configurations of power, facilitates systematic analysis into settlement-specific tensions and developmental collective-action problems. Table 3.2 summarizes these relationships by indicating the four basic quadrants, distinct developmental paths for each of the concentrated-power quadrants; and for each classification, key attributes, tensions, and associated developmental collective-action problems. These features constitute principal elements of political/economic contexts that shape a society's prospects for development, by pointing to pertinent constraints and possibilities. This approach facilitates interpreting specific environments and their developmental barriers, outcomes, and possibilities.

Table 3.2 A summary of political settlement types, characteristics, and key collective-action challenges

PS type	Hypothesized characteristics	Key collective-action challenges
Q1: Broad-dispersed	• Governing elite largely failed to resolve internal collective-action problems; • Broad but unequal distributions of immediate benefits across and within incohesive clientelistic networks; • Some substantive accountability, but weak state capability; • Weak to moderate performance on economic development; • Moderate performance on social development; • Social inclusion makes civil war/coup threat comparatively low	◦ Concentrating authority without resorting to repression/social foundation narrowing; ◦ Moving beyond short-term patronage to long-term policy planning and state capability enhancement; ◦ Reducing clientelism without undermining political stability.
Q2: Narrow-dispersed	• Governing elite has largely failed to resolve internal collective-action problems; • High levels of corruption and dysfunctionality; • Poor performance on economic and social development; • Serious coup threat due to elite disunity and generally poor performance; civil war threat if excluded elites can arm themselves.	As above, plus: ◦ Maintaining peace and stability generally; ◦ Concentrating authority without triggering a coup by potentially marginalized elites; ◦ Broadening the social foundation without triggering increased repression by fearful insider groups.
Q3: Narrow-concentrated	• Governing elite has largely resolved internal collective-action problems via either force or consensus; • Some potential for building state capability, more likely to be deployed for exclusionary forms of economic development; • Potential for rapid economic development with some potential spillover to social performance; • In the absence of a resource constraint or shared threat perception, kleptocracy is the most likely result; • Civil war threat if excluded groups can arm themselves.	◦ Broadening the social foundation without undermining elite unity, triggering increased unproductive rent-seeking, repression and/or civil war; ◦ In predatory variants, increasing elite commitment to development of any kind; ◦ In proto-developmental variants, increasing elite commitment to social development; avoiding policy disasters made more likely by weak societal feedback mechanisms;

Continued

Table 3.2 *Continued*

PS type	Hypothesized characteristics	Key collective-action challenges
Q4: Broad-concentrated	• Governing elites have largely solved internal collective-action problems; • Potential for building state capability for development; • Broad social foundation incentivizes elites to distribute benefits widely; • In face of resource constraint this is likely to lead to a potential developmental state, with strong economic and social performance, provided policies are good; • In cases of resource abundance, a stable patronage state may result, with moderate to strong social performance but erratic economic performance; • Chance that broad social foundation will give birth to violent conflict if not provided democratic outlet.	° Maintaining concentrated authority in the face of a broad range of powerful groups, especially in procedural democracies; ° In less democratic variants, maintaining autocracy without provoking violent contestation, or increasing democracy without undermining concentrated authority; ° Ending the exclusion of any marginalized groups without weakening the settlement; ° In proto-developmental variants, avoiding policy blind spots/mistakes; ° In patronage variants, injecting a developmental impetus.

Source: Adapted from (with modification) Ferguson 2020, Appendix 8B, Table 8B.1, pp332–333.

Because political settlements underlie configurations of institutions and ulti-mately social orders, effective policy approaches need to account for context-specific distinctions implied by broad vs. narrow social foundations and dispersed vs. concentrated configurations of power, the corresponding categories of political settlements, distinct developmental paths within the concentrated-power quad-rants, and the presence or absence of resource constraints and compelling internal or external threats to elite political survival. Put differently, the basic ways in which powerful groups succeed or fail to resolve their second-order collective-action problems, has a powerful bearing on how development practitioners should tackle first-order collective-action problems, such as the supply of public goods and the preservation of the commons. Developmental policy analysis should then consider underlying tensions within each designated category and the specific collective-action problems that accompany it, as a lens for examining the prospects and pitfalls of potential developmental remedies. Such analysis should permit policy-makers to make 'first bets' on reform approaches, that is options most likely, but far from guaranteed, to succeed, given the current configuration of power and reform path of least resistance. This 'working with the grain' approach (Levy 2014) is arguably most likely to maximize aid effectiveness. But even if reformers are intent on working against the grain, PSA can help them situate themselves in a politi-cal context and field of power, seeing the interstices and opportunities for action. We discuss the implications for policymakers and reformers at greater length in Chapter 8.[21]

---

[21] The approach to collective-action and political settlements presented here also offers a foundation for designing more detailed models that could amplify particular components, such as vertical power dimensions within insider coalitions which could amplify the analysis of specific contexts and imply additional testable hypotheses.

PART II
MEASUREMENT AND TESTING

In Part Two we explain and illustrate how to operationalize our new approach and test it against some hypotheses about the relationship between political settlements and economic and social development.

4

Measuring Political Settlements

Constructing the PolSett Dataset

The last chapter spelled out our new typological theory of political settlements and provided a set of associated characteristics and hypotheses. In this chapter we show how we can begin to test and refine these hypotheses. We do so by describing the construction of ESID's PolSett Dataset,[1] then move on to explain how we operationalized our key power configuration and social foundation variables, before providing a preliminary mapping of political settlements. Note that in the interests of putting PSA on a sounder scientific footing, parts of this chapter are quite specialized. While general readers may wish to skim some of the more technical details, the chapter as whole is important to an understanding of our later findings.

As we have seen, political settlements comprise agreements, institutions, a distribution of benefits, and a configuration of powerful groups. Numerous databases exist that provide various indicators for the first three of these dimensions. However, it is by providing a framework for analysing the configuration of powerful groups that PSA's greatest claims to distinction lie, and for this there are no good databases. Hence, the need to create the Political Settlements (PolSett) Dataset (PSD).

To appreciate the composition and geometry of a society's more and less powerful groups, an in-depth knowledge of its political history is required. For this reason, we chose an expert survey as our approach to capturing data. For each country, three to four experts in its political economy and/or political history were identified through personal networks or web searches and invited to participate in our survey. We surveyed a total of forty-two countries in the Global South, shaded darker in Figure 4.1. Limited in the number of experts we could pay[2] and thus countries we could code, we selected only countries that were coastal, that in the 1960s had predominantly rural populations above 5 million, with an agricultural sector that contributed at least 10 per cent of GDP and a GDP per capita (in 2010 constant US dollars (USD)) less than USD3,500. In this way, the dataset allows

---

[1] For the dataset, codebook and illustrative paper, see Schulz and Kelsall (2021a, 2021b, 2021c).
[2] Given the considerable time invested in the survey, coders were compensated with a small honorarium.

Political Settlements and Development. Tim Kelsall et al., Oxford University Press.
© Tim Kelsall et al., (2022). DOI: 10.1093/oso/9780192848932.003.0004

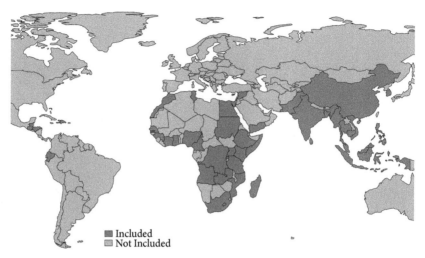

Fig. 4.1 Surveyed countries
Source: Authors' own

the users to study the covariation of political settlement variables with development and other outcomes while already holding some variables fairly constant by construction. There is a slight caveat to this: the dataset also includes an additional handful of countries that did not meet the selection criteria but which were particularly important to the ESID research programme. These were Rwanda, Zambia, Uganda, Ethiopia, and South Africa.[3]

Readers will readily appreciate that the ineffable nature of political settlements means that many of our codings are based on expert coders' educated guesstimates or 'judgement calls'. We also recognized that it was perhaps a tall order to expect coders to have detailed knowledge of all of the granular and sometimes difficult-to-discern phenomena across all the political periods we asked about. Consequently and herein following other large-scale expert-survey designs (e.g. Coppedge et al. 2019), for each question coders were asked to record their degree of confidence in their answer. While not a fail-safe method for eliminating error and bias, we felt this provided some indication of where the evidence was stronger or weaker, and a safeguard against making exaggerated claims for our data. Moreover, we could employ these confidence ratings as weights during the aggregation of our country-coder-period scores to single country-period scores.[4]

---

[3] Please note that our core findings from the regression analysis in Chapter 7 are robust to excluding these countries.
[4] Note that we weighted country-expert codings lower the less confident they were with their assessment, and lower the more distant their coding was from the simple-average coding of all country-experts.

These caveats noted, the survey nevertheless generated a wealth of data on the internal structuring of political settlements within and across countries. As we explain in more detail later, building on the Khanian approach of dividing society into three basic blocs or groups, we found out about the size and strength of the blocs relative to one another, their sociological composition, their internal cohesion, the relationship between leaders and followers, whether their agreement to the settlement was secured primarily through co-optation or coercion, and the distribution of material benefits both between and within them. While it is important to acknowledge the limitations of the data, we are confident that this represents a significant advance over previous political settlement approaches which have taken a less systematic approach to evidence and sometimes sought to secrete de facto quantitative judgements about the size and relative strength of different political groups under the guise of a qualitative methodology. In the following, we will delve deeper into how specifically the survey and our key variables of interest were constructed.

Creation and classification of political periods

The expert survey itself was conducted in two phases. To explore the developmental impact of different types of political settlement over time, it was first necessary to divide country histories into different political 'periods' in **Phase 1**. To do this, we took the view that a political settlement could be said to have changed or evolved when there was a major change either in the degree of agreement around the settlement, in the configuration of power, or in political and economic institutions. Our approach was to provide an initial periodization based on various databases and web resources, before asking our coders to corroborate this (more detail can be found in the PolSett Codebook) (Schulz and Kelsall 2021a). To be clear, we do not comment on whether each period represents a change or merely an evolution in the settlement, as the criteria for determining this are fiendishly difficult to specify. What we can, *ex post*, say with confidence, is when a political settlement crosses from one *type* to another.

Because we were only interested in a detailed understanding of countries *with* a political settlement, we then classified the periods according to whether the country did or didn't have one. If a political settlement is a conflict-ending agreement among powerful groups over the basic rules of the political and economic game, it should be indicated by a certain type and level of peace, that is to say, an absence of all-out civil war or disorder. However, we needed to add certain caveats to that.

Firstly, as discussed in Chapters 2 and 3, agreements among the most powerful groups may be compatible with substantial violence against or repression of less powerful groups; they may also be compatible with considerable levels of 'tolerated' violence, for instance in the domestic or criminal sphere. Further, a political settlement may exist even though there are some less powerful groups engaging in competitive violence. Somehow, we needed to find an indicator for a civil war that is so serious that is signifies a lack of agreement among the country's most powerful groups over prevailing political and economic institutions. Our solution was to devise three main categories: 'settled', 'unsettled', and 'challenged'.[5] To this we added a fourth category: 'transitional', which we used to denote periods in which there is a formalized transition from one set of institutional arrangements to another, for example from apartheid to majority rule in South Africa in the 1990s, or from autocracy to democracy in Spain after the death of General Franco. Our codebook explains the precise empirical thresholds and cut-off points we applied.

Dividing country histories in different periods in this way would make it possible for us to test the basic hypothesis that a settlement is necessary for economic and social development, which we do in Chapter 7. It would also allow us to assess any economic and social impacts of having a political settlement that was 'challenged'.

Many countries in their history will have periods in which they adopt a new leader or new set of institutions only for them to be replaced after just a short period, despite there being neither a war nor a generalized state of disorder. In a few countries such periods are the norm. We adopted a working assumption that such changes indicated a lack of basic agreement among powerful groups over who should lead and/or the rules of the political game. Consequently, we coded any periods which saw a new leader, major institutional change, or serious escalation in violence/disorder less than two years after they came into being as 'semi-settled'. Unsettled and semi-settled periods were not coded.

Structure of the main survey questionnaire

Having established when countries had a political settlement, in **Phase 2** of the survey we asked experts to characterize them in more detail via a set of twenty-eight mostly close-ended questions. Implemented using the Qualtrics online software, the survey took experts a full day of work to complete on average and resulted in a total of 103 raw variables. The reason we have significantly more variables than questions is primarily due to our decision to have experts answer half of our questions for three distinct political blocs. As stated previously, political settlements' major claim to date in making a distinctive contribution to politics and

---

[5] Note that this category, especially when it follows an externally brokered peace agreement, may have a substantial overlap with Bell and Pospisil's (2017) idea of a 'formalised political unsettlement'. Normally, this takes the form of an internationally backed peace agreement which has been formally signed by at least some of the most powerful actors, but which they are constantly trying to change to their advantage, including through the use of violence.

development studies rests on the way it dissects these groups in a way that goes beyond conventional regime theory and other approaches in political science.

Previous work in the field, notably Khan (2010), has revolved around the strength of the ruling coalition, relative either to oppositional groups in general, or to its own 'lower level factions'. While intuitively attractive, a key problem with this approach is the lack of a clear definition of 'the ruling coalition' (see Appendix A). We wanted an approach that would allow us to test the hypotheses at the heart of the Khan approach, plus our own, while avoiding its definitional ambiguities.

Our solution was to divide the polity initially into three blocs:[6]

- **The leader's bloc (LB)**: That is, the segment of the population whose political loyalty the current de facto leader can be reasonably assured of, at least in the short-term (by political loyalty, we mean a determination to defend the leader against challenges and/or to not defect from or make serious political trouble for him/her, where serious political trouble refers to deliberate actions that might directly or indirectly threaten the leader's political survival);
- **The contingently loyal bloc (CLB)**: The segment of the population that is currently aligned with the de facto leader (and therefore has some representation in government) but whose political loyalty s/he cannot be assured of (in other words, there is a *realistic* possibility that it could defect from the leader and/or make serious political trouble for him/her); and
- **The opposition bloc (OB)**: The segment of the population that is not currently aligned with the LB or the CLB and does not feel represented by government. Note that this will include both members of the official and outlawed political opposition, including those in exile. For convenience, it is also where we place individuals who have no political alignment, no interest in politics, and no prospect of being mobilized into politics.

The ruling coalition, then, would comprise those members of the LB and the CLB that 'control political authority and state power', but not the OB. As in Khan, this solution maintains the idea of a ruling coalition that, in addition to facing external opposition, may be internally fractured. However, unlike in Khan, our solution admits of the possibility that the ruling coalition itself may be both horizontally (in terms of rival elites) and vertically (in terms of elites vs non-elites) fractured (cf. Whitfield et al. 2015).

This bloc-based structure is the basis for all indicators used to construct our two key independent variables: the power concentration index (PCI) and the social foundation size (SFS) index. In the next sections we elaborate in

---

[6] Note that these are 'etic' analytical categories that may or may not correspond to empirically self-conscious entities with a unity of purpose. Later questions were designed to establish whether the blocs had the ability to act 'for themselves'.

more detail how they and their sub-components were operationalized. More detail on these indices can also be found in the dataset's codebook (Schulz and Kelsall 2021a), included online in the supplementary material. The dataset's respective variable names are written in brackets and/or italics in the subsequent description.

Power concentration index

As illustrated in Figure 4.2, the PCI is the aggregate of two sub-indices—corresponding to Khan's vertical and horizontal power indices—which themselves were derived from five indicators. The simpler of the two is the **horizontal power index** (*x_horizontalpower*). As described earlier, the horizontal power dimension in Khan's political power configuration refers to the ruling coalition's holding power vis-à-vis the opposition. To approach this measure, Q2 of our survey asked: 'Given the repressive capabilities of the LB, please estimate how powerful each bloc would likely have appeared to the Leader to be':

a. **Extremely powerful:** it could single-handedly change the settlement or prevent it from being changed by others.

b. **Quite powerful:** it could not single-handedly change the settlement or prevent it from being changed, but would likely make a big difference in struggles over the settlement.

c. **Somewhat powerful:** it could not single-handedly change the settlement or prevent it from being changed, but would likely make a significant difference in struggles over the settlement.

d. **Somewhat powerless**: it would likely make only a small difference in struggles over the settlement.

e. **Powerless:** it would likely make virtually no difference in struggles over the settlement.[7]

To construct our horizontal power variable, we simply invert the power level of the OB (*q2_power_ob*). Consequently, the ruling coalition is stronger the weaker the OB.[8] These values are further scaled so that they range from 0 to 1 and are comparable with the equally ranged vertical power index. Higher values in this

---

[7] These questions involved coders making judgements about how things might reasonably (or in some cases unreasonably) have appeared to leaders at the time. We chose this route so as to allow us to test the relationship between leadership perceptions and policy commitment. As such, power that was not perceptible to the leader or that was only perceived *ex post* was not of interest to us. Granted, this creates some methodological difficulties as the perceptions of the leader are not entirely transparent. However, we asked coders to consider as evidence speeches, statements, or policy documents by the leader/ruling coalition; commentaries by contemporary observers identifying the relative size and strength of the blocs; convincing historical accounts of the leader/ruling coalition's mindset; etc.

[8] This variable correlates highly (0.88) with more complex—but we found not more construct valid—indices, like the ratio *q2_power_lb* or *q2_power_clb* (whichever is higher) versus *q2_power_ob*.

variable indicate a more powerful ruling coalition vis-à-vis the opposition. To provide a hypothetical example, a country with a 'quite powerful' OB would be scored a low 0.15 on the horizontal power scale, i.e. the governing coalition's power vis-à-vis the OB is low compared to other countries in our sample.

Note that this is a slightly different approach to Khan. Khan assesses the strength of the ruling coalition by reference to its ability to 'hold out' in struggles against the opposition. These struggles are always relative to some issue or other, famously the distribution of rents from industrial policy. What Khan does not really acknowledge, however, is that this opens the possibility that the ruling coalition's strength can vary depending on the precise issue under consideration—for example, it may be weak on the issue of industrial policy rents, but strong on the issue of patriarchal property rights, and somewhere in between on the identity of the state religion. Khan thus fails to provide a method for assessing the overall strength of the ruling coalition. Our approach consequently asks a more general question about strength in respect of changing the settlement itself; in other words, in changing the settlement's foundational institutions, configuration of power, or distribution of benefits, and we ask coders to make an average assessment. This ensures that our typological variables are derived more clearly from our core

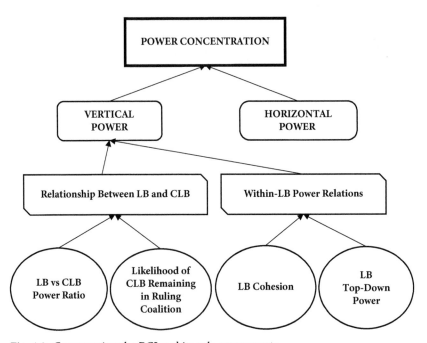

Fig. 4.2 Constructing the PCI and its sub-components
Source: Authors' own

political settlement concept. This approach is consistent with Khan's, we believe, and arguably an improvement on it.

Measuring Khan's vertical axis is a little more complicated. Here, we made a composite index based on four variables and indices: The power ratio between the LB and the CLB (*x_lbvsclbpowerratio*), the likelihood that the CLB would split from the LB (*q3_clbsplit*), the hierarchical power concentration of LB (*q8_hierarchy_lb*) and the internal cohesiveness of the LB (*q9_cohesiveness_lb*). The weights for the four sub-components of the index were derived via principal component analysis (PCA).[9] The resulting value is then scaled, where 0 equals the lowest level of vertical power in the dataset and 1 the highest. Or to put it differently, higher scores indicate a leadership that is stronger vis-à-vis the ruling coalition's support base and lower scores indicate a leadership that is weaker.

For a worked example, let us return to the previously introduced hypothetical governing coalition, and assume that while it has fairly weak horizontal power, its vertical power is rather strong.[10] Specifically, the LB is twice as strong as the CLB (the ratio score equalling 2), the likelihood that the CLB leaves the coalition is low (equalling a maximum score of 3), de facto power in the LB rested exclusively with the highest leadership (equalling a maximum score of 6), and the LB was very cohesive (again, equalling a maximum score of 4). The factor loadings of the PCA's first component for each variable provide weights to join the standardized variables in one index. Overall these weights are fairly similar at 0.50, 0.52, 0.41, and 0.54 for the LB-CLB ratio, CLB-Remainer-Likelihood, LB-Power-Hierarchy, and LB-Cohesion variables respectively. A final scaling provides this example a high 0.82 (1 being the maximum), indicating, as intended, that this country has a high concentration of vertical power.

The two operations described earlier provide us with a systematic means for measuring Khan's variables. However, given our scepticism about the distinct causal mechanisms Khan posits for these variables, our own typology collapses Khan's vertical and horizontal axes into the **PCI** (*x_powerconcentration_add*). Concretely, both sub-components are weighted equally before they are added to each other.[11] And for easier interpretability, this score is scaled so that values in our dataset range from exactly 0 to 1. Higher values indicate a greater concentration of power in the de facto leader. Thus, in our worked example—where horizontal

---

[9] The idea of PCA is to reduce the dimensionality of the dataset into underlying components, which represent a common source to the variation in the original variables. The standard procedure is then to use the respective variables' factor loadings to the first component (which represents the greatest source of common variation) as weights for the indicator. This procedure ensures that the theoretically chosen sub-components are combined in a mathematical way that reflects a coherent concept that can be empirically distinguished from other concepts of interest. Overall, the PCA led to fairly equally weighted sub-components.

[10] Note that these scores for vertical power are taken from the Cameroonian 1962 to 1966 period.

[11] The equation is: *x_powerconcentration_add* = 0.5 * *x_horizontalpower_nor* + 0.5 * *x_verticalpower*. This simple additive approach is therefore equal to a simple averaging of the two values.

power scored a low 0.15 and vertical power a high 0.82—the average power score lies at 0.615 which after scaling results in a final PCI score of 0.648. With a full sample average of 0.52, our hypothetical country would be among the countries with a relatively high degree of power concentration.

Note that we have been at pains to stress that power concentration is not the same as autocracy. By examining its constitutive components, we can see that a democracy with some combination of a ruling coalition or party with a large popular majority, unifying vision, and internal party mechanisms for resolving disputes and generating consensus and discipline, could also qualify. In fact, of all its component parts, it is only arguably *q8_hierarchy_lb*, 'LB Top-down power', that is likely to have a particularly strong association with autocracy; and even here, a particularly skilled or charismatic democratic leader might score highly.

Social foundation size index

Deriving a value for our second variable, the social foundation, was also some-what complicated. True to our definition of a good concept, we wanted to tie the causal properties of distinct political settlements back to the idea of a political set-tlement as an agreement among powerful groups that maintains relative peace and stability. The key groups then are those that have the potential to disrupt peace and stability by overturning existing political arrangements, often by means of vi-olence, but also by means of economic pressure, and occasionally by means of peaceful revolutions, e.g. through the ballot box. Readers will recall from the dis-cussion around Figure 3.1 in Chapter 3 that when describing the configuration of a political settlement, there are three key categories: the social foundation, that is, potentially disruptive groups that are co-opted by the political leadership (in practice, this also includes 'liminal groups' that are equally subjected to both co-optation and repression); groups with disruptive potential that are repressed by the leadership, that is 'repressed groups'; and groups that lack disruptive potential, which we call 'marginal groups'.

Importantly, whether a group is co-opted, liminal, or marginal does not per-fectly predict the extent to which it is aligned with the leadership. For example, marginal groups with no disruptive potential may align with the leadership, and liminal groups may be at least contingently aligned. Even co-opted groups may be part of the political opposition, especially in political democracies. As such, these categories do not map neatly onto the 'political blocs' we asked about in our ques-tionnaire. How then did we estimate the size of the social foundation? Our solution was to construct a composite variable based on three different questions. Recall that the aim is to assess what percentage of the population is both potentially dis-ruptive *and* co-opted. To do this we needed to find out first, what population share was represented by each of the LB, the CLB, and the OB, which is specifically what we asked coders in the first question of our survey.[12] Then for each bloc we wanted to know what percentage of the groups in it was powerful (a number derived from inverting coders' replies to Q7 in our survey).[13] By multiplying these two numbers together we got an estimate of the total share of the potentially disruptive population commanded by each bloc (e.g. the *x_lbpowerfulshare*, abbreviated 'PowPop' in Figure 4.3).

We then multiplied each bloc's powerful population share by a 0-to-1 scale estimate of whether the bloc's followers and leaders were primarily co-opted or

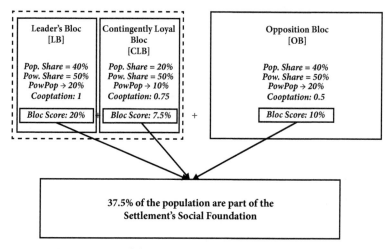

Fig. 4.3 Construction of the social foundation variable
Source: Authors' own

---

[12] Obviously, this required some educated guesswork on the part of coders. Firstly, because affiliations are not entirely transparent and secondly because allegiances shift over time. On the first problem, we asked coders to make rough guesstimates based on such evidence as internal party, leadership, and general elections; putsches, coups, and attempted coups; reports of purges, political factionalism, and infighting; the breadth and depth of political repression, etc. On the second problem, and because it would be too cumbersome to ask for data month by month or year by year, we asked coders to make a judgement about the average or 'typical' alignment of the population with these blocs for each of our political (settlement) periods. For example, if the leader was tremendously popular in his first year in office, but then extremely unpopular for the remainder of a ten-year period, we would expect coders to enter a low percentage for the LB.

[13] Specifically, in Q7 we asked coders what percentage of each bloc was accounted for by relatively powerless groups. Examples of such groups might be women, youth, poor people, specific ethnic minorities, or other political, economic, or sociological categories which may be noteworthy on account of their marginalization; such groups need not be either organized or self-conscious. The threshold for inclusion was that it would require a big stretch to imagine the group making a significant difference in political struggles either within or between blocs. To provide an example, coders may feel that under the LB were a certain percentage of poor women, but that this group would not make a significant difference in struggles either within the bloc or between the bloc and others. As such, 'poor women' should be listed as a relatively powerless group. As before, we expected these power attributes to have been perceptible to the ruling coalition.

repressed as a means of incorporating them under the settlement.[14] This bloc average co-optation score was constructed in several steps, illustrated here with the answers given for the OB. The general idea of this variable was to create an index out of two equally weighted components: repression and co-optation. These themselves are created out of several sub-components, namely our questions Q10a–g and 11a–g from the survey (see Appendix G). The components are first constructed separately for Q10 (relating to the bloc's leaders) and Q11 (relating to the bloc's followers), before later being averaged with equal weighting.

Let us focus first on Q10 (leaders) to illustrate the construction process. First, the repression component is made up of violent (Q10a) and non-violent repression (Q10b). After their scales were inverted (so that low values mean higher repression and lower co-optation), both variables were added and weighted at 0.3 and 0.2 respectively (reflecting our assumption that violent repression is more important than non-violent repression). Similarly, the co-optation component is made up of two sub-components. One, the highest value of co-optation measured in one of the co-optation variables (Q10c–g) and the other is the average of all co-optation variables, both being equally weighted in the index (at 0.25). Doing so acknowledges that a country's leader might validly focus primarily on one form of co-optation, but at the same time that the general mix of co-optation also matters. These variables are then joined into one index for the OB's leaders' co-optation, using the following formula (and using the respective variables from our dataset):

$$X\_obcooptjoinedleaders = 0.3^* \ [inverted] \ q10\_violrepresslead\_ob + 0.2^*$$

$$[inverted]q10\_nonviolrepresslead\_ob + 0.25^* \ x\_obcoopthighleaders + 0.25^*$$

$$X\_obcooptaverageleaders$$

The exact same is done for the followers, only that the respective values of Q11 are used. The final index joins these two sub-indices on equal weighting, creating the final OB average co-optation score:

$$X\_obgencooptindex = 0.5^* \ x\_obcooptjoinedleaders + 0.5^*$$

$$x\_obcooptjoinedfollowers$$

Lastly, each bloc's co-optation was normalized by its theoretical minimum (1) and maximum (4). As a result, the score ranges between 0 and 1, making

---

[14] By co-optation, we mean securing of agreement or acquiescence by means of ideological affinity or symbolic or material benefits, such as status, recognition, rights, offices, jobs, goods, services, income, economic opportunities, entitlements; and by repression we mean that a group's agreement or acquiescence to the settlement is directly or indirectly secured by means of force, the threat of force, or by deliberately blocking or withholding access to economic resources.

its multiplication with the total share of the population that is powerful and the resulting SFS index more interpretable.

By multiplying this co-optation score with our previously derived power population share, we get a number that represents the percentage of the population that is both potentially disruptive, and co-opted: that is, the SFS. For example, in Figure 4.3, the LB accounts for 40 per cent of the population, of whom 50 per cent are powerful or potentially disruptive. Members of the LB are incorporated under the settlement entirely by means of co-optation, giving a composite bloc score of 20 per cent. The CLB, meanwhile accounts for 20 per cent of the population, of whom half have some disruptive potential. The CLB is incorporated primarily by means of co-optation, giving a bloc score of 7.5 per cent. Finally, the OB accounts for 40 per cent of the population, of whom half, again, have some disruptive potential. They are subject to an equal mix of co-optation and repression, giving a bloc score of 10 per cent. Adding all the bloc scores together, we find that the settlement's social foundation comprises 37.5 per cent of the population, and thus would tend to be a slightly broader-than-average case on the social foundation spectrum (our population average being 33.98 per cent).

Careful readers may note an element of circularity in the way we have constructed the social foundation variable. Specifically, we argue that the breadth of the social foundation affects the distributive goals of the ruling coalition, and thus its commitment to various types of development policy. However, the way we measure the social foundation is by counting the share of the population that leaders try to co-opt. A critic might say that this is tantamount to saying that leaders will distribute benefits broadly when there are a lot of people they are trying to co-opt, which is virtually tautologous.

We have a number of responses to this criticism. First, PSA is an approach that is aimed predominantly at policymakers, especially foreign donors. It is easy for foreign donors to see whether a government has signed up to some inclusive policy, such as the Millennium Development Goals, or other. It is less easy for them to predict whether they will follow through on those goals with a high level of commitment. PSA, by identifying the underlying social foundation of the settlement, provides a read on that. It thus remains a method for identifying non-obvious features of a polity with causal consequences.

Second, our approach is not based on an analysis of the social foundation alone. Our argument is that the social foundation, as per our typological theory, produces novel and interesting causal effects in its interaction with the power configuration. Any circularity in the social foundation variable is thereby obviated.

Finally, our survey also includes data that allows us to test the relationship of the social foundation to upstream variables. For analysts who prefer a more straightforwardly structural variable, we have found a strong association between the share of the population that is powerful and the breadth of the social foundation.[15] We, however, wish to preserve the intuitive idea that a settlement is at least in part an agreement among powerful groups about who, in the interests of preserving peace and stability, needs to be taken seriously, and which of them are insiders (to be co-opted) and outsiders (to be repressed).

Sticking to our original coding, we see that our worked example, with a social foundation and power concentration a little above the survey means, illustrated by the data point 'Example' in Figure 4.4, lies just inside the 'broad-concentrated' quadrant. Other things being equal, and reflecting the hypotheses developed in Chapter 3, we would expect the political leadership in such a settlement to demonstrate some commitment to and implementation capacity for inclusive growth and social policies, but not an exceptional one.

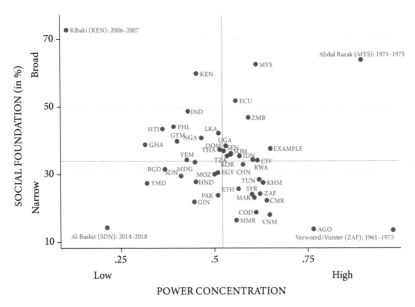

Fig. 4.4 Position of selected cases and historical country-averages in the ESID political settlement typology space

Source: Authors' own calculations using data from Schulz and Kelsall (2021c)

[15] For example, we are able to test whether, or in what specific circumstances, settlements that have a broad distribution of disruptive power in society also have broad social foundations (i.e. broad co-optation). We call the former variable the total powerful population share (*x_totpowerfulpopshare*), which is generated by (1) multiplying a bloc's population share with the percentage of its powerful members and (2) adding the three blocs' values. It thus covers the social foundation's powerful population size dimension while excluding its co-optation dimension, hereby avoiding the potential circularity described. As expected, these two variables correlated very highly at 0.81. Moreover, in Appendix F we re-run all our major regressions using the total powerful population share variable and find a strong robustness of our results.

Illustrating the Effective States and Inclusive Development typology using the PolSett dataset

In Figure 4.4, we illustrate how our data maps onto the ESID typology, with the cross-hairs representing the respective dimensional survey sample means, which we treat as the thresholds for our political settlement types. We show two types of data points. First, the historical averages of all our forty-two countries. Readers are urged to handle these with caution. Most countries over the course of a sixty-year history will have experienced more than one type of settlement; some, like South Africa, have experienced all four. For that reason, plotting the country 'average' is potentially misleading. Nevertheless, for many countries, especially those on the outer edges of the distribution, the quadrant in which they are placed usually provides an indication of where they have spent a good part of their political history. It might be considered, then, their 'modal' political settlement type. It is also important to note that only country-years in which a country had a political settlement (and was therefore coded) is included in the average. Hence, for countries like Somalia that have experienced large parts of their histories since 1945 or independence in states of unsettlement, the respective dimensional scores are likely to jar with popular perceptions. More detailed country mappings, illustrating the evolution of political settlements across time, are provided in Appendix C.

Second, in each quadrant we provide data points for one illustrative, 'archetypal', country/leader period, the scores for which ranked above the 70th or below the 30th percentile for each dimension of our dataset.

One of the broadest, most dispersed settlements we have in our dataset is Mwai Kibaki's Kenyan regime between 2006 and 2007. This was a period in which Kibaki's National Alliance Rainbow Coalition (NARC), a tenuous 'super-alliance' formed from a collection of ethnic parties in the run-up to the 2002 election, had split over the allocation of posts in the new regime and proposals for a new constitution. After losing the constitutional referendum, Kibaki expelled from government followers of his most powerful rival, Raila Odinga, creating a new Party for National Unity from his own loyalists and some former opposition members of parliament (MPs). However, the new coalition was weak, with a high perceived likelihood that it would split again. Moreover, Raila's supporters, having joined forces with the opposition Kenya African National Union (KANU) party in the Orange Democratic Movement, retained a high degree of mobilizational capacity, which the regime was unable or unwilling to repress.

Readers will see from our social foundation survey data in Table 4.1 that although the distribution of the population among blocs was fairly typical, that is, close to the survey means, the percentage of the population with the power to disrupt the settlement was higher than average, especially for the OB. Moreover, Kibaki for the most part used co-optation, not least the promise of free and

Table 4.1 Social foundation in illustrative settlements

Leader period	Survey mean	Kibaki 2	Al-Bashir 6	Verwoerd/ Vorster	Abdul Razak 2
Social foundation					
Size (% population)	34	73	14	13	64
Leadership bloc					
Size (% population)	36	37	17	13	60
o/w powerful %	21	36	15	10	48
Co-optation score	0.7	0.8	0.5	0.9	0.9
Contingently loyal bloc					
Size (% population)	27	17	23	8	13
o/w % powerful	10	12	12	3	10
Co-optation score	0.7	0.8	0.2	0.8	0.7
Opposition bloc					
Size (% population)	37	36	60	80	27
o/w % powerful	19	49	24	10	22
Co-optation score	0.5	0.7	0.2	0.1	0.7

Note: Social foundation, bloc sizes and the percentage of which are powerful, are rounded to the nearest per cent. Co-optation scores to the nearest tenth of a per cent.
Source: Schulz and Kelsall (2021c)

fair elections, to try and incorporate these groups into his settlement and fore-stall the eruption of violence. When it comes to power concentration, as Table 4.2 shows, Kibaki's own bloc was rather incohesive, but more importantly, there was a high likelihood that the CLB would split, making the leadership very weak vis-à-vis the opposition, signalling dispersed power. Together, this made for a very broad-dispersed settlement, and, when Kibaki did not deliver on the promise of free and fair elections in 2007, to serious violence and settlement breakdown (Chege 2008).

For a narrow-dispersed settlement, we turn to the regime of General Omar al-Bashir in Sudan from 2014–2018. Taking power in a coup in 1989, Bashir had originally been a front man for an Islamist state project under the tutelage of ideologue Sheikh Hassan-al-Turabi. However, in 1999, al-Bashir split with the latter. After a brief oil boom, in which al-Bashir proved adept at managing what Alex de Waal has called a 'centralized kleptocracy' around Khartoum, furnishing

Table 4.2 Power concentration in illustrative settlements

Leader period	Survey mean	Kibaki 2	Al-Bashir 6	Verwoerd/Vorster	Abdul-Razak 2
Power concentration	0.52	0.02	0.06	0.98	0.81
Horizontal power					
Leadership bloc power relative to opposi-tion (1–5; 5 = maximum)	3.4	1.9	1.7	4.7	4.7
Vertical power					
Top-down decision-making power within the LB (1–6; 6 = maximum)	5.4	5	5.7	6	5.6
LB cohe-sion (1–4; 4 = maximum)	3.1	2.5	2	4	4
Passivity of CLB (1–3; 3 = no defection risk)	2.2	1	1.3	3	2.8
Power of LB relative to CLB (1–3; 3 = maximum)	1.4	1.1	0.6	2.3	1.8

Note: Scores for horizontal and vertical power are rounded to the nearest tenth of a per cent.
Source: Schulz and Kelsall (2021c)

rents which were used to buy protection in a 'political marketplace' of competing paramilitary groups in the outer regions, al-Bashir's power began to wane (De Waal 2019).[16] By 2014, after the secession of the South, an indictment by the International Criminal Court (ICC), falling oil revenues, and a split in his ruling National Congress Party, he found himself increasingly embattled. The opposition's mobilizational potential had grown and was manifested in recurring street protests,

---

[16] We note in passing that we regard the political marketplace approach, which also considers the configuration and composition of different powerful groups and their modes of incorporation in the polity, as complementary to PSA. Indeed, we believe our dataset could provide greater precision to political marketplace analysis.

yet al-Bashir failed to broaden the base of his settlement, responding mainly with repression.

The main takeaway from the social foundation survey data in Table 4.1 is that while the percentage of the population with the power to disrupt or change the settlement is about average, it tilts away from al-Bashir's bloc. Moreover, al-Bashir does not try very hard to absorb these elements, with a much lower than average co-optation score. Meanwhile, when it comes to power concentration (Table 4.2), the LB is smaller and weaker vis-à-vis the OB than the average, and al-Bashir's own bloc is incohesive and exceptionally weak vis-à-vis the CLB. Together, this makes for a very narrow, dispersed settlement, which was to prove unsustainable. In April 2019, with protest escalating, political rivals in the Sudanese armed forces removed al-Bashir from power.

Our narrow-concentrated settlement, meanwhile, is represented by the South African apartheid regime of Hendrik Verwoerd and John Vorster. Crystallized in the National Party, this settlement grew out of a social movement among Afrikaner settlers, anxious to protect their own privileges against the perceived threat of the native population and the former colonial power. It completely marginalized and repressed the majority black population, while gaining the contingent support of most English-speaking whites, including the business community.

The social foundation survey data in Table 4.1, shows the OB to be very large in this period, yet its members for the most part lacked power. With a very low co-optation score, it was for the most part forcibly incorporated under the settlement by means of repression. When it comes to power concentration, Table 4.2 shows that the LB was extremely cohesive, the CLB extremely passive, and that the LB was uncommonly strong vis-à-vis both the CLB and the OB. As we detail in the following chapter, this narrow-concentrated type of settlement was to survive for many years.

Finally, we have an archetypal broad-concentrated settlement represented by Abdul Razak Hussein's Malaysia between 1971 and 1975. Abdul Razak first assumed the premiership in 1970, during a period of National Emergency, after serious communal riots in 1969. When Malaysia returned to parliamentary rule in 1971, Razak continued as prime minister and leader of the ruling Alliance Party, a coalition of Malay, Chinese, and Indian ethnic parties. In 1973 he broadened the settlement still further by brokering the creation of the Barisan Nasional or National Front, which incorporated an additional six, initially rivalrous parties. Within the Barisan Nasional, diverse political elites largely set aside their differences to promote a New Economic Policy, aiming to eradicate poverty and end the association between race and economic position in society which had threatened political stability. This cemented a form of elite solidarity that had already developed in response to Chinese communist mass mobilization in the late colonial period. As the leader of the Parti Islam Se-Malaysia (PAS) stated when urging its members to support the Barisan Nasional in 1972, 'United Malays National Organ-isation (UMNO) [the main Malay party] shared similar views on the two crucial issues of security and development. Communism and communalism represented an immediate serious threat to security, and their containment required greater national unity.'[17]

Social foundation survey data in Table 4.1, show that the ruling coalition in this period was supported by over 70 per cent of the population, while a very high 80 per cent were regarded as powerful enough to make a difference in struggles over the settlement, and were heavily co-opted. When it comes to power concentra-tion, Table 4.2 shows that the ruling coalition was strong relative to the OB and that the passivity of the CLB and the cohesion of the LB were exceptional. Given the diversity of the ethnic coalition that comprised the Barisan Nasional, this co-hesion is quite remarkable, signalling a highly successful resolution of intra-elite collective-action problems around mutual protection and Abdul Razak's vision for national development. With Abdul Razak dying in 1976, this was the apogee of broad concentrated power in Malaysia; nevertheless, the settlement remained in this typological category for another twenty years.

A more extensive list, conforming to the same specifications, follows in Appendix D.

Having explained how we have created a dataset and constructed our variables, as well as providing a mapping of our countries, in subsequent chapters we move to more detailed description and analysis. Chapter 5 provides a detailed case study of South Africa, Chapter 6 a comparative analysis of Ghana, Guinea, Cambodia, and Rwanda over the past two decades, and Chapter 7 provides a large-*n* regression analysis.

---

[17] Slater (2010: 155).

5

Describing Political Settlement Evolution in a Single Country

The Case of South Africa

Working on South Africa with the PolSett Dataset

This chapter applies the theoretical framework laid out in earlier chapters to a single country—South Africa.[1] The primary goal is to use a single, well-known country case to illustrate how the framework can be operationalized. The case explores the extent to which the causal propositions laid out in Chapters 3 and 4 are consistent with the observed South African patterns, and also adds detail and country-specific intuition into the construction of the key variables and their sub-components.

A secondary goal is to explore the extent to which 'quantification' along the lines laid out in Chapter 4 brings to the forefront aspects of political settlements which might otherwise have received less attention. The intent is not to provide a new account of South Africa's political settlement, but rather to explore what value added there might be in working at a different point along the quantitative-qualitative spectrum than is the case for most country-level political settlement analyses.[2]

Two variables—power concentration and social foundation—are central to the approach to political settlements laid out in this book. As per Chapter 3, the variables are defined as follows:

---

[1] This chapter is based on the expert analyses of political settlements in South Africa, in each of their responses to the ESID survey, by Alan Hirsch, Brian Levy, and Jeremy Seekings. In an extended meeting, Hirsch, Levy, and Seekings discussed differences in their analyses and overall interpretation of the data, based on a collation of the data prepared by Levy. Levy subsequently further analysed the data and wrote this chapter. Levy is solely responsible for the chapter's interpretations and takes full responsibility for any weaknesses in the chapter.

[2] A complementary paper (whose lead author is the lead author of the present chapter) explores in a more encompassing, qualitative way the drivers of political change in South Africa subsequent to 1994. See Brian Levy, Alan Hirsch, Vinothan Naidoo, and Musa Nxele, 'South Africa—when strong institutions and massive inequalities collide', Carnegie Endowment for International Peace, April 2021.

Political Settlements and Development. Tim Kelsall et al., Oxford University Press.
© Tim Kelsall et al., (2022). DOI: 10.1093/oso/9780192848932.003.0005

- *The social foundation* designates who are the socially salient included groups (insiders), as opposed to the excluded (outsiders), along a spectrum which extends from broad to narrow. Insider groups are those which (i) have the potential to disrupt the settlement, and (ii) are co-opted by the ruling coalition.

- *The concentration of power* focuses on how power is organized—the extent of coherence in the allocation of decision-making procedures and authority among insiders, ranging from concentrated (highly coherent) to dispersed (lacking in coherence), and proxied by the presence or absence of powerful groups that are likely to make serious political trouble for the leadership.

The two right-hand columns of Table 5.1 report the South African scores for social foundation and power concentration for each of eight time periods. Accounting for these scores, and their variations across periods, is a central focus of this chapter.

As Chapter 4 described, the empirical point of departure for characterizing a country's political settlement in terms of the power concentration and social foundation variables is the grouping of the population into three blocs:

Table 5.1 Applying the ESID political settlements framework to South Africa, mid-1960s–2019

	LB (%)	CLB (%)	OB (%)	Social foundation (%)	Power concentration
Peak apartheid (mid 1960s)	12.5	7.5	80	13	0.98
Post-Soweto uprising (circa 1980)	9.0	9.0	82.0	14.0	0.55
Deepening crisis (mid-1980s)	8.0	9.0	83.0	14	0.23
Transition (1990–1993)	8.5	18.0	73.5	35	0.20
Mandela (1994–1996)	65.0	14.0	21.0	38.5	0.57
Mandela/Mbeki (1997–2007)	48.0	20.0	32.0	37.5	0.77
Zuma (2009–2017)	41.0	21.0	38.0	37.5	0.57
Ramaphosa (2018–)	44.0	27.5	28.5	52.5	0.42
ESID average	*36*	*27.5*	*37*	*34.0*	*0.52*

Note: First four columns are rounded to nearest 0.5 per cent.
Source: Schulz and Kelsall (2021c)

- *The leader's bloc (LB)*—the segment of the population whose political loyalty the current de facto leader can be reasonably assured of, at least in the short term;
- *The contingently loyal bloc (CLB)*—the segment of the population that is currently aligned with the de facto leader (and therefore has some representation in government) but whose political loyalty cannot be assured, in the sense that there is a realistic possibility that it could defect from the leader and/or make serious political trouble; and
- *The opposition bloc (OB)*—the segment of the population that is not currently aligned with the LB or the CLB and does not feel represented by government.

The first three columns of Table 5.1 distribute South Africa's population across the three blocs for each of eight time periods, using averages of the responses to the ESID survey of three country experts. (Averages of the three expert responses are used throughout the chapter; for the most part, the responses of the three experts to the ESID survey were very similar to one another.) The time period covered by Table 5.1 encompasses two distinct political settlements: the apartheid political settlement, with governmental power monopolized by the country's white minority, and the 1960s as the moment of peak apartheid; and the new political settlement which took shape in the mid-1990s, in which governmental power shifted to the African National Congress (ANC), elected by a non-racial majority of the country's voters. The bottom row provides an overall benchmark, the mean scores for each variable across all 2,718 observations, for forty-two countries in the ESID dataset.

In addition to grouping the population into blocs, the country experts also responded to a variety of supplementary questions. As the discussion which follows details, responses to these supplementary questions both provide the basis for generating empirical estimates of the social foundation and power concentration measures and turn out to be of intrinsic interest in themselves.

The next section of the chapter uses the ESID measures to examine how the apartheid political settlement changed over time, with particular attention to the initially very high, and then subsequently rapidly declining power concentration score. The subsequent section contrasts the ESID scores across the two political settlements—with particular attention to what are the core features which differentiate the settlements. Then the ESID measures are used to interpret the difficult evolution of South Africa's political settlement in the quarter century subsequent to the country's seemingly miraculous transformation from racist minority rule to constitutional democracy. The chapter's final section reflects more broadly on both the strengths and limitations of the ESID empirical approach.

Peak apartheid and its demise

The distribution of population across the LB, CLB, and OB provides a starting point for understanding South Africa's apartheid polity. 'Peak apartheid' comprises the period between the 1964 Rivonia trial of Nelson Mandela and associates, and the 1976 Soweto uprising. The Soweto uprising, which began with spontaneous protests by adolescent schoolchildren, set in motion an almost two-decades-long mass mobilization—a popular movement which culminated in a negotiated end to apartheid in 1994.

As per Table 5.1, during the peak apartheid period, the LB comprised about 13 per cent of the population, and the CLB 7 per cent. These numbers are almost identical to the white share of the South African population as of the mid-1960s (about 20 per cent), and the share (about 60 per cent of white voters) who supported the Afrikaner nationalist government. The OB comprised the overwhelming majority of South Africa's population.

During peak apartheid South Africa's social foundation score was 13.5 per cent and its power concentration score 0.98. Comparing across the ESID forty-two-country sample, this social foundation score was among the lowest, and the power concentration score among the very highest, almost the maximum feasible. South Africa's mid-1960s 'peak apartheid' regime thus turns out to be an almost perfect approximation of a 'narrow social foundation with a high concentration of power' (quadrant 4 in Figure 3.2 of Chapter 3) political settlement. Drilling into the components which underlie these scores illustrates the logic of the ESID approach, highlighting the way in which the data direct attention to some striking aspects of how the apartheid polity functioned, and the sequence via which the struggle against apartheid resulted in the regime's weakening, and eventual demise.

As laid out in Chapter 4, and considered further in the discussion of South Africa's political settlement since 1994, the construction underlying the social foundation, and the methodology for its measurement, is complex. Without yet getting into all of the complexities of the measure, the reason for the low social foundation score emerges clearly in Table 5.2: as per Table 5.1, the large majority of South Africa's population was in the OB—and the mode of 'incorporation' of this bloc was overwhelmingly through relentless repression. During 'peak apartheid', repression was 'successful' in the sense that it rendered the opposition powerless.

Over time, the OB was able to exercise increasing power. Its post-Rivonia trial revitalization began in the early 1970s with efforts to organize black workers and with the emergence of the black consciousness movement. Subsequent to the 1976 Soweto uprising, momentum for mass mobilization built within the country, and accelerated with the formation of the United Democratic Front in 1983. There also was some intensification of armed struggle (especially by the ANC's military wing,

Table 5.2 The changing social foundation in late-apartheid

	Peak apartheid (mid 1960s)	Post-Soweto uprising (circa 1980)	Deepening crisis (mid-1980s)	Transition (de Klerk)
Social foundation				
Size (% population)	13	14	14	35
OB				
o/w % powerful	10	30	40	36
Co-optation score for OB (0-1; 1 = maximum)	0.1	0.1	0.1	0.5
Repression as mode of co-optation (1–4; 4 = maximum)	4	4	4	3

Note: Social foundation and bloc sizes are rounded to the nearest per cent. Co-optation scores to the nearest tenth of a per cent.
Source: Schulz and Kelsall (2021c)

Umkhonto we Sizwe), plus important support from a global anti-apartheid movement. However, prior to the transition period which began in 1989, the response to the rising tide of opposition was continuing repression. The result was that the social foundation remained narrow as per the logic of its construction.

Table 5.3 details the scores for the components which make up the power concentration measure, organizing them according to the way they align with each of the OB, LB, and CLB. As the second row of the table signals, relentless repression meant that during peak apartheid the power of the LB relative to the OB was overwhelming. As the third and fourth rows of the table suggest, the 'peak apartheid' LB was overwhelmingly hierarchical in its mode of decision-making, and highly cohesive. The source of this cohesion was white Afrikaner nationalism, a highly motivated, ethnically mobilized social movement (O'Meara 1983).

The role of the CLB during apartheid was somewhat more ambiguous. It was comprised principally of English-speaking white South Africans (including the predominantly Anglophone business class). As the fifth and sixth rows of the table signal, during peak apartheid the CLB largely acquiesced to the Afrikaner Nationalist government's racist and repressive policies; the risk of defection to the anti-apartheid (overwhelmingly black) opposition movement was limited. The CLB was not powerless, however its interests (especially business interests) were in large part catered to by government.

Note that the combination of high power concentration, narrow social foundation and an ideologically unified leadership bloc comprises precisely the set of conditions which were identified in Chapter 3 as providing a basis for a 'proto-developmental state' (albeit, a repressive, racially exclusionary one in the

Table 5.3 Unbundling power concentration over time, apartheid era

Leader period	Peak apartheid	Post-Soweto uprising (circa 1980)	Deepening crisis (mid-1980s)	Transition (1990–1993)
Power concentration **OB, relative to LB**				
LB power relative to opposition (1–5; 5 = maximum)	4.7	3.3	2	2
Within LB				
Top-down decision-making power within the LB (1–6; 6 = maximum)	6	5.7	6	5.3
LB cohesion (1–4; 4= maximum)	4	3.5	2.3	3
CLB relative to LB				
Passivity of CLB (1–3; 3 = no defection risk)	3	2.3	2	1.7
Power of LB relative to CLB (1–3; 3 = maximum)	2.3	1.5	1.1	1.3

Note: Scores for horizontal and vertical power are rounded to the nearest tenth of a per cent.
Source: Schulz and Kelsall (2021c)

South African context). Two predictions followed in that chapter (and are supported by the regression analysis in Chapter 7): relatively rapid economic growth, and limited provision of socially inclusive policies. Indeed, between 1933 and 1973 the South African economy grew at a real average annual rate in excess of 5 per cent—with the rate exceeding 5.5 per cent annually in the 'peak apartheid' years of the 1960s.

Meanwhile, as discussed further in subsequent sections, social and economic conditions for the majority of the population were abysmal.

Things changed in the 1970s, beginning in 1973 with a series of strikes by black workers, followed by the 1976 Soweto uprising. These events provided the sparks for a continually growing and increasingly powerful opposition movement, which culminated in the unbanning of opposition parties in late 1989, a three-year process of negotiation, and the first non-racial democratic election in 1994.

How and why all of this happened, and the details of each step in the process, have been comprehensively documented elsewhere.[3] The ESID measures provide a parsimonious way of tracking the unfolding sequence through which power

---

[3] For detailed treatments, see Mandela (1994), Sparks (1996), Waldmeir (1997), Seekings (2000), and Welsh (2010).

was transformed, becoming progressively less concentrated—and, in the process of tracking the sequence of change, the measures hopefully shed some additional insight into a story the broad contours of which are well known.

An early step in the decline in power concentration came with the Soweto uprising—an assertion of power among some of those who hitherto had seemed powerless. This assertion of power is signalled in the increase in the immediate aftermath of the Soweto uprising in the percentage of the OB rated in Table 5.2 as at least 'somewhat powerful' (though, as per the table, the assertion of power was met by repression)—and in the corresponding decline in the power of the LB relative to the OB evident in the second row of Table 5.3. As the table signals, the rising tide of mass mobilization by the OB resulted in a continuing decline in the power of the LB relative to the OB over the course of the 1980s.

Mass mobilization also led to a decline in power concentration via a second, indirect channel—increasing restiveness on the part of the CLB, which became less willing to sustain its passive stance vis-à-vis repressive apartheid rule. This is evident in the bottom two rows of Table 5.3, which show a post-Soweto rise in CLB relative power, and an associated reduction of CLB passivity. This change had two aspects. One aspect, of modest political impact, was that an increasing share of the subset of whites who were not supporters of the ruling National Party shifted their support to more avowedly 'progressive' political parties, who were less willing to ignore the brutalities of the apartheid regime.

Of more profound consequence than the modest electoral shift within the white population was the way in which the establishment business community inserted itself into the political discourse (Hirsch and Levy 2018). Within the country, it became increasingly vocal in its support for improving the living conditions and opportunities for the urban black population; this was contrary to the 'peak apartheid' vision of confining the black population to rural so-called bantustans, except as migrant workers. Even more far-reaching was the pioneering role played by the establishment business community in initiating and influencing dialogue between the apartheid government and the banned, underground and exiled ANC.

In time, as a third step in the decline of power concentration, the new assertiveness of both the OB and the CLB resulted in internecine struggles within the LB. Hard-line apartheid ideologues increasingly were challenged by a more pragmatic wing within the ruling National Party (and in the white Afrikaner community more broadly) who recognized the large gap between the ideological vision, and the practical reality of extreme poverty and rising social conflict.[4] This trend is captured in Table 5.3 in the decline in the mid-1980s in the LB 'cohesion' score.

Overall, by the mid-1980s the combination of declining power of the LB relative to both the OB and the CLB, and the loss of cohesion within the LB, added up to a massive decline in the power concentration index from 0.98 in the mid-1960s

---

[4] Giliomee (2016) provides a useful perspective on this 'broadertwis' (conflict between brothers).

to 0.23 by the mid-1980s. Strikingly, even as the various structural aspects of power weakened, the top-down character of leadership decision-making remained hierarchical.

In 1989, following a bout of ill-health, South Africa's hardline president P. W. Botha (who had previously served for fourteen years as minister of defence before acceding to party and national leadership) left office. He was succeeded by the lawyerly F. W. de Klerk, who ushered in a move away from repression and towards new modes of political incorporation of the majority of the country's population. This step is captured by the rise in the co-optation component in the third row of Table 5.2 (more on the co-optation measure a little later)—and by a corresponding rise in the social foundation index, from 13.8 per cent in the mid-1980s to 35.5 per cent during the political transition. South Africa was en route to a new 'political settlement'.

A new political settlement

By the latter 1980s, the apartheid political settlement was in tatters; South Africa seemed deep in a downward spiral towards civil war. Then came the celebrated 'rainbow miracle': the unbanning of the ANC and other political parties; the freeing of political prisoners, including Nelson Mandela; agreement in 1993 on an interim constitution; non-racial democratic elections in 1994; and the 1996 promulgation by an elected parliament of a new constitution.

As this sequence of events suggests, at the heart of the rainbow miracle was negotiation and agreement on a new set of formal institutions—a constitutional democracy. As laid out in Chapter 3, institutions feature centrally in the ESID definition of a political settlement. However, the empirical measures which are the focus of this chapter focus less on institutions and more on the constellations of power within which institutional arrangements are negotiated. The power dynamics underlying South Africa's new political settlement will thus be the focus of this section; the role of institutions will be discussed further in the chapter's conclusion.

To characterize South Africa's new political settlement, two time periods need to be considered together—the 1994–1996 period designated in Table 5.1 as 'Mandela', and the 1997–2007 period designated as 'Mandela/Mbeki'.[5] This is for two reasons. For one thing, while the country held its first non-racial democratic election in 1994, it was only in 1996 that a new constitution was approved by parliament.[6] Further, prior to the 1996 approval of the new constitution, South

---

[5] Thabo Mbeki succeeded Nelson Mandela as South Africa's president in 1999. From 1994–1999, as deputy president, he played a very active governing role.

[6] A painstakingly negotiated interim constitution had been approved in 1993, and provided sufficient surety to all to enable elections to proceed in 1994.

Africa formally was governed by a 'government of national unity'; only subsequently was the new political settlement consolidated under ANC leadership.

As per the three left columns of Table 5.1, there was a massive difference between the peak apartheid years and the new political settlement in the distribution of the population between the LB, CLB, and OB. The LB's size increased from under 10 per cent of the population in the latter apartheid years to 48 per cent/65 per cent in the new constitutional dispensation. In their responses to the ESID survey, the three expert respondents described the new LB in similar terms, as (to quote each):

- 'the umbrella ANC alliance';
- 'the ANC; black trade unions in the Congress of South African Trade Unions (COSATU); the South African Communist Party'; and
- 'the ANC; the black middle class; the black working class; the rural black population; Anglican etc. churches'.

Subsequent to 1994, most of the apartheid-era leaders were in either the CLB or OB; the new LB overwhelmingly comprised people who previously had been part of the (repressed) OB.

The ways in which these shifts in bloc composition translate into changes in the social foundation and power concentration scores are not straightforward. Consider, first, the 'social foundation' scores for the new political settlement. Paralleling the shift of affiliation of a large fraction of the population from the OB to the LB (and, to a lesser extent CLB), the social foundation scores for the latter periods are about three times as high as they were for peak apartheid. Strikingly, though, the 1994–2007 social foundation scores amount to only about half the share of the population who were included as part of either the LB or the CLB. Why?

Looking beyond the details of how the social foundation is constructed,[7] at the broadest level the reason why the social foundation is so much smaller than the LB-plus-CLB share is that citizens who are powerless are not included as part of the social foundation, regardless of their bloc. Indeed, as the bottom row of Table 5.4 shows, relative to the ESID average, a disproportionately large share of the ANC LB was in practice powerless. The unshakeable loyalty to the ANC of this 'part-of-LB-but-powerless' sub-bloc meant that their support could be taken for granted, independent of the actual policies pursued.[8] As will be discussed further below, the implications for South Africa's subsequent economic and political evolution were profound.

---

[7] For these details, see Chapter 3.
[8] The principal author of this chapter is indebted for this insight and its implications to a February 2020 conversation with Alan Hirsch and Jeremy Seekings.

Table 5.4 Changes in the ANC leadership bloc, 1994–2007

Leader period	Survey mean	Mandela (1994–1996)	Mbeki (1997–2007)
Social foundation			
Size (% population)	34	39	37
LB			
Size (% population)	36	65	48
o/w powerful (% population)	21	30	19
Share of LB that is powerful	0.6	0.5	0.4

Note: Social foundation and bloc sizes are rounded to the nearest per cent. Share of LB that is powerful to the nearest tenth of a per cent.
Source: Schulz and Kelsall (2021c)

Now consider the power concentration index. As per the top row of Table 5.5, the power concentration score for the new political settlement—0.57 for 1994–1996, and 0.77 for 1997–2007—was well below the 0.98 score for peak apartheid. However, both the 1994–1996 and 1997–2007 scores were above the power concentration mean of 0.52 across all observations included in ESID's forty-two-country dataset. Again, unbundling the power concentration score into its components reveals the reason for these variations.

The OB's influence on the power concentration score is summarized in the second row of Table 5.5. The OB was marginalized during both peak apartheid and post-1994 (especially 1997–2007), though for very different reasons. During peak apartheid, the OB comprised a very large share of the population—but, as discussed earlier, was comprehensively repressed. Subsequent to 1976 (indeed, until the government of national unity), repression continued; however, as the discussion of Table 5.3 highlighted, the OB's resistance made it powerful. During the 1994–1996 period, the OB continued to have quite significant power—though now the threat was of violent resistance from right-wing white elements within the society. Strikingly, in the 1997–2007 period, the OB was almost as powerless as it was during peak apartheid—though now because of its political irrelevance, not because of repression.

Within the LB, there turn out to be some striking parallels in how leaders wielded power in the peak apartheid years and in the first decade of democracy. As per the third row of Table 5.5, both the ANC and National Party were deferential to their leaders. Both also were political parties with deep roots in social movements. In consequence (as the fourth row of the table signals), in both there was a high degree of cohesion within the LB, at least on the surface. However, within the ANC this seemingly high degree of cohesion was fragile. The ANC was a broad tent, not only formally (it described itself as an 'alliance', with the Congress of South African Trade Unions and the South African Communist Party), but in

Table 5.5 Unbundling power concentration

Leader period	Peak Apartheid (mid 1960s)	Mandela (1994–1996)	Mbeki (1999–2007)
Power concentration	0.98	0.57	0.77
Horizontal power			
LB power relative to opposition (1–5; 5 = maximum)	4.7	3.3	4.3
Vertical power			
Top-down decision-making power within the LB (1–6; 6 = maximum)	6	5.7	5.7
LB cohesion (1–4; 4 = maximum)	4	3.3	3.7
Passivity of CLB (1–3; 3 = no defection risk)	3	2.7	2.3
Power of LB relative to CLB (1–3; 3 = maximum)	2.3	1.3	1.6

Note: Scores for horizontal and vertical power are rounded to the nearest tenth of a per cent.
Source: Schulz and Kelsall (2021c)

terms of the wide range of interests and ideologies which gathered under its umbrella (Lodge 2003; Booysen 2011, 2015). As will be explored below, this made it vulnerable to subsequent fragmentation.

The CLB comprises an intermediate category between the LB and the OB. As such, it can be the fulcrum of power within a political settlement. Indeed, the CLB played a central role in South Africa's democratic transition, as discussed earlier. Once democracy was established, the CLB was 'reconstituted' to include many of the most powerful actors from the late-apartheid era—both the apartheid-era political leadership, whose historical task was to negotiate their exit from power, and organized business whose role had been key in facilitating and influencing negotiations. In their responses to the ESID survey, the three expert respondents independently described the (at least 'somewhat powerful')[9] 1994–1996 CLB in very similar terms, as (to quote each):

- 'Broederbond-linked, "elite" white Afrikaners organized in the National Party, participating in a government of national unity. Organized business which was supportive of the new constitutional order. Zulu nationalists incorporated into the government of national unity'

[9] The survey asked respondents to distinguish between bloc sub-groups who had at least some power, and sub-groups who were powerless.

- 'The National Party; the Inkatha Freedom Party; most of organized business; trade unions other than those affiliated with COSATU; traditional leaders; security forces; rights-oriented civil society groupings; non-Calvinist churches'
- 'Military; bureaucracy; "independent" trade unions; traditional leaders; "English" capital; National Party; Inkatha Freedom Party'.

As per the bottom row of Table 5.5, the CLB remained powerful subsequent to 1994 (especially so in the initial period). However, having successfully achieved agreement on a set of institutional arrangements which they believed were capable of constraining the arbitrary exercise of governmental authority, they were content to revert (as in the apartheid-era) to a relatively passive role. More on this in the final section of this chapter.

One final contrast between South Africa's power concentration scores for peak apartheid and for the post-1994 political settlement is noteworthy. A score as high as apartheid South Africa's is likely only in a strongly unipolar authoritarian setting. However, the power concentration scores for South Africa's post-1994 political settlement signal that, outside of the upper extreme, there is no necessary association between whether or not a regime is authoritarian, and whether it has a high power concentration score. South Africa's settlement was negotiated among multiple stakeholders; it was multipolar; its relatively high 1997–2007 score signalled high national cohesion around the settlement, not top-down dominance.

South Africa's constitutional democracy—from hope to disillusion

For the first fifteen years, South Africa's new political settlement seemed to provide a viable platform for economic and social turnaround. Economic growth gradually accelerated, reaching a peak of a little over 5 per cent in 2007. Further, as predicted by the ESID framework, the broadening of the social foundation (albeit to a more limited extent than might superficially have seemed to be the case) resulted in major gains in social provisioning. As Table 5.6 summarizes, the percentage of the population that lived in poverty with daily hunger declined from 28 per cent in 1996 to 11 per cent in 2010; access to public services expanded rapidly; lifeline social grants were provided to 15 million people, close to 30 per cent of the population.

Then things began falling apart. The economy stopped growing. Inequality remained massive; a distributional 'cliff' left those outside the top one-third of the population poor, with little opportunity for upward mobility. Control over public resources (procurement contracts, high-paying jobs) became the most

Table 5.6 Changes in the provision of public services

	1996	2011
Absolute poverty, with daily hunger	28%	11%
Access to:	58%	85%
—electricity		
—piped water	56%	91%
Immunization coverage	68%	98%
Secondary school enrolment	50%	75%
Access to social grant (old age, child support, disability)	2.4 million	15 million

Sources: Levy, Hirsch, and Woolard (2015). The data, drawn from official statistics, were collated in Goldman Sachs, *Two Decades of Freedom—A Twenty-Year Review of South Africa*, 2013. Available at http://www.goldmansachs.com/our-thinking/outlook/colin-coleman-south-africa/20-yrs-of-freedom.pdf

available avenue for accumulating power and resources. Formal institutions (the bureaucracy, checks and balances) came under increasing pressure.[10]

Paralleling the earlier discussion of the demise of apartheid, what insight does ESID's empirical framework offer as to the causes of this reversal? As a first step in answering this question recall that, as per Table 5.4, the proportion of the LB that was at least somewhat powerful was strikingly low (especially during the Mbeki period). One plausible consequence is that the elite within the LB had unusually wide scope for setting the trajectory of governance and policy—including (given South Africa's proclivity for top-down decision-making) a disproportionate influence of leadership. This indeed turned out to be what happened. To see this, it is helpful to examine closely another set of ESID's building-block sub-components—the mode of co-optation.

The ESID survey asked respondents to weight the relative importance of a variety of ways of taking bloc members' concerns into account. Table 5.7 groups the responses into three categories: repression, clientelism, and programmatic co-optation.[11] As the table suggests, one of the great successes of South Africa's new political settlement, evident in the table, was that subsequent to 1994 repression has played almost no role in South African politics. Beyond that, however, the modes of co-optation varied across the four presidencies, with Jacob Zuma a marked outlier.

[10] For more in-depth analyses, see Mbeki (2009); Levy, Hirsch, Naidoo, and Nxele (2021); and Seekings and Nattrass (2015).

[11] These three categories are themselves aggregates: the survey elicited specific responses for each of violent and non-violent repression; and material and non-material clientelistic co-optation. It also distinguished between programmatic material legitimation, universalistic ideological legitimation, and procedurally democratic legitimation—all three of which are aggregated (by simple averaging) into the 'programmatic' category in the table.

Table 5.7 Changing modes of co-optation (1 = not important; 4 = very important)

	Verwoerd/ Vorster (1963–1975)	Mandela (1994– 1996)	Mbeki (1997– 2007)	Zuma (2009– 2017)	Ramaphosa (2018–)
LB and CLB					
Programmatic	3	3.4	3.3	2.1	3.3
Clientelism	3	2.5	2.4	3.6	2.5
Repression	1	1	1	1.6	1.1
OB					
Repression	4	1	1	1	1

Note: The survey elicited separate responses for each type of co-optation for each of the LB and the CLB, and (within each bloc) separately for leaders and followers. The responses were sufficiently similar for the four sub-categories that, for convenience, for each co-optation type, they were averaged into a single score.
Source: Schulz and Kelsall (2021c)

As per Table 5.7, though clientelism played some role during the Mandela and Mbeki periods, co-optation was predominantly programmatic—the promise (as per the ANC's campaign slogan) of 'a better life for all', underpinned by a strong ideational commitment to constitutional democracy. Indeed, Mbeki's unwillingness to cater to many of the ANC's factional interests was his downfall.

Jacob Zuma won power, defeating Mbeki's preferred successor, by skilfully exploiting resentment at Mbeki's top-down, technocratic, imperious approach to leadership. As Table 5.7 summarizes, upon acceding to power Zuma scaled back on programmatic ways of sustaining support and gave increasing emphasis to clientelism—both material (including explicit corruption) and non-material (ethno-nationalist, including a growing rhetorical assault on 'white monopoly capital') clientelistic co-optation. This U-turn from programmatic to clientelistic co-optation was associated with a decline in power concentration.

As shown in Table 5.8, South Africa's power concentration measure declined steadily from the Mbeki presidency (with a power concentration of 0.77), to Zuma (0.57) to Ramaphosa (0.42). The reason for this decline was not principally that the individual leaders varied in their willingness to assert power. Indeed, as the second row of the table signals, both Jacob Zuma and Thabo Mbeki, schooled as they were in the disciplines of the ANC-in exile, continued a longstanding South African pattern of making decisions from the top-down. Rather, unbundling the power concentration components reveals that a central reason for the decline in measured power concentration was that the complexity and brittleness of the elite bargain which underlay South Africa's political settlement increasingly became manifest.

As the third row of Table 5.8 signals, the bitter leadership struggle which led to Jacob Zuma's accession undermined the cohesion of the LB. Some ANC cadres, disaffected by Jacob Zuma's heightened emphasis on clientelism, no longer gave

Table 5.8 Unbundling power concentration over time, democratic era

Leader period	Mbeki (1999–2007)	Zuma (2009–2017)	Ramaphosa (2018–)
Power concentration	0.77	0.57	0.42
Vertical power			
Top-down decision-making power within the LB (1–6; 6 = maximum)	5.7	5.7	5.0
LB cohesion (1–4; 4 = maximum)	3.7	2.0	2.7
Passivity of CLB (1–3; 3 = no defection risk)	2.3	2.0	2.3
Power of LB relative to CLB (1–3; 3 = maximum)	1.6	1.3	0.9
Horizontal power			
Power of LB relative to OB (1–5; 5 = maximum)	4.3	4.1	3.3

Note: Scores for horizontal and vertical power are rounded to the nearest tenth of a per cent.
Source: Schulz and Kelsall (2021c)

their undivided loyalty, and became part of the CLB. Many who remained within the LB opposed Zuma's turn—signified by the decline in the intra-LB cohesion score in Table 5.8 from 3.7 to 2.0. Portions of the established business community became less passive. As per the bottom three rows of Table 5.8, the relative power of both the CLB and OB rose somewhat.

When Ramaphosa won the battle to succeed Jacob Zuma, the hope was that he would restore the Mandela/Mbeki approach to governance. Indeed, as per Table 5.7, Ramaphosa gave more emphasis than Zuma to programmatic approaches, with a corresponding scaling back of clientelism. He also generally was less top-down in wielding authority than either Mbeki or Zuma—as evident in the lower top-down decision-making score in Table 5.8. While these shifts resulted in a modest rise in the cohesion of the LB (from 2.0 to 2.7), they were offset (for reasons explored further later) by a decline in the influence of the LB relative to both the CLB and OB. Taken together, the cumulative consequence was a further decline in power concentration.

Disaggregation of the social foundation indicator and its components offers an additional perspective on the complexity and brittleness of the 'bargain' underlying South Africa's post-1994 political settlement. As per the top row of Table 5.9, the 'headline' measure of social foundation barely changed between the Mandela, Mbeki, and Zuma periods, but then increased sharply when Ramaphosa became president. Beneath these aggregate patterns is a more complex story.

Table 5.9 Unbundling the social foundation over time, democratic era

Leader period	Survey mean	Mandela (1994–1996)	Mbeki (1997–2007)	Zuma (2009–2017)	Ramaphosa (2018–)
Social foundation					
Size (% population)	34	39	37	38	53
LB component (% population)	15	27	17	15	19
CLB component (% population)	10	6	13	9	20
OB component (% population)	9	5	8	13	15

Note: Each cell comprises the per cent powerful in the bloc weighted by the bloc's co-optation score, rounded to the nearest per cent.

The ESID average co-optation scores for each of the LB, CLB, and OB are 0.72, 0.66, and 0.46. As detailed in Appendix E, for all but one of the cells in the table, the South African co-optation weights were above 0.80 (the Zuma period OB score was 0.71).

Source: Schulz and Kelsall (2021c)

As laid out in Chapter 4, the social foundation uses a weighting system to designate who are the socially salient groups that have the potential to disrupt a settlement which does not adequately incorporate them. Table 5.9 lays out the (weighted) distribution of these influential groups across the LB, CLB, and OB for each of the four periods; Appendix E provides disaggregated detail as to the weights.[12] The data in the table suggest that between 1994 and 2019 influence progressively shifted away from the LB towards the OB and CLB. The paragraphs which follow drill down into these shifts.

Part of the explanation for the rise in the social salience of the OB is straightforward: in 2013, a disgruntled faction of the ANC, motivated by a mix of grievances (some ideological, others self-serving) broke away to establish a new political party, the Economic Freedom Front (EFF). The EFF has been moderately successful electorally, winning 5–10 per cent of the popular vote, and has been an ongoing, vocal thorn in the side of both the Zuma and Ramaphosa administrations. Once Ramaphosa succeeded Zuma, the OB's size declined from 38 per cent of the population to 28.5 per cent (Table 5.1) yet, paradoxically, its contribution to the social foundation score increased—a result of Cyril Ramaphosa's more inclusive, co-optation-oriented approach to leadership.

---

[12] The bloc-specific components in Table 5.9 are calculated from three sub-measures: bloc size; the proportion of each bloc that is relatively powerful; and the co-optation scores. Only for the first of these is there a one-to-one correspondence between a decline in the measure for one bloc, and a rise in the measure for the others. In large part, actual power dynamics, not arithmetic correspondences, thus account for the Table 5.9 patterns.

Turning to the CLB, as Table 5.9 signals, its social salience has fluctuated throughout South Africa's democratic era. This fluctuation was shaped in part by how various sub-blocs chose to position themselves in relation to power, and in part on the degree to which LB leadership chose (or was successfully pressured) to attend to their concerns. In the immediate aftermath of 1994 rainbow miracle, the CLB's social salience was low—most sub-blocs with influence chose to bask in the glow of South Africa's rainbow miracle and cooperate with power. By the 2010s, established business elites (a longstanding part of South Africa's CLB) had become more distant from government. In addition, the composition of the CLB had shifted to incorporate also sub-blocs who broadly were part of the ANC's big tent, but had become distant from the inner circle of power.[13]

Jacob Zuma and Cyril Ramaphosa responded to the concerns of CLB sub-blocs in very different ways. Zuma was less attentive to their concerns than Thabo Mbeki, reducing their power. Cyril Ramaphosa, by contrast, chose (insofar as he had a choice which, given the hair-breadth intra-party victory which brought him to power, is itself uncertain) to respond not by ignoring the concerns of potential rivals and of business but by engaging them, working to incorporate them into a ruling coalition.

In sum, at 52.6 per cent, the social foundation during the Ramaphosa period was much higher than in earlier periods (and also high relative to the average of all countries in the ESID sample). However, this high social foundation was not reflective of support from an increasingly unified, broad-based political organization. Instead, a disproportionate share of the social foundation reflected the influence of socially salient and potentially disruptive sub-blocs within the CLB and OB. Especially noteworthy is the rise in the social salience of CLB sub-groups who had been close to Jacob Zuma, and now were estranged from power, but could not be ignored by President Ramaphosa. By 2020, the optimism of the rainbow miracle was gone. Increasingly, South Africa's difficult historical legacy, deep-seated inequality, limited opportunities for upward mobility, and contestation for influence among emergent elites was taking a toll. The combination of a relatively broad social foundation and a relatively low power concentration made the country difficult to govern.

As laid out in Chapter 3, the ESID framework predicts that a decline in power concentration would have an economic cost, in the form of slower growth. South Africa's growth pattern from 2000–2019 (see Figure 5.1) is consistent with this prediction. Over the course of the Mandela/Mbeki era, economic growth had been accelerating. As with most countries the world over, growth was knocked off track by the global financial crisis. At first, the country seemed to recover

---

[13] Throughout the 2010s, both of the ANC's 'alliance' partners—the South African Communist Party and the Congress of South African Trade Unions (COSATU)—were careful to maintain some distance from ANC leadership. COSATU was itself quite divided, with different factions aligning themselves differently (even to the point of a split during the Zuma period).

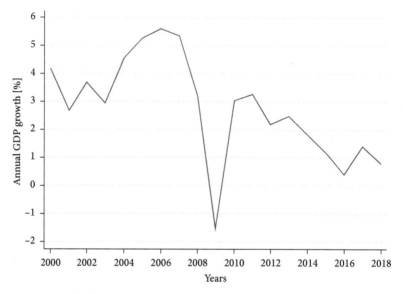

Fig. 5.1 South African economic growth, 2000–2019

Source: Our illustration using World Bank data (data.worldbank.org).

quite rapidly. Subsequently, however, contrary to other middle-income countries (MICs), the South African economy failed to build momentum, and became mired in stagnation.

Applying the ESID political settlement framework at the country level—some reflections

This chapter has applied the ESID political settlements framework and measures to the experience of a single country over time, South Africa. The effort reveals a mix of strengths, ambiguities, and limitations.

As a first strength of the framework, South Africa's development experience is consistent with the two causal hypotheses presented in Chapter 3 and tested econometrically in Chapter 7. As per these chapters, higher power concentration is hypothesized to be associated with higher growth rates, and higher social foundation is hypothesized to be associated with broader social provisioning. Both patterns are evident in the South Africa case.

Along with affirmation of the core causal relationships, the South Africa case study points to a further strength—the insights which the measures and trends of each of power concentration and social foundation offer into power, and its evolution. At its peak, apartheid South Africa was an extreme outlier across the forty-two-country ESID dataset—at the upper limit in power concentration, and near the lower limit in the breadth of its social foundation. This power progressively decayed. Strikingly, a parallel pattern of decay was evident for the post-apartheid democratic political settlement. As this chapter has detailed, the ESID measures provide a basis for linking this decay to very specific, clear-cut sequences of change in the relationship between the LB and the OB, in how the contingent leadership bloc positioned itself vis-à-vis the LB, and in the internal cohesion of the LB itself.

Some ambiguities in the ESID approach emerge from the country-specific application—but they turn out to be analytically intriguing. One ambiguity concerns the longstanding challenge in political settlements analysis (PSA) of how to decide what type of political settlement prevails in a specific country. Chapters 3 and 4 use the power concentration and social foundation variables to identify four characteristic types of political settlement. Table 5.1, at the outset of this chapter, reported South Africa's power concentration and social foundation scores for each of eight distinct sub-periods from the mid-1960s to the late 2010s. Applying these scores cross-sectionally to each period, it might seem as if, over the course of the half-century, the country inhabited each of the four political settlement cells laid out in the earlier chapters. Considered intertemporally, a different interpretation emerges, one with two distinct political settlements, each of which 'enjoyed' a peak period of authority, but then subsequently decayed.

A second ambiguity concerns the place of institutions in PSA. Institutions are, of course, central to the ESID approach—as per the definition of a political settlement laid out in Chapter 3 as 'an ongoing agreement (or acquiescence) ... to a set of political and economic institutions'. The South Africa case study reveals powerfully an additional function of institutions in a political settlement—the case directs attention to the role which pre-existing institutional capability can play in shaping a political settlement by helping (as per Chapter 3) to resolve second-order collective-action problems. Pre-existing institutional capabilities turn out to be crucial in accounting for South Africa's transition from one settlement to another: inherited institutional strengths gave established elites from the apartheid era confidence that agreements negotiated in the transition would be effectively monitored and enforced going forward; this enhanced their willingness to cede control over government and its coercive apparatus.

Institutions aside, leadership and ideas comprise two further variables to which the ESID political settlements framework gives limited attention, but which turn out to play a crucial role in accounting for South Africa's political dynamics. The role of leadership is vividly evident in three South African transitions: the shift from the hard-line leadership of P. W. Botha to the pragmatic leadership of F. W. de Klerk; the visionary, reconciliation-oriented leadership provided by Nelson Mandela; and Jacob Zuma's turn, subsequent to assuming power, away from the broad-based, programmatic, and non-racial ethos which had characterized the ANC.

'Ideas' played an important independent role in South Africa's political evolution via their roles both in social mobilization to win power and, power having been won, in the extent of cohesion of the leadership bloc. These roles are evident in the highly cohesive Afrikaner nationalist movement which underpinned the coming to power and rule of the National Party, in the longstanding ANC commitment to non-racialism which underpinned South Africa's rainbow miracle political settlement, and in emerging efforts (which so far have had only limited success) to use ethno-populism as a basis for transforming South African politics.

A further limitation concerns the extent to which the ESID approach provides a causal explanation of changes over time (as distinct from simply tracking trends). The principal purpose of PSA generally has been more static/cross-sectoral than dynamic/inter-temporal. The aim has been to show how distinctive settlements give rise to distinctive patterns of incentives and constraints—and how these, in turn, affect growth, public-sector capability and social provisioning.[14] The approach was not designed to shed much light on key inflection points, why they arise—and why, in the immediacy of the moment, leaders and organizations reacted to these inflection points in the way they did. Indeed, a political settlements approach adds little to our understanding of the reasons for South Africa's 1970s uprising of the black majority, or of why the country was able to effect its successful, rainbow miracle turnaround from a seemingly inexorable descent into civil war to a constitutional democracy. But, perhaps unexpectedly, it does offer some fresh insight into how and why, in the aftermath of these critical junctures, things unfolded the way they did.

Application of ESID's empirical methodology to the South African case highlights cascading declines of power concentration: the cumulative disintegration of the ruling coalition in the late apartheid-era; and the ways in which the brittleness of ANC governance—internecine conflict within the LB and between the LB and CLB—put pressure on institutional capabilities.[15] These insights signal all-too-vividly how daunting is the challenge South Africa confronts if it is to, once again, turn things around. While a purely qualitative methodology may also have yielded similar insights, the addition of a quantitative component throws them into particularly sharp relief, while opening new possibilities for rigorous intra-country and international comparison.

---

[14] For a sustained application along these lines to South Africa's education sector, see Levy, Cameron, Hoadley, and Naidoo (2018).

[15] For a detailed exploration of these dynamics see Levy, Hirsch, Naidoo, and Nxele (2021).

6

Analysing Political Settlements and Development in Four Countries

Ghana, Guinea, Cambodia, and Rwanda

In the previous chapter we illustrated how our approach to variable construction and survey data could be used to describe and illuminate the political history of a single country. In this chapter we show how the approach can be used to analyse the comparative politics of development. We select four countries that over the past two decades provide good representations (see Figure 6.1) of the different quadrants of our typology, and trace the links between our typological variables and economic and social development. Specifically, we discuss Ghana as a broad-dispersed settlement, Guinea as a narrow-dispersed settlement, Cambodia as a narrow-concentrated settlement, and Rwanda as a broad-concentrated settlement.

In the following pages we explore the relationship between political settlement type, elite commitment, state effectiveness, and development outcomes in three policy areas: economic growth, maternal mortality reduction, and quality education, effectively making twelve cases. As Table 6.1 illustrates, of these twelve, eight conform to the predictions of our typological theory, and four conform partially. In the chapter's final section we invoke the idea of the 'policy domain', a meso-level field of power relations which interacts with the political settlement and within which actors promote competing policy agendas, to help explain this.

Note that our case selection was driven by two factors: countries that lie towards the outer edge of the distribution for each type and/or countries where the Effective States and Inclusive Development research centre (ESID) had already conducted extensive multi-sectoral fieldwork. Ghana and Rwanda satisfy both criteria; Cambodia satisfies the second, and Guinea the first. Regarding the latter, note that ESID did not conduct any primary research in narrow-dispersed settlements and, with the present book being completed during the lockdown conditions of the Covid-19 pandemic, it has not been possible to conduct additional, gap-filling research. In the case of Guinea we have thus had to rely on secondary materials, which do not exist in abundance. However, such materials as we have been able to find do appear to support our hypotheses.

Political Settlements and Development. Tim Kelsall et al., Oxford University Press.
© Tim Kelsall et al., (2022). DOI: 10.1093/oso/9780192848932.003.0006

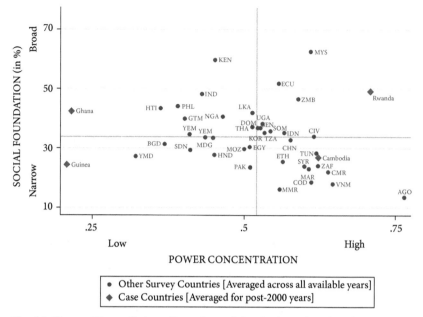

Fig. 6.1 Recent Ghana, Guinea, Rwanda, and Cambodia political settlement codings relative to other survey countries

Source: Authors' illustration using data from Schulz and Kelsall (2021c)

Political settlements in the four countries

We turn now to a discussion of political settlements in our four countries, the evolution of which is shown in Figure 6.2, illustrating for each how we arrived at our codings.[1]

Broad-dispersed Ghana

Ghana, formerly known as the Gold Coast, gained independence from Britain in 1957. In the ensuing six decades it has swung between periods of democracy and authoritarianism, broader and narrower settlements; yet no regime has concentrated power to a high degree.

Since the year 2000, the period on which ESID research has concentrated, the country has witnessed periodic electoral swings between the two political traditions that predate independence: the 'Danquah-Busia' liberal tradition, associated with the New Patriotic Party (NPP) (Kufuor, 2000–2008; Akuffo-Addo, 2016–)

---

[1] Note that the text that follows draws on a combination of referenced published sources and the PolSett survey data.

Table 6.1 Summary of country findings with respect to development performance and political settlement type

Country/Settlement	Economic growth	Maternal health	Education
Ghana/Broad-dispersed	*Conforms to type:* moderate growth performance with low structural transformation.	*Conforms to type:* high spending but poor performance, except in pockets.	*Conforms to type:* high spending but poor performance, except in pockets.
Guinea/Narrow-dispersed	*Conforms to type:* low growth with no structural transformation.	*Partially conforms to type:* low spending and poor performance, though with recent spending increases.	*Conforms to type:* low spending and low performance.
Cambodia/Narrow-concentrated	*Conforms to 'proto-developmental' sub-type:* high but somewhat exclusionary growth with significant structural transformation.	*Partially conforms to type:* low spending but very good performance, explained by policy domain dynamics.	*Partially conforms to type:* low spending and poor performance but signs of improvement that can be explained by political settlement/policy domain dynamics.
Rwanda/Broad-concentrated	*Conforms to 'proto-developmental' sub-type:* fairly high and reasonably inclusive growth with some structural transformation.	*Conforms to type:* high spending and excellent performance.	*Partially conforms to type:* high spending but poor performance. Can be explained by political settlement/policy domain dynamics.

Source: Authors' Own

and the more left-leaning 'Nkrumah/Rawlings' tradition, represented by the National Democratic Congress (NDC) (Atta-Mills/Mahama, 2008–2016). The settlement is premised on a constitutional agreement that the government will be formed by the winner of a competitive struggle for the people's vote, and an informal understanding that the government will use its power to reward its own supporters, while trying to curry favour with others.

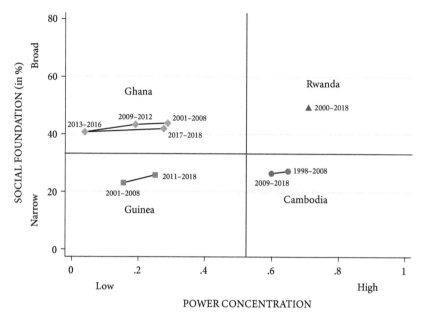

Fig. 6.2 Political settlements in Ghana, Guinea, Cambodia, and Rwanda, *c.*1998–2018

Source: Authors' illustration using data from Schulz and Kelsall (2021c)

Each of the parties has its regional and or/class heartlands. Strongly loyal to John Kufuor, for example, were ethno-regional elites of the Ashanti and Eastern regions, professional and southern elites, mainly from the South, established and younger business elites, as well as the established churches and NPP political appointees in District Assemblies and Executives. For the NDC's Atta-Mills it was 31st December Women's Movement, transport workers, local youth associations in small towns, elites from the Volta, Northern and Upper Regions, in addition to NDC political appointees.

To win power and govern, however, each was also dependent on winning favour from substantial, only contingently loyal swing constituencies. These included private business clients, cocoa farmers in parts of Ashanti and the East, ethno-regional elites, and voters in parts of the Western, Central, and Brong-Ahafo regions as well as Accra.[2] In an attempt to capture these constituencies, each party typically mobilizes its local-level supporters in colourful and sometimes rowdy election campaigns. Concretely, party 'footsoldiers' and business backers, especially in these regions, have the power to demand patronage in the shape of cash, government jobs, and contracts. Meanwhile most senior public-sector bureaucrats

---

[2] Ghana previously had ten regions until after 2018 when a referendum in four regions culminated in the creation of six additional regions.

Table 6.2 Unbundling power concentration in Ghana, 2000–2018

Leader period	Survey mean	Kufuor	Atta-Mills	Mahama	Akufo-Addo
Power concentration	0.52	0.29	0.19	0.04	0.27
Horizontal power					
LB power relative to opposition (1–5; 5 = maximum)	3.4	2.3	2.3	1.7	2.7
Vertical power					
Top-down decision-making power within the LB (1–6; 6 = maximum)	5.4	4.5	4.1	4.1	4.1
LB cohesion (1–4; 4 = maximum)	3.1	3	2.3	2.3	2.7
Passivity of CLB (1–3; 3 = no defection risk)	2.2	2.7	2	1.7	2
Power of LB relative to CLB (1–3; 3 = maximum)	1.4	1.2	1.2	1.1	1.2

Note: Scores for horizontal and vertical power are rounded to the nearest tenth of a per cent.
Source: Schulz and Kelsall (2021c)

are said to be 'appointed by presidential fiat, largely on the basis of partisan political criteria rather than merit' (Gyimah-Boadi and Yakah 2012).

This is reflected in our survey results in Table 6.2, which show that all the ruling coalition's vertical power components are a little lower than average, while horizontal power is much lower, signifying a dispersed configuration. When it comes to the social foundation (Table 6.3), the data suggests that the leader's bloc (LB) in Ghana tends to be quite large, with a smaller contingently loyal bloc (CLB) and larger opposition bloc (OB), with the percentage of bloc members that are powerful close to the survey mean. It is the comparatively high levels of co-optation, especially for the OB, that contribute to Ghana being coded as having a broad social foundation.

Narrow-dispersed Guinea

Since gaining independence from French colonial rule in 1958, Guinea's political settlement has had a narrow social foundation consisting primarily of the ruling president's and related clans. During the Marxist dictator Sekou Touré's regime

Table 6.3 Unbundling the social foundation in Ghana, 2000–2018

Leader period	Survey mean	Kufuor	Atta-Mills	Mahama	Akufo-Addo
Social foundation					
Size (% population)	34	44	43	41	42
LB					
Size (% population)	36	47	47	46	49
o/w powerful %	21	21	19	21	22
Co-optation score	0.7	0.9	0.9	0.9	0.9
CLB					
Size (% population)	27	17	17	13	15
o/w % powerful	10	12	12	10	10
Co-optation score	0.7	0.9	0.9	0.9	0.9
OB					
Size (% population)	37	36	36	41	35
o/w % powerful	19	18	19	17	17
Co-optation score	0.5	0.8	0.8	0.8	0.8

Note: Social foundation and bloc sizes are rounded to the nearest per cent. Co-optation scores to the nearest tenth of a per cent.
Source: Schulz and Kelsall (2021c)

(1958–1983), political power was concentrated in the LB, dispersing over time. After Touré died, a military dictatorship took control, led by Lansana Conté as head of the Military Committee for National Recovery. Conté held multi-party elections in 1993, yet from the early 2000s, the country experienced increased political instability as his legitimacy waned and the opposition grew stronger.

In 2008, Conté died, an event which was immediately followed by a military coup. After a period of extreme instability, elections were held in 2011, with Alpha Condé being declared the new president.[3] Many Guineans welcomed the return to civilian rule, yet support for Condé was lukewarm. The LB was small and the CLB consisted of diverse groups that supported Condé mainly to prevent his opponent, Diallo, from taking power. The OB was also more substantial than during Conté's rule since political parties had now had time to develop.

The subsequent decade has seen intense periods of opposition protest and government crackdown, postponed and disputed elections. Condé's approach to leadership is similar to Touré and Conté in the way that he tightly controls his party and resists political opposition despite it now being legal. Like Conté, he uses material clientelism and force to co-opt and repress, while also utilizing narratives around ethnic identity to marginalize or co-opt social groups. Only those closest to the leader benefit from state resources. Trade unions, civil society, and

---

[3] Note that these sections draw heavily on qualitative data in the ESID survey.

Table 6.4 Unbundling power concentration in Guinea, 2000–2018

Leader period	Survey mean	Conté	Condé
Power concentration	0.52	0.15	0.25
Horizontal power			
LB power relative to opposition (1–5; 5 = maximum)	3.4	2.9	2
Vertical power			
Top-down decision-making power within the LB (1–6; 6 = maximum)	5.4	4.5	5.7
LB cohesion (1–4; 4 = maximum)	3.1	1	2.6
Passivity of CLB (1–3; 3 = no defection risk)	2.2	1.3	2
Power of LB relative to CLB (1–3; 3 = maximum)	1.4	0.9	1.3

Note: Scores for horizontal and vertical power are rounded to the nearest tenth of a per cent.
Source: Schulz and Kelsall (2021c)

independent media meanwhile are subject to state harassment. This has resulted in violent and volatile politics as all three regime leaders have struggled to maintain their position of power.

Our Table 6.4 data show that not only has the ruling coalition been weak relative to the opposition in terms of horizontal power, but that on most dimensions of vertical power, the leadership has also been weak, with a higher-than-average likelihood that the CLB would split, weak LB cohesion, and somewhat-low top-down decision-making power. This apparently endemic fractiousness helps explain why we code Guinea's power configuration as dispersed.

When it comes to the social foundation, the Table 6.5 data shows that LB and CLB supporters combined constitute a minority of the population under Conté. The OB are in the majority, with the regime's preference for repressing over co-opting them, keeping the social foundation narrow. The ruling coalition broadens a little under Condé, yet it is still some distance below the survey mean.

Narrow-concentrated Cambodia

Cambodia was led to independence from France in 1953 by the charismatic Prince Norodom Sihanouk. Initially, Sihanouk's power was highly concentrated and narrow, but over time it began to disperse as opposition grew. He was displaced by a coup in 1970, and there followed thirty years of dictatorship and civil war, including the genocidal Khmer Rouge regime (1975–1979). In 1993, a power-sharing agreement followed multi-party elections, and since 1998, the country has been

Table 6.5 Unbundling the social foundation in Guinea, 2000–2018

Leader period	Survey mean	Conté	Condé
Social foundation			
Size (% population)	34%	23%	25%
LB			
Size (% population)	36	25	31
o/w powerful %	21	12	19
Co-optation score	0.7	0.7	0.7
CLB			
Size (% population)	27	21	24
o/w % powerful	10	9	10
Co-optation score	0.7	0.6	0.6
OB			
Size (% population)	37	53	44
o/w % powerful	19	22	16
Co-optation score	0.5	0.4	0.4

Note: Social foundation and bloc sizes are rounded to the nearest per cent. Co-optation scores to the nearest tenth of a per cent.
Source: Schulz and Kelsall (2021c)

dominated by Hun Sen's Cambodian People's Party (which has in effect been in power since 1979).

Hun Sen's support base includes domestic and foreign capitalists, most CPP cadres, CPP aligned unions, civil-society organizations (CSOs), and religious organizations, as well as significant numbers of peasants and civil servants. Other peasants, some workers, and foreign donors—including, increasingly—China, can be categorized as contingently loyal. The main opposition has come from former royalists, students, and those displaced by the government's economic policies (Kelsall and Heng 2014a). Although the CPP has faced tough tests at the polls in 2003 (continuing, nominally, to share power with the royalist party FUNCINPEC until 2008) and 2013, after which there were around three months of anti-CPP demonstrations, its domination of the security forces and its willingness to use repression when necessary to maintain its rule, have disempowered the majority of the population. In 2017, the courts dissolved the main opposition the Cambodia National Rescue Party (CNRP), resulting in a landslide victory for Hun Sen at elections in 2018.

Table 6.6 shows that on most indices the horizontal and vertical power of the ruling coalition has been above the survey means, explaining its 'concentrated' coding.

When it comes to the social foundation, Table 6.7 shows that although the three blocs are relatively evenly matched in size, a significant proportion of the LB's

Table 6.6 Unbundling power concentration in Cambodia, 1998–2018

Leader period	Survey mean	Hun Sen 4	Hun Sen 5
Power concentration	0.52	0.65	0.59
Horizontal power			
LB power relative to opposition (1–5; 5 = maximum)	3.4	4	3.2
Vertical power			
Top-down decision-making power within the LB (1–6; 6 = maximum)	5.4	5.5	6
LB cohesion (1–4; 4 = maximum)	3.1	3	3.2
Passivity of CLB (1–3; 3 = no defection risk)	2.2	2.5	2.5
Power of LB relative to CLB (1–3; 3 = maximum)	1.4	1.4	1.9

Note: Scores for horizontal and vertical power are rounded to the nearest tenth of a per cent.
Source: Schulz and Kelsall (2021c)

Table 6.7 Unbundling the social foundation in Cambodia, 1998–2018

Leader period	Survey mean	Hun Sen 4	Hun Sen 5
Social foundation			
Size (% population)	34	27	26
LB			
Size (% population)	36	31	30
o/w powerful %	21	17	16
Co-optation score	0.7	0.6	0.6
CLB			
Size (% population)	27	33	28
o/w % powerful	10	10	7
Co-optation score	0.7	0.5	0.5
OB			
Size (% population)	37	35	40
o/w % powerful	19	28	33
Co-optation score	0.5	0.4	0.4

Note: Social foundation and bloc sizes are rounded to the nearest per cent. Co-optation scores to the nearest tenth of a per cent.
Source: Schulz and Kelsall (2021c)

supporters are relatively powerless. And while a greater percentage of opposition supporters are powerful, they are more than averagely repressed. It is this combination of powerlessness and repression that explains Cambodia's narrow coding. At the same time, it should be stressed that the codings for Cambodia are averaged or 'typical' for the twenty-year duration of a political settlement that began in 1998. There have been episodes within that long period, for example around elections in 2003 and 2013, when the opposition has appeared rather strong.

Broad-concentrated Rwanda

Rwanda gained independence from Belgium in 1962. Since that date the country's politics has been dominated by dynamics between the minority Tutsi ethnic group, bearers of the royal lineage and collaborators with the Belgians for much of the colonial period, and the majority Hutu, with in-group cleavages playing a secondary role. Simplifying, first president Gregoire Kayibanda established a narrow-concentrated settlement around Hutus from the Central-Southern region; the regime's centre of gravity swung to Hutu in the North after he was displaced in a coup by General Juvenal Habyarimana in 1973. This settlement unravelled in 1990, when Tutsi exiles invaded the country, leading to a period of civil war, political transition, and ultimately a genocide of Tutsi by extremist Hutu elements. Despite the genocide the Tutsi-dominated Rwandan Patriotic Front (RPF) took power in 1994. The RPF installed as president Pasteur Bizimungu, a Hutu, though many believed Paul Kagame, leader of the Rwandan Patriotic Army (RPA) and vice-president, was the man really in charge.

In 2000, Bizimungu resigned and Kagame was elected president by MPs and ministers. This followed a period in which political elites disagreeing with Kagame's basic vision and behavioural precepts were progressively excised from the party, and began a period of dominance that has lasted until the present day. With a seven-year presidential mandate, Kagame has secured re-election twice, albeit in conditions widely criticized by international observers. Partly because of this, perceptions of the current regime are contested, including among our coders. However, there is a consensus that loyal to Kagame are much of the Ugandan old guard, military and security officers, and that his support base may extend to allied political parties, an ethnically diverse business community, and even former Hutu extremists who have returned to the country. In the CLB, meanwhile, are Hutu in official positions, development partners, plus ordinary Hutu and Tutsi peasants, with whom the government tries to legitimate itself through both clientelistic and programmatic co-optation. Meanwhile the opposition is comprised of recalcitrant Hutu extremists and former fractions of the RPF that have fallen out with Kagame, most of which are now in exile. Also included in this bloc have been opposition parties such as the Democratic Greens.

Institutionally, the RPF has chosen to govern in combination with smaller pro-regime parties, among whom great care is taken to generate consensus. Apparently, robust policy debates occur behind closed doors, but once decisions have been made, the focus shifts to implementation, with little tolerance for dissent. The party has established hierarchical governance structures characterized by strong

Table 6.8 Unbundling power concentration in Rwanda, 2000–2018

Leader period	Survey mean	Kagame
Power concentration	0.52	0.71
Horizontal power		
LB power relative to opposition (1–5; 5 = maximum)	3.4	4.05
Vertical power		
Top-down decision-making power within the LB (1–6; 6 = maximum)	5.4	5.6
LB cohesion (1–4; 4 = maximum)	3.1	3.6
Passivity of CLB (1–3; 3 = no defection risk)	2.2	2.1
Power of LB relative to CLB (1–3; 3 = maximum)	1.4	1.74

Note: Scores for horizontal and vertical power are rounded to the nearest tenth of a per cent.
Source: Schulz and Kelsall (2021c)

top-down accountability measures, more common in states at much higher levels of income (Chambers 2012; Chambers and Golooba-Mutebi 2012).

When it comes to coding, Table 6.8 shows that the leadership has high horizontal power, being much stronger than the opposition, and that power is also higher than average on all components of the vertical dimension, with the exception of CLB passivity, which is just below average. The combined strength of horizontal and vertical power provides Rwanda with its highly concentrated power coding.

Social foundation-wise, Table 6.9 suggests that in Rwanda, the LB and CLB comprise a small majority, with the OB being quite large. The balance of co-optation over repression is actually close to the country means. What distinguishes Rwanda and makes its social foundation broad, is the high percentage of all bloc members who are deemed to have some power. This is somewhat contrary to popular perceptions of Rwanda as a country with a largely quiescent population. But remember that we are dealing with leadership perceptions here. Rwanda's ruling coalition, living with the memory of genocide, may perceive the population to be potentially powerful, even in the face of apparent passivity.

Economic growth and transformation

In Chapter 3 we laid out several hypotheses about the relationship between political settlement types and development. When it comes to economic growth, we argued that, generally speaking, concentrated settlements will have an advantage for two potential reasons (the balance between which will likely vary according to the precise character of their 'power concentration'). First, being in most

Table 6.9 Unbundling the social foundation in Rwanda, 2000–2018

Leader period	Survey mean	Kagame
Social foundation		
Size (% population)	34	49
LB		
Size (% population)	36	31
o/w powerful %	21	29
Co-optation score	0.7	0.6
CLB		
Size (% population)	27	25
o/w % powerful	10	23
Co-optation score	0.7	0.6
OB		
Size (% population)	37	44
o/w % powerful	19	39
Co-optation score	0.5	0.5

Note: Social foundation and bloc sizes are rounded to the nearest per cent. Co-optation scores to the nearest tenth of a per cent.
Source: Schulz and Kelsall (2021c)

cases more politically secure, political elites will be more likely to have a long time-horizon, and thereby incentivized to make short-term sacrifices for bigger long-term pay-offs, for example in the 'stationary bandit' scenario hypothesized by Mancur Olson, and the reasoning that informs Mushtaq Khan's 'horizontal' power dimension (Olson 1993, Khan 2010). Not only might this lead to higher rates of investment over consumption, and more productive over less productive forms of rent-seeking, it should also provide governing elites the breathing space to build the disciplined state capacity needed to enable technological learning and upgrading. Second, and corresponding more closely (though not exactly) to Khan's 'vertical power' dimension, the relative political strength of governing elites will make it easier for them, other things being equal, to enforce growth policy on potential losers, whether that be rent-seeking elites or expropriated popular classes.

The way power concentration plays out, however, will also be influenced by the breadth of the social foundation. We hypothesized that where the social foundation is broad, governing elites will be incentivized to try and promote a more inclusive growth pattern. Growth might not be as rapid as in narrow settlements, but it will arguably be more equitable, with fewer instances of expropriation and dispossession. That does not mean that growth in narrow-concentrated settlements cannot have inclusive effects; however, these are more likely to be the result of positive externalities and trickle-down effects than deliberate policy.

In dispersed power configurations, by contrast, governing elites are likely to have shorter time-horizons since they are more focused on immediate political survival. Since they are less sure that they will benefit from economic growth in the future, they will have less incentive to try and promote it. Even if they try, they will have less breathing space in which to build state technical capacity, and less political strength to enforce policy on losers.

The breadth of the social foundation does, however, have a role to play. In broad-based settlements the elite may at least try to promote some general, income-raising economic growth as a means of being seen to be responsive to the mass of the population and with a view to funding broad-based social benefits. In narrow settlements there is less of an incentive even to try. Such growth as exists is more likely to be confined to enclaves from which governing elites can extract short-term profits, especially, perhaps, in the form of kick-backs and corruption.

One final point is in order when it comes to economic development. In all types, where point-source resources are abundant this is likely to weaken elites' motivation to foster transformative growth. The temptation will be to use rents for populist or patronage purposes, instead of undertaking the hard slog of productivity enhancement. Nevertheless, where elites are far-sighted and have a mutual understanding of a compelling threat, point resources may prove to be a transformative resource.

Putting it slightly differently, concentrated settlements, whether narrow or broad, have the ability to focus leadership efforts on building state capacity and consequently, in the absence of abundant and easily available resources, societies of this type are often in a better position to pursue growth objectives than are societies with dispersed settlements. With either type of power configuration, a broad social foundation encourages broad distribution of associated benefits, whereas a narrow settlement tends to permit or encourage the hoarding of benefits among a small group of elites and their supporters. Figure 6.3 provides a summary of the main hypotheses with respect to economic development.

Our four country case studies bear out these hypotheses. As Figure 6.4 and Table 6.9 show, our fastest growing country was narrow-concentrated Cambodia, with 6.02 per cent annual growth, the next fastest was broad-concentrated Rwanda at 5 per cent growth, then broad-dispersed Ghana at 3.64 per cent, and bringing up the rear, narrow-dispersed Guinea, with 2.29 per cent.[4]

Growth changes are also reflected in economic complexity data. As Table 6.10 shows, in 2003 Cambodia was the least complex of the four economies; by 2018, it was the most. There is no OEC data for Rwanda, though the African Centre for

---

[4] Note that we have removed 2009 and 2010 from the equation in Guinea, since they were coded as 'unsettled' and 'transitional'. If we include them, average growth is less than 2 per cent.

Broad dispersed: Moderate elite commitment to promote inclusive growth but less interest in or capability to promote long-term productivity enhancement, especially if natural resources are abundant.

Broad concentrated: Moderate to strong elite commitment to promote inclusive growth and long-term productivity enhancement, with potential to build requisite state capability, esp in cases of well-understood threats. Incentives weaker where natural resources are abundant.

Narrow dispersed: Weak elite commitment to and capability for inclusive growth and long-term productivity enhancemnet. Growth, if it occurs, more likely to be exclusionary and limited to enclaves with easy rent extraction.

Narrow concentrated: Strong elite commitment to promote economic growth and long-term productivity enhancement (weaker or non-existent in resource abundant contexts), with potential to build requisite state capability. Growth pattern more likely to be exclusionary.

Fig. 6.3 Political settlement types and predicted economic development performance
Source: Authors' own

Economic Transformation adjudge it to be outperforming Ghana on economic diversification, productivity gains, and technological upgrading.[5] Ghana's economic complexity had improved in absolute terms, but it was falling behind relatively speaking. Guinea, meanwhile, was regressing on both fronts.

Narrow-concentrated Cambodia

Behind these figures lies a story that further supports our hypotheses. Take Cambodia. Since 1998 when Hun Sen decisively consolidated power, Cambodia has overseen an impressive structural transformation. The changes were seeded in the

---

[5] See http://africantransformation.org/2014/02/13/d-diversification/.

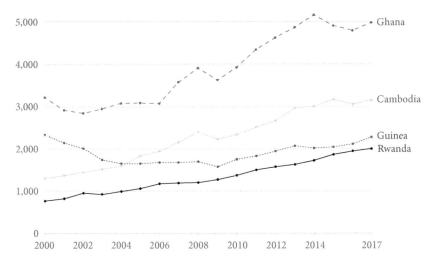

Fig. 6.4 GDP per capita levels and growth (2000–2017) in Cambodia, Ghana, Guinea, and Rwanda

Source: Illustration using data from Feenstra et al. (2015) via Roser (2013).

Table 6.10 Economic complexity in Cambodia, Rwanda, Ghana, and Guinea, 2003–2013.

Economic complexity, 2003–2013		
	2003 Economic complexity index (ECI) score/rank (out of 140)	2018 ECI score/rank
Cambodia	−1.72/108	−0.69/100
Rwanda	No data	No data
Ghana	−1.59/106	−1.12/122
Guinea	−1.65/117*	−1.67/134

Note: *2006.
Source: Observatory of Economic Complexity (OEC) https://oec.world/en/rankings/eci/hs4/hs02.

mid-1980s, when the young Hun Sen, leading a Vietnamese-backed regime under threat from Khmer Rouge and loyalist guerillas, apparently made a calculation that private-sector-led growth was crucial to regime survival, whereupon he began to nurture and ally himself with influential businessmen (Gottesman 2004, Slocomb 2010).

Growth improved, albeit erratically, until 1998 when the CPP was able convincingly to sideline FUNCINPEC, its rival. Since then, the settlement has evolved to create a balance between technocrats and rent-seekers within the inner circle of power. Technocrats are given just enough latitude to support growth industries such as garments, tourism, electronics, and rice; rent-seekers (*oknha*) are given the political backing to generate profits, a proportion of which are funnelled back to the political elite, and thence to the masses in the form of CPP-backed patronage projects.[6] A mixture of formal and informal institutions, meanwhile, has helped to resolve industry problems and injected increasing amounts of order into the business environment, while a repressive state apparatus has more or less kept the lid on political fallout from the growth process (Hughes and Un 2011, Kelsall and Heng 2014a).

In the case of garments, for example, private businesses created the Garment Manufacturers' Association of Cambodia (GMAC) in the mid-1990s, which all garment makers were later instructed to join. Working with government, it has progressively simplified, streamlined, and made export procedures more transparent. In addition, preferential access to the American market has been obtained and sustained with the help of the 'Better Factories' programme, a multi-stakeholder initiative between the International Labour Organization (ILO), government, GMAC, and unions, which monitors factories and facilitates collective bargaining (Ear 2011). State capacity building around garments has had positive feedback effects for other export industries. According to one well-placed source, 'We opened the road for many other exporting industries, we cleared the path really, clarifying certain issues ... [the government] look[s] to us and says, "ok, this is being done for [the garment] industry and it should apply to other industries"' (Kelsall and Heng 2014a: 34). The Government-Private Sector Forum (G-PSF), to some extent institutionalizes these trends (Cambodian Federation of Employers and Business Associations (CAMFEBA) n.d.).

The economy has also boomed in agri-business and construction, albeit controversially. According to NGOs, since 2000 Cambodia has granted more than 2 million hectares in Economic Land Concessions to more than two hundred firms, around 28 per cent of that area being held by a handful of CPP senators (Vrieze and Kuch 2012). Also growing have been monopolistic or semi-monopolistic areas of the domestic economy, not to mention a number of large urban development projects. Since 2013, with the government moving closer to China, there has been a huge boom in casino-building, especially around the coastal town of Sihanoukville—a mixed blessing for the local population. Other large domestic industries include banking, telecoms, brewing, and petrol supply, all of which are dominated by a few large players, with a smattering of smaller operators. Prominent in most are the biggest Cambodian tycoons or *oknha*, large East Asian foreign companies, or both. All this growth has had some spillover

---

[6] According to Ear (2011), 'The title of "*oknha*" comes from Cambodia's peerage system and is bestowed by His Majesty the King. It is designated for individuals whose "Contributions [to national reconstruction] values in excess of $100000". The title of *oknha* is the preserve of businessmen interested in formalizing their relationship with the state (and by extension the CPP). As of April 2008 there were officially 220 *oknha* of whom less than ten were women.' See also Hughes and Conway (2003), Pak et al (2007), Un (2005: 203–30), Hughes and Un (2011: 1–26).

benefits for small and medium enterprises, which operate in a relatively open, semi-ordered environment (Kelsall and Heng 2014a).

Economic growth has been accompanied by significant structural transformation. In 1995, agriculture accounted for 44.7 per cent of total GDP and 81.4 per cent of the labour force, while in 2010 its share had fallen to 27.4 per cent of GDP and 57.5 per cent of the labour force. Industry, meanwhile, had risen from 15.1 per cent of GDP and 16.3 per cent of the labour force, to 26.4 per cent and 27.4 per cent, respectively (National Institute of Statistics 2011). Within industry, manufacturing has led the way, rising from 8.9 per cent to 20.5 per cent of GDP. Cambodia was thus the only one of our study countries to make a breakthrough into manufacturing. Between 1998 and 2008, its economic complexity growth was in the top 20 per cent of countries globally (Hausmann et al. n.d. : 83) and by 2015 it was beginning to experience another wave of structural transformation, with the arrival in the country of bicycle manufacturers, electronics, and light engineering firms, transferring the most labour-intensive aspects of their production from higher-wage China and Thailand (Kelsall and Heng 2018).

Characteristic of a narrow-concentrated settlement, however, not too much attention has been paid to growth's distributional consequences. NGOs claim that over 400,000 people have been displaced or involved in land conflicts since 2000 (Vrieze and Kuch 2012), while some estimate that more than 10 per cent of Phnom Penh's population has been displaced. As a senior economic advisor told us in 2013, 'We knew there was a gap developing, but we thought we could get another decade of growth before we would have to address it' (Kelsall and Heng 2017). In that year there was a disputed election, strikes, and anti-government demonstrations. Yet once the state flexed its repressive muscles, firing on crowds and killing four demonstrators in January 2014, protest melted away. After moving closer to China and becoming more repressive of the opposition, the 2018 election was barely even a contest.

Broad-concentrated Rwanda

Rwanda's growth, meanwhile, has been less dynamic but also arguably less rapacious in nature. It can be attributed to a combination of sound macroeconomic management and concerted attempts to diversify the economy. With respect to the latter, the RPF has taken a dual approach to economic policy. The first strand, doubtless heavily influenced by donors, follows conventional wisdom about creating a stable macroeconomic environment and cutting red tape to create a predictable and transparent business environment. With its efforts centred around the Rwandan Development Board, the country has been ranked by the World Bank as the third best country in sub-Saharan Africa in which to do business (Kelsall 2013, Booth and Golooba-Mutebi 2012).

If the first approach rests on encouraging investment via an open, arm's length form of regulation, the second, facilitated by Rwanda's concentrated power configuration, involves an approach that addresses critical market failures by working arm-in-arm with the ruling party. Prominent here have been party-linked holding companies or consortia. For example, Tri-Star Investments (later Crystal Ventures Ltd.), a company with close links to the ruling elite, has invested in metals trading, road construction, housing estates, manufacture of building materials, fruit processing, mobile telephony, and printing. Other examples have been the army-linked Horizon Group, and Rwanda Investment Group, a consortium of well-connected businessmen who have invested in, among other things, a Kigali industrial park (Kelsall 2013: 127–8). According to a spokesman, 'We invested where no-one else would invest, like in the tourism sector. It is this model of going in where others will not that has spurred the growth of the Rwandan economy' (Behuria and Goodfellow 2017: 227).

The approaches can be illustrated further by means of sector examples from coffee and mining. Prior to the genocide, the coffee sector was a relatively closed and largely stagnant space in which investors needed close personal ties to the political regime. When the RPF took over, the coffee sector was opened up. New, mainly international, firms entered the market, bringing with them improved knowledge and technology, leading to value addition. The mining sector was also subject to a rapid, somewhat chaotic, liberalization in the mid-2000s. As with coffee, however, the government has gradually built the capacity to regulate and order the sector, and to deliver on promises made to investors. In 2013, mining was described as, 'a redoubt of arm's length facilitation' (Kelsall 2013: 137). Yet in both sectors, the government retains an interest in economic transformation. For example, when it comes to exports of packaged, single-origin coffee, 'only certain local firms (with close relationships with the government) are entrusted with risky value-addition attempts' (Behuria and Goodfellow 2017: 233). Meanwhile in strategically important mining sectors such as beneficiation, private company Phoenix Metals has been offered benefits that other firms would not enjoy, such as guaranteed electricity supplies (Behuria and Goodfellow 2017: 237).

Overall, the Rwandan economy has made modest progress on economic diversification, productivity gains, and technological upgrading.[7] Agriculture as a proportion of GDP has declined—although given its importance to poverty reduction, plans are being implemented to revive it (Booth and Golooba-Mutebi 2014)[8]—while services and industry (mainly construction) have increased, with some increase in employment—admittedly from a very low base—in the manufacturing and extractive industries (Behuria and Goodfellow 2017). The trends are reflected to some extent in its export figures. In 2000, coffee accounted for 57.3 per

[7] http://africantransformation.org/2014/02/13/d-diversification/.
[8] Booth and Golooba-Mutebi (2014).

cent of exports; by 2018, this had fallen to 6.85 per cent, even though the value of coffee exports had doubled. Tea, while only 5.8 per cent, had expanded massively in value. Another 79.8 per cent was accounted for by gold and a variety of other metal ores, which had expanded from almost nothing in the year 2000.[9]

There had been no significant breakthrough, however, into manufacturing exports. Part of this can be explained by the severe disadvantages Rwanda faces here. Landlocked, with a tiny domestic market and an inexperienced local capitalist class, it is structurally a much less desirable manufacturing investment location than our other countries, especially Cambodia.[10] Perhaps recognizing this, the RPF's economic plan puts the emphasis on a service-oriented knowledge economy, reflective also of the powerful idea of 'leap-frogging' (Behuria and Goodfellow 2019).

To sum up, broad-concentrated Rwanda is trying, as our model predicts, to encourage economic growth and transformation and has enjoyed some modest progress, made more impressive by its challenging context. However, it appears not to be going for broke, with fewer reports of displacement and dispossession than in narrow-concentrated Cambodia.

Broad-dispersed Ghana

As in Rwanda, growth in Ghana has been positive, though structural transformation has lagged behind. Ghana has spent most of its post-independence political history in the 'broad-dispersed' quadrant of our typology. Since 2000, its intensely competitive political settlement has put a premium on campaign funding. The literature on state–business relations under multi-party democracy is full of examples of businesses providing finance to political parties in exchange for lucrative government contracts; there are also numerous examples of the renegotiation of contracts coinciding with a change in the party in power (Kelsall 2013: 82–3, Opoku 2010, Otchere-Darko 2011). The symbiosis between politicians and businessmen, the former reliant on political campaign contributions, the latter on government handouts, makes it difficult to craft an industrial policy that will both support and discipline capitalists. Nor has the government necessarily felt the need to invest in a really credible industrial policy, given the point-source resources it has access to. The government agencies that have been created ostensibly for this purpose tend to be weak and underfunded, and areas of industrial policy, for

---

[9] Source: https://oec.world/en/visualize/stacked/hs92/export/rwa/all/show/2000.2018/. Note there has been some controversy about the origins of Rwandan mineral exports, with at least some alleged to originate in the Democratic Republic of Congo (DRC). https://cdn.globalwitness.org/archive/files/congo's%20minerals%20trade%20in%20the%20balance%20low%20res.pdf.

[10] Attempts to encourage growth in areas like apparel and cement production have also been weakened by an unstable trade-preferences regime, plus vigorous regional competition (Behuria 2019).

example, in textiles, palm oil, and industrial starch production, have been politically captured and/or have underperformed (Kelsall 2013: 74–93; Whitfield 2010, 2011; Osei et al. 2018.). Non-traditional exporters lack weight within the political settlement and have been unable to pressure government to create an effective, enabling policy framework (Osei et al. 2018.).

Arguably the biggest economic success story of post-independence Ghana, with significant poverty-reducing effects, has been the rehabilitation of the cocoa industry under the regime of Jerry Rawlings (1982–1992). Recognizing that a thriving cocoa industry was crucial to his long-term political survival, Rawlings set about reforming the cocoa marketing board from being a vehicle for parasitic rent-extraction to an organ that would provide an enabling environment for growth in the cocoa industry (Wiggins and Leturque 2011; Whitfield 2011). The creation of a pocket of effectiveness around cocoa was matched by one in the Ministry of Finance (Abdulai and Mohan 2019), and at least one successful initiative in horticulture (Whitfield 2011). It is notable, however, that these changes took place under a narrower, more concentrated settlement. While cocoa has continued to perform well, its importance apparently being acknowledged by all subsequent regimes, these other initiatives have foundered under broader, more dispersed multi-party political settlements. Oil discoveries have also been subject to intense political pressures, with Ghana arguably securing poor deals for a resource with potentially transformative effects (Hickey et al. 2020).

These trends are reflected in the figures, which are consistent with our 'growth without transformation' predictions for broad-dispersed settlements, especially one in which there are fairly abundant natural-resource rents to hand. In 2018, more than 80 per cent of Ghana's exports were accounted for by primary commodities, mainly gold, petroleum, and cocoa.[11] There has been something of a boom in service industries, yet most of these are at the lower-productivity end of the spectrum, and there has been no breakthrough into higher value-added production. As such, Ghana's economic fortunes remain vulnerable to changes in the global prices of its key export commodities, calling into question the sustainability of its economic trajectory, not to mention its ability to provide good jobs for the majority of the population.

Narrow-dispersed Guinea

Guinea's economic growth has been erratic and, on average, low since independence. A largely closed economy under the socialist dictatorship of Sékou Touré in the 1960s and 1970s, matters began to change after Lansana Conté took power

---

[11] Observatory of Economic Complexity (https://oec.world/en/visualize/stacked/hs92/export/gha/all/show/2000.2018/).

in 1984. Conté reconnected with the international finance institutions (IFIs) and opened Guinea's market to international trade. Bauxite exploration was accelerated but major industries, all of which were linked to bauxite, were owned by foreign companies and allowed to operate with little state interference (Schulz and Kelsall 2021c). These industries have been an important source of wealth for the ruling regime. Corruption scandals in the mining sector that involved Rio Tinto and Conté and then BSG Resources and Conté's widow Mamadie Touré indicate how closely the mining industry supported Conté and his clans' personal enrichment (Balint-Kurti 2017). Mining scandals have continued under Alpha Condé's rule. In 2015, Condé's son was charged with stealing public funds and accepting gifts from French mining companies looking to invest in Guinea (Louw-Vaudran 2015). In 2016, Rio Tinto admitted to having paid bribes to politicians close to Condé to secure access to the Simandou iron ore operation (France24 2016). The subsequent arrival of Chinese investment in Guinea has also meant that the regime has been less reliant upon Western donors and their ideas about good governance and democracy.

Generally speaking, there appears to be a symbiosis between Guinea's minerals-based economy and its narrow political settlement. The abundance of point-source resources has meant that successive regimes have had little interest in growing and strengthening the economy beyond these sectors which largely supply their own, enclave infrastructure, and which can be closely controlled. At the same time, the domination of resources by a narrow elite provokes political opposition and unrest. Tellingly, the 2016 Enterprise Survey found that 38 per cent of Guinean firms cited political instability as the main constraint to business, whereas, on average, only 5 per cent of firms in sub-Saharan Africa named this as a significant problem (World Bank 2016). The government has so far been able to stay in power by using repression, but this type of settlement is inherently unstable.

Guinea's economy is actually going backwards in terms of structural transformation, a fact that is nevertheless consistent with its status as a narrow-dispersed settlement. In 2018, 92.2 per cent of its exports were accounted for by gold and aluminium ore. Guinea remains highly vulnerable to changes in commodity prices, with little technology or infrastructure to support more complex manufacturing or services (Doumbouya 2008).

Social development

When it comes to social development, the story is somewhat similar to that with growth. Concentrated settlements have an advantage when it comes to incentivizing elite long-horizon thinking about the benefits of investing in health and education. It also provides them, as in the case of economic growth, with the breathing space to build state capacity around planning and provision, and the political strength to triumph over the potential blockers of health and education reforms, for example doctors' associations or teachers' unions.

And as with growth, the breadth of the social foundation will influence how widely, other things being equal, governing elites attempt to supply health and education. Where the social foundation is broad, there should be an attempt to supply services more inclusively. This is because elites are likely to feel the demand of popular classes for these services more keenly. Where the social foundation is narrow, by contrast, there will, on average, be more of a focus on elite-level provision, and/or leaving social provision to development partners, the private or non-state sector.

It should be noted that where resources are scarce, as they almost always are, there are likely to be trade-offs between inclusion and quality. This tension is likely to be particularly evident in broad-dispersed settlements, where there is political pressure to expand the scope of social benefits yet little political incentive or state capacity to do so judiciously.

As an addendum, we also hypothesize that, if we contrast broad and narrow settlements in general terms, elites in broad settlements are more likely to be committed to social development than economic development, and vice versa. This is based on an assumption that popular classes in poor countries are likely to have shortish time-horizons and therefore likely to prefer easily visible, immediately consumable health and education benefits to long-term growth policy, which may require sacrifices in consumption in the short term and an uncertain and/or uneven distribution of benefits in the long term. Popular classes in broad settlements are thus likely to demand health and education more vociferously than they do economic growth.

In narrow settlements, by contrast, the reverse preference is likely to be found. In concentrated configurations especially, governing elites may be able to impose the burden of consumption sacrifices on popular classes in the short term, while reaping the majority of the benefits for themselves in the long term. Figure 6.5 summarizes the hypotheses. In the following sections we illustrate these hypotheses with case studies of maternal health and education.

Maternal health

Examining overall public expenditure on health as a percentage of GDP (Figure 6.6), it is no surprise to find Rwanda and Ghana, with their broad social foundations, occupying the top places for most of the period. It is also not surprising that Cambodia, with its narrower social foundation, spends a comparatively low percentage of GDP on health. Somewhat surprising is Guinea, which begins, as we might expect, from a very low base, but then experiences a sharp rise from

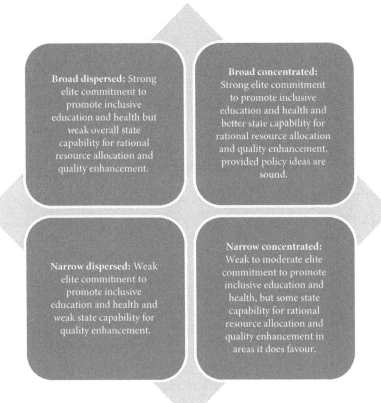

Broad dispersed: Strong elite commitment to promote inclusive education and health but weak overall state capability for rational resource allocation and quality enhancement.

Broad concentrated: Strong elite commitment to promote inclusive education and health and better state capability for rational resource allocation and quality enhancement, provided policy ideas are sound.

Narrow dispersed: Weak elite commitment to promote inclusive education and health and weak state capability for quality enhancement.

Narrow concentrated: Weak to moderate elite commitment to promote inclusive education and health, but some state capability for rational resource allocation and quality enhancement in areas it does favour.

Fig. 6.5 Political settlement types, commitment, and performance on social policy
Source: Authors' own

2008.[12] Official development aid for health in Guinea more than doubled between 2009 and 2010, but that does not entirely explain the rise.[13]

When we examine the reduction in maternal mortality (Figure 6.7), we find that Rwanda, as we might predict, has the steepest decline, reducing the ratio by 72 per cent, followed by Cambodia at 67 per cent, Ghana significantly behind at 31 per cent, and Guinea bringing up the rear at 30 per cent.

Rwanda also does exceptionally well when it comes to share of births attended by skilled health staff (Figure 6.8), with the percentage rising from 31.3 per cent in 2000 to 90.7 per cent in 2015. Cambodia shows the next best increase from 31.8 per cent in 2000 to 89 per cent in 2014. Then Ghana, from 47.1 per cent in 2003

---

[12] Note that the World Health Organization (WHO) data records a much smaller increase and far lower figures: $3.93 per capita in 2000 to $2.6 per capita in 2010 (WHO 2012).

[13] https://ourworldindata.org/grapher/gross-oda-for-medical-research-and-basic-heath-sectors.

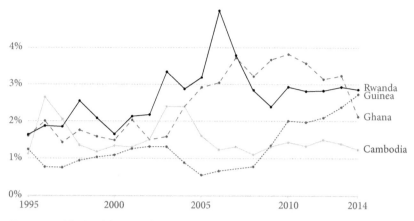

Fig. 6.6 Public health expenditure (% GDP) in Cambodia, Ghana, Guinea, and Rwanda (1995–2014)

Source: Illustration using data from from WHO (2021) via Ortiz-Ospina and Roser (2017)

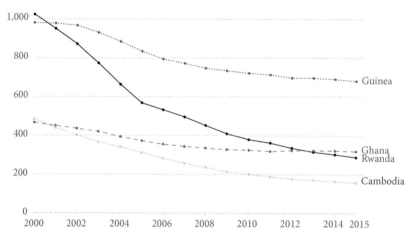

Fig. 6.7 Maternal mortality per 100,000 live births in Cambodia, Ghana, Guinea, and Rwanda (2000–2015)

Source: Illustration using data from World Bank (2021a) via Roser and Ritchie (2013).

to 70.8 per cent in 2014, and finally Guinea, from 48.7 per cent in 2003 to 62.7 per cent in 2016.

In the following section we illustrate how Rwanda, Ghana, and Guinea have more or less conformed to type when it comes to maternal mortality, and how the particularities of Cambodia's health policy domain have arguably led to better-than-expected results.

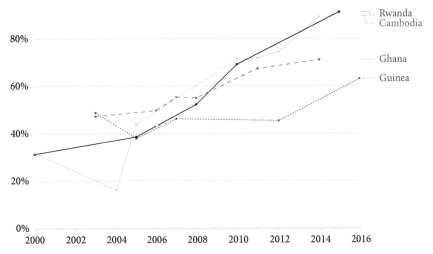

Fig. 6.8 Share of births attended by skilled health staff in Cambodia, Ghana, Guinea, and Rwanda (2000–2016)

Source: Illustration using data from World Bank (2021a) via Roser and Ritchie (2013)

Broad-concentrated Rwanda

Characteristic of broad-concentrated settlements, Rwanda has demonstrated both a high level of elite commitment to solve health problems and the state capacity to do so. The health policy domain in Rwanda is dominated by the president and the Ministry of Health, scrutinized by the Rwandan Patriotic Front's Commission on Welfare, and generously funded by development partners. Local authorities are the main implementing agents, under the watchful eye of local RPF cadres. Unlike in some of our other cases, neither professional associations nor the private sector emerged as significant actors, allowing government greater control over the sector and more capacity to implement reforms (Golooba-Mutebi and Habiyonizeye 2018).

Implementation is strengthened via strong top-down accountability mechanisms. The president signs performance contracts with local mayors, who in turn sign them with local health officials, all the way down the line to community health workers, employed to encourage expectant mothers to seek antenatal care and have facility births. There are strict reporting requirements, salaried staff are paid bonuses related to performance, while community health workers have access to grants and other perks. In addition, health indicators are regularly monitored and localities ranked in local or national performance. This has engendered a spirit of competition among districts, with mayors and local health officials conscious of the fact that good performance will cause their careers to blossom. Conversely, 'the prospect of identification as a non-performer and being held to account for performing below expectation compels lower-level officials to take their obligations seriously' (Golooba-Mutebi and Habiyonizeye 2018).

Health facility inspections are regular and frequent. In addition, the ministry periodically sends inspectors to conduct thorough audits that cover general hygiene, staff punctuality, prescription and management of medicines, and the use and management of assets such as equipment—including furniture, power generators, vaccine refrigerators, beds in wards, vehicles, and other things.

The health sector has also responded creatively in a problem-solving way to aspects of the local context. For example, traditional birth attendants were banned, but then trained and encouraged to become community health workers. They have been given mobile phones and use SMS services to alert health workers to cases requiring emergency response within communities. Before women had been sensitized to the importance of facility births, they were fined for delivering at home; and to reduce the probability of women giving birth before they are able to reach a facility, special wards have been created where pregnant women close to their due date can stay free of charge (Chambers and Golooba-Mutebi 2012).

Bottom-up accountability measures are also significant, with local citizens represented on health-centre management committees, well-used suggestion boxes present in health centres, and health officials' photographs and phone numbers prominently displayed. That most Rwandans are locked into the public health system through community health insurance, together with the comparative dearth of private facilities, contributes to local people voicing their health concerns.

As a result of measures such as these, health units open their doors to users promptly at the designated times, are clean, and under normal circumstances well stocked with drugs and sundries. Facilities have all the equipment they need to carry out their allotted duties, including vehicles and fuel. Reports of misconduct by health staff are rare. These factors have contributed to an upsurge in facility births and to improvements in emergency obstetric care, which have surely contributed to the country's rapidly declining maternal mortality ratio (MMR).

Despite excellent performance, it was not apparent that maternal health was accorded special status within the health policy domain, or at least not relative to other Millennium Development Goals (MDGs), which the RPF tends to make a point of trying to exceed. Rather, a focus on maternal health appeared to be a by-product of two main factors: first, a general determination to earn political trust by delivering benefits to the population, leaving no one behind; and, second, to lay the foundations for middle-income status by creating the conditions for a healthy workforce (Golooba-Mutebi and Habiyonizeye 2018). Both these trends are consistent with our predictions for a broad-concentrated settlement.

Broad-dispersed Ghana

The situation in Ghana is similar and different in important ways. As we might expect for a broad-based political settlement, spending on health in Ghana, at least until the recent macroeconomic crisis, has been comparatively high. Moreover, maternal health has also been something of a priority for the government, at least in spirit. President Nkrumah introduced free antenatal care services as early as 1963, and in 2008, the NPP government declared maternal mortality a national emergency. The NDC was equally enthusiastic, with President Mills declaring in 2010 that 'no woman should die while giving life'. A special fund was created to reduce the MMR, and in 2013, the government announced a 10 per cent voluntary pay cut in the salaries of the president and other members of the executive, with the objective of constructing 'special purpose Community Health-Based Planning Services (CHPS) compounds focusing on maternal and neonatal health' (Republic of Ghana 2013: 5). Indeed, since 2000, Ghana has adopted numerous initiatives aimed at reducing maternal mortality, the most recent being the 2010 MDG Acceleration Framework (MAF)—Ghana Action Plan. All have been laudable on paper; implementation has been lacking in practice.

As we have seen, Ghana's political settlement puts a premium on political appointments and short-termism. To give a few examples, there were seven different ministers of health between 2009 and 2015, disrupting policy continuity, while many senior officials were kept in 'acting positions', making them increasingly vulnerable to political interference and pressure. Despite there being a hierarchical system of performance management in place, rewards and sanctions were rarely enforced. According to one informant: 'Have I been ever called and asked, "Director, this is your contract with me what have you done?" No! There is no follow through. You sign, and you take pictures and they sign, but then what else? Nothing!' (Abdulai 2018). Promotion is largely dependent on seniority or political connections.

Large numbers of health staff have been trained: Ghana exceeds internationally recommended midwife/nurse-to-population ratios, yet maldistribution of resources means that many facilities remain chronically understaffed. Some doctors and nurses remain on the central payroll even though they never show up to their official place of work, with schemes to remedy this, such as putting salaries under the control of local assemblies, vigorously opposed by the Ghana Medical Association, whose members resist being posted to particularly remote districts. There has been, and continues to be, a huge drive to build highly visible CHPS compounds, yet many are lacking basic equipment and staff, while an initiative to expand massively the number of ambulances in the country has not been matched by resources to equip emergency rooms (Abdulai 2018).

Another populist policy is the National Health Insurance Scheme. Introduced to great fanfare in advance of the 2004 elections, it was rapidly expanded on the insistence of the president, against technical advice. Its financial problems have all but crippled some health facilities, leading them to reintroduce unofficial user fees that deter poorer patients. Expert recommendations to scale back the scheme to target the most underprivileged contradict political imperatives, which are to spread resources as widely as possible (Abdulai 2018). Here, then, is another example of an inclusive policy, introduced with a view to satisfying a broad social constituency, yet undermined by a lack of rational resource allocation and coherent implementation, as predicted for configurations with dispersed power.

It is interesting to note, however, that performance on maternal health is not geographically uniform, as we might predict for a dispersed power context. We studied two local districts at opposite ends of the performance spectrum: Upper East and Volta Region. Upper East District, one of the most impoverished regions of the country, nevertheless had some of the best maternal-health figures. This could be attributed to the creation of an island of excellence under the dynamic leadership of the regional director for health, who inspired others with his vision and conduct, introduced a variety of staff-pleasing innovations, at the same time as subjecting them to performance checks and audits. All health staff were aware that the regional director treated every maternal death as a preventable tragedy, and were motivated accordingly (Abdulai 2018). By contrast, our research in the Volta Region showed that many of the same systems as in Upper East were in place, but they failed to function because of poor supervision and monitoring, permitting absenteeism and hostile staff–patient attitudes to flourish.

Narrow-dispersed Guinea

The situation in Guinea, as far as we can tell, is somewhat similar. For example, Doumbouya reports that fees in health centres vary and do not follow official policy and the distance for women to access a health centre is reported as a significant barrier to maternal care (Doumbouya 2008). Access to health care is better in urban areas, primarily the capital where there are more health centres and health professionals than in other parts of Guinea (Doumbouya 2008). Private health-care provision increased as the economy was liberalized and state provision has not met health-care needs. Private health expenditure in 2000 was $17.15 per capita and this rose to $20.41 by 2009 (WHO 2012); this is unlikely to be meeting the needs of the poor, however. Meanwhile, the Ebola epidemic in 2014 placed enormous strain on the limited public health service and there are reports that some Guineans stopped accessing health care, including for maternal care due to fears of contagion in health facilities (World Bank 2018). International Crisis Group reported a higher frequency of attacks on aid workers during the epidemic in Guinea than occurred in Sierra Leone or Liberia at the time. This may reflect Guinea's history of political purges, repression, and generally feckless government, which has led citizens to distrust state officials (Foucher 2015).

Nevertheless, maternal-health outcomes have been gradually improving. Official development assistance (ODA) disbursements to Guinea for health care increased between 2000 and 2010 by 166 per cent. The proportion of this money that was spent on reproductive health and family planning also increased from

17 per cent in 2000 to 46 per cent in 2010 (WHO 2012). This increase may have contributed to the gradual improvement in infant, child, and maternal mortality.[14]

Although we cannot prove that Guinea's modest health improvements are mainly attributable to development partners, this would be a predictable consequence of its narrow-dispersed settlement type.

Narrow-concentrated Cambodia

As we might expect for a narrow-concentrated settlement, health for all has not been a priority for the government. Until 2008, the health portfolio was held by coalition partner FUNCINPEC, and footed the table of spending ministries. As late as 2010 only 6 per cent of health funding came from the national government.[15] Cambodia's health sector continued to be afflicted by rent-seeking, absenteeism, nepotism, and moonlighting, with many health staff very poorly qualified (World Bank 2014). In spite of this, health outcomes have shown significant progress. Mortality rates, especially infant, and under-5 mortality, as well as the MMR, have dramatically declined. Health MDGs 4 and 5 were comfortably met (United Nations Development Programme (UNDP) 2014).

There are three potential explanations. The first is simply the spillover effects of strong economic growth. Road infrastructure, private health facilities, availability of medicines, family planning, and incomes have all increased, and this has likely had an impact on health outcomes.

The second, and somewhat paradoxical explanation, is that the government's comparative lack of interest in health has given remarkably free reign to development partners and a few key allies within the health ministry, to experiment and innovate. For example, there has been a drive to introduce internal and external contracting into local health provision, as well as various new public management techniques (Keovathanak and Annear 2011). A significant minority of health districts are now semi-autonomous 'Special Operating Agencies' (SOAs), a model adapted from the British National Health Service in which a chain of performance-linked contractual relationships links national, provincial, district, and facility health managers. There have also been a number of schemes aimed at increasing access for the poor, the most important being Health Equity Funds (HEFs), which facilitate free health care for millions (Annear and Ahmed 2012, Net and Chantrea 2012, Kelsall and Heng 2014b).

Third, over time, some of these initiatives have gained the attention of high-level elites and received their backing. The prime minister has signalled his support for a number of health campaigns designed by development partners and Ministry

---

[14] Aid per capita to Guinea has increased substantially in recent years, surpassing Ghana in 2014 and Cambodia in 2016. Nevertheless, in 2018 it was at just over half the level of Rwanda.
[15] Connell (2011).

of Health (MOH) technocrats, including HEFs, child malnutrition, and reducing maternal mortality. The first lady, a midwife by training, has been enrolled by the UN as a national champion for safe motherhood, turning it into something of a cause célèbre (Jones et al. 2012). Apparently the prime minister and first lady lost their first child when he was dropped, at only a day old, by a Khmer Rouge nurse, which might explain some of their interest in the issue. From the year 2000, in particular, training of midwives has been a priority for the government, with estimates suggesting that all health centres have at least one primary midwife and most a secondary midwife. In 2007 the government introduced a midwifery incentive scheme, which provided $15 to health centres and $10 to hospitals for every live birth, while deliveries by traditional midwives have been banned. Minister for health Mam Bun Heng apparently stated that he wished to be remembered as the 'Minister of Midwifery'![16] Birth-spacing has also increased with increased use of contraception and legal abortion (Dingle et al. 2013), while in some areas expectant mothers have been provided vouchers for delivering in health facilities (Van de Poel et al. 2014, Liljestrand and Sambath 2012).

Hun Sen has always been a leader with an eye both on earning popular legitimacy and squashing opposition, so it is difficult to say to what extent this relatively recent elite commitment to health has been driven by an attempt to bolster CPP support, a recognition of its importance to human capital and growth, or purely idiosyncratic factors. Whatever the precise explanation, however, the case of maternal health in Cambodia demonstrates that with the right constellation of actors and circumstances, channels of effectiveness can be created in narrow-concentrated settlements, in areas our model would not entirely predict.

Education

When it comes to education, spending figures are broadly in line with our model's predictions. As Figure 6.9 shows, our broad settlements, Ghana and Rwanda, have been spending a higher proportion of their budgets on education than our narrow settlements, Guinea and Cambodia.

On the indicator of total net enrolment in primary education (Figure 6.10), Ghana and Rwanda, as expected, also perform well, with Guinea lagging significantly behind. Cambodia is arguably doing better than expected.

Comparative indicators for the quality of education are harder to find. However, ESID conducted field research on this subject in three of the four countries, with interesting results, and we have also reviewed the secondary literature on Guinea.

---

[16] https://core.ac.uk/download/pdf/71422333.pdf.

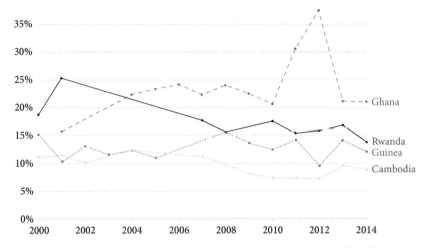

Fig. 6.9 Share of education in government expenditure in Cambodia, Ghana, Guinea, and Rwanda (2000–2014)

Source: Illustration using data from World Bank (2021a) via Roser and Ortiz-Ospina (2016).

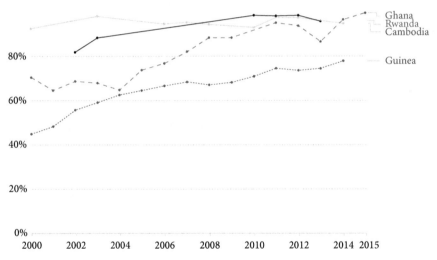

Fig. 6.10 Total net enrolment rate in primary education in Cambodia, Ghana, Guinea, and Rwanda (2000–2015)

Source: Illustration using data from World Bank (2021b) via Roser and Ortiz-Ospina (2013)

Broad-concentrated Rwanda

Other things being equal, our model would predict Rwanda to have made the greatest strides on all social policy indicators. Whereas this is borne out by our account of maternal health, an analysis of education reforms injects some complexity into the picture, illustrating some of concentrated power's pitfalls. To summarize, a regime that has solved its internal collective-action problems is able to act rapidly and purposively to achieve its intended aims. However, such single-mindedness brings dangers if the policies on which it settles are wrong-headed. Such has arguably been the case with Rwandan education.

Like many countries in the region, Rwanda has made great strides in expanding educational access, however, and perhaps surprisingly, it has been less successful in promoting learning. Recent figures show that a majority of primary students failed to meet basic reading and arithmetic standards (Williams 2019: 111). There are a few reasons for this.

To begin with, the main thrust of education policy was to expand access and to supply the infrastructure conducive to doing so. Only more recently has quality also been identified as a goal. In 2014, the government's annual leadership retreat called for a monitoring and evaluation system for tracking educational quality and an education quality strategic plan with a baseline and desired targets (Honeyman 2015 in Williams 2019: 89). As discussed in the section on maternal health, Rwanda has an elaborate system for performance monitoring which in most cases has been highly effective. However, in the case of education, the bias towards easily measurable accomplishments, has tended to skew efforts towards infrastructure and access. 'Performance outcomes that were more difficult to measure and improve, such as learning outcomes, were assigned lower priority' (Williams 2019: 90). This was reflected in ESID's fieldwork at local level, where district officials, 'linked education priorities to the improvement of access and provision of infrastructure as their primary targets [...] District, sector-, and school-level officials understood the training of teachers as a centralized affair' (Williams 2019: 97).

Perhaps the most serious impediment to improving quality, however, has been the 2008 decision to shift the medium of instruction from French to English. The decision is consistent with two features of Rwanda's political settlement. First, its domination by former Anglophone exiles in Uganda, who have wanted to distance the country from France and Belgium. Second, a policy of increased regional integration, given Rwanda's membership of the East African community, whose other members are English-speaking.

Higher political logics notwithstanding, the decision has had disruptive effects. It came at a time when perhaps only half of the teaching workforce was actually competent in English: 'The switch was made so quickly that it has left the quality of the education system in a perpetual state of catch-up' and has been described as 'an immense challenge for teachers in government schools' (Williams 2019: 91). Decentralized in-service training, which might have been geared to the pedagogical needs of local teaching staff, has been recentralized and almost entirely commandeered for purposes of English training (Williams 2019: 92). With non-English speaking teachers struggling to learn English, it is no wonder that other initiatives to improve teaching have fallen by the wayside.

To understand how this could happen, it is useful to examine the politics of the education policy domain. Although there is an inner circle of power comprising the Ministry of Education, the Finance Ministry, the Ministry of Local Government and DFID, and an outer circle which includes such actors as the Rwandan Education Board, Parliament, USAID and the Rwandan Education NGO Coordination Platform (Williams 2019, 88), the important thing to note is the overwhelming power of the president. On occasions he has been able to dictate policy to education-sector actors, the decision to move to English as a medium of instruction being a case in point.

The process behind which this decision was reached is opaque, but judging by the disquiet it has caused among other education-sector stakeholders, they were either not extensively consulted, afraid to speak their minds, or their concerns were dismissed. One suspects that in a more dispersed settlement, sectoral stakeholders would have had more power to resist, and a policy better calibrated to the realities of the sector might have emerged. Williams concludes, 'the strong political will of the country's principal and elite, coupled with a lack of real opposition or pushback, enabled it to introduce transformative educational policies in line with its developmental ambitions, but which may be at odds with the present-day realities of classroom learning' (Williams 2019: 100).

The importance of a knowledge-based economy to the Rwandan elite's vision for the country, plus its track record of successful problem-solving, suggests that these problems are likely to be recognized and addressed over time. Until then, however, the education sector provides a salutary tale of what can happen in contexts of over-concentrated power.

Broad-dispersed Ghana

Like most developing countries, Ghana has witnessed a significant expansion in access to education over the past two decades. To the extent that data is available, quality has also risen, though not by nearly as much. A 2014 study found that 75 per cent of those leaving school after five or six years could not read (Rose 2014, cited in Ampratwum, Awal, and Oduro 2019: 44).

This disappointing performance is in spite of the fact that Ghana has instituted some of the basic reforms that might be expected to improve quality, namely a fairly thoroughgoing decentralization of educational provision and accountability. In particular, the Education Act of 2008 deepened the decentralization of education service delivery, creating new mechanisms and structures to empower regional- and district-level stakeholders (Ampratwum, Awal, and Oduro 2019: 48). Nevertheless, broad features of the political settlement feed into the power dynamics of the policy domain. For example, 'ensuring that critical constituencies such as the teaching force and district-level bureaucracies are appeased is essential, with a strong union focused on teacher salaries and welfare issues, and not (unlike the professional teacher associations) on teacher performance' (Ampratwum, Awal, and Oduro 2019: 47).

How this plays out in terms of educational outcomes, however, is strongly influenced by political factors at a local level. ESID studied two comparable districts in the Central Region of the country, with a specific focus on teacher attendance. Teacher absenteeism was considerably lower in one, anonymized as TM, than the other, AK. ESID's research explained this by reference to the phenomenon of political dominance or power concentration locally. In the better-performing district, the NDC had a virtual hegemony over political representation, and intra-party competition was comparatively weak as well. This had allowed the NDC MP for the district to work cooperatively with the district assembly, district education director, and the circuit supervisor to solve local problems and ensure that most of the time teachers were in post. In some cases, this involved deductions from salary or salary embargoes for unsanctioned absence, facilitated by community monitoring and complied with by unions (Ampratwum, Awal, and Oduro 2019: 58). This incentivized teachers to stay in post and/or prepare proper handovers to untrained teachers when they had a valid reason for absence. Teacher unions had even been brought into a cooperative alliance with district education and political elites and provided with financial and logistical support. Meanwhile, stand-in teachers were drawn from a pool of patronage in the gift of the district political elite: 'a political alliance between the MP, District Chief Executive (DCE), and officials at the District Education Directorate (DED) … ensured the appointment of party loyalists and activists through the National Youth Employment Programme' (Ampratwum, Awal, and Oduro 2019: 57). The elite had also formed links with non-state actors such as faith-based organizations and traditional authorities, who played an active role at school level and supported head teachers in improving learning outcomes.

In the neighbouring district, by contrast, the NDC was a much more fractious organization which had in the past lost power to the NPP. The district education director (DED) was said to covet the MP's job, with a detrimental effect on elite-level coordination in and around the education sector. For example, 'mistrust between the MP, District Chief Executive (DCE) and DED in AK resulted in the appointment of trainee teachers who had loyalty either towards the MP or the DCE. These teachers were often difficult to control, decreasing the ability to reduce absenteeism' (Ampratwum, Awal, and Oduro 2019: 47). Moreover, school committees became infected by clientelist competition, while the district education director seemed more focused on visible infrastructure provision than teacher attendance. In this competitive arena, teacher unions acquired increased leverage and ability to resist, such attempts as there were, to hold teachers to account (Ampratwum, Awal, and Oduro 2019: 59).

As mentioned earlier, uneven national performance with an augmented role for localized power constellations is a predictable consequence of dispersed power configurations.

Narrow-concentrated Cambodia

Our discussion in Chapter 3 hypothesized that even proto-developmental governments in narrow-concentrated settlements would emphasize economic growth over social development. However, if they came to appreciate the contribution of human capital to growth, they might be able to translate their concentrated authority into improved performance here too. Our case study of education in Cambodia seems to bear this out.

Until recently, and as our model predicts, Cambodia has devoted relatively little attention to education, and the attention it has devoted has focused on access. The modern education system was all but destroyed during the Khmer Rouge period, with the majority of the teaching workforce either murdered or fleeing into exile. When its current rulers took power and began rebuilding, they had in mind the creation of a cohort of dutiful socialist workers. With the departure of the Vietnamese, increased space was opened for collaboration with Western donors (Sloper 1999).

Post-1998, the CPP-dominated settlement coincided with a period of increasing alignment between the party's desire for popular legitimacy, and donor efforts to expand education access under the Education for All initiative and the MDGs. Between 2000 and 2014, the number of primary schools increased from 5,468 to 6,993, and the number of teachers from 45,152 to 55,958 (Ministry of Education, Youth, and Sport (MoEYS) 2014; United Nations Educational, Scientific and Cultural Organization (UNESCO) 2010). There were also numerous schemes to improve educational quality. These schemes failed, however, to make a big impact on overall learning outcomes. For example, the 2010 Early Grade Reading Assessment of grades 1–6 found that 33 per cent of children could not read, and that 47 per cent of those who could had difficulty comprehending what they had read. A recent impact evaluation found that grade 9 schoolchildren performed no better in maths and vocabulary than children who were not in school (cited in Tandon and Fukao 2015: 1).

In the light of these results, teacher quality was recognized as a major obstacle to better outcomes, but until recently it had not received the highest priority. Teacher standards that were recommended by a 2008 World Bank report, piloted, and adopted as national policy in 2010, were not given sufficient political backing or resources to prioritize their introduction in teacher training colleges and schools (Tandon and Fukao 2015, Kelsall et al. 2015).

Impending Association of Southeast Asian Nations (ASEAN) economic integration, and a budding jobs crisis among school leavers, has begun to change this, however. As of the end of 2015, ASEAN nationals were theoretically able to take jobs in Cambodia, with Cambodians able to take jobs elsewhere. Concerns about educational quality have also been voiced by employers and business associations (Kotoski 2015, *Global Times* 2013). The response has been an increased interest in adopting ASEAN educational norms, for instance a 12+4 teacher training system. The CPP-led political settlement has always been premised in part on earning legitimacy through ongoing economic growth, and there is a realization among elements in the leadership that better quality education is necessary to this. In addition, a community of interest that includes employers' associations, underemployed youth (a politically volatile group), international donors, and education NGOs are directly or indirectly applying pressure on the government, contributing to the appointment of a new education minister and a sweeping programme of reform, with quality at the centre.

2015's Teacher Policy Action Plan (TPAP) aimed to establish a new vision for the teaching profession, improve educational quality at all school levels, reform teaching education institutions, raise the status of teachers, change teaching and learning practices, and lay the foundation for even deeper reforms post-2020. A myriad of activities was undertaken with the learning agenda in mind, including strengthening a quality assurance department, creating a national assessment framework, providing additional training for monitoring and inspection, and beginning to administer standardized tests. As of 2017, most of these initiatives were taking place on a small scale and were not yet translating into improved learning in the classroom (MoEYS 2016, 2017). The ministry did, however, secure a large increase in its budget (Sokhean 2017), and teacher salaries were again raised.

A visit to Cambodia in 2019 revealed that the government was ploughing significant resources and attention into what were called 'New Generation Schools' (Supporting Economic Transformation 2020). These were an attempt to raise the quality of education and bring it up to date with the needs of a modern digital economy in a small selection of public schools. The policy had received a mixed reaction from development partners and teachers, however, partly because of its elitist overtones. Whether or not one agrees with the criticism, it is consistent with a narrow-concentrated political settlement which prioritizes elite gains over more broad-based social provisioning.

Narrow-dispersed Guinea

After Guinea gained its independence, Sekou Touré embarked on widespread education reforms, making primary school compulsory and free, removing French as the teaching language and banning missionary schools. Promoting education for all fitted with Touré's revolutionary ideals and was also an effective tool for establishing state presence and control across the country, where the state had previously been largely absent. Despite these efforts, the proportion of primary-school-age children who were enrolled in school barely improved.

When Conté came to power, in a reversal of Touré's policies, he reinstated French as a language of tuition. While this aligned with Conté's attempt to co-opt Touré's opposition and re-engage with Western markets and finance, few teachers or pupils were able to teach and learn in French, which inevitably undermined any potential improvements (Barry 2010). The donor-promoted structural adjustment programmes (1989–2000) that Conté embraced included improving education equity, financing, quality, and policy: they attracted donor funding, but the results were limited. The education sector remained highly centralized with little state funding and ineffective at improving education quality (Barry 2010). The later Education for All programme had similarly disappointing outcomes (Diallo 2019). However, enrolment evidently increased substantially during Conté's rule and the rise has continued into Condé's rule, too. Guinea increased the construction of schools and classrooms by 81 per cent between 2010 and 2017, which facilitated the rise in enrolment rates (World Bank 2019). Yet, in 2017 an estimated 44 per cent of school-aged children were out of school (World Bank 2019). Primary-school completion rates are improving but disparities persist between male and female access to education and between urban and rural areas (World Bank 2019).

The increase in pupil enrolment rates may be due in part to the proliferation of private schools. Between 2002/3 and 2006/7, the number of public primary schools increased by 20 per cent compared to the number of private primary schools which increased by 280 per cent (Barry 2010), suggesting that the state was failing to meet a high demand for primary schooling. During this period, the education budget fluctuated between 2.6 per cent of GDP (2000) and 3.69 per cent of GDP (2010), reflecting low government interest in supporting education (World Bank 2014). Education accounted for between 15.5 per cent (2008) and 9.4 per cent (2012) of public expenditure (World Bank 2014). The fluctuations in government spending on education also closely followed the fluctuations in public expenditure overall, which indicates that the ruling regime had little interest in investing in the public sector (World Bank 2014b), consistent with predictions for a narrow social foundation where there is little incentive to broaden access to state resources.

The proportion of the education budget spent on primary education is also low. This has risen from 30 per cent in 1992, peaking at 43 per cent in 2012 but dropping to 38 per cent in 2014 (Census Economic Information Center (CEIC) Data 2014). This is especially low compared to the high proportion of Guinean pupils who are in primary school. In 2010, for example, 23.3 per cent of the education

budget was spent on higher education despite only 1.3 per cent of pupils studying at this level (Barry 2010). Forty-nine per cent of this funding was allocated to
scholarships (Barry 2010), which is far more conducive to clientelist distribution of
resources than funding primary-level education. Again, this reflects a political settlement maintained through the personalistic distribution of resources to co-opt
potentially disruptive groups while being largely unaccountable to those without
disruptive power.

There have clearly been implications for quality. In 2019, a World Bank report pointed to the comparative lack of resources available to schools, pointing
to a 'chronic lack of recurrent resources at schools, which leaves them unable
to make even the most basic expenditures such as the procurement of essential teaching-learning materials or building maintenance'. In addition, resource
constraints made key inputs to improving teaching and learning, such as adequate education planning, supervision, coaching, and training within schools,
impossible. There was also a lack of accountability and limited orientation
around learning outcomes. In sum, 'the fragmented system and poor operational
and resource management contribute to disconnects between funding decisions
and policy goals, policies and needs, and policies and implementation' (World
Bank 2019: 4).

Poor educational outcomes, it reported, were a major concern, with almost 90
per cent of children in grades 2 and 3 unable to read simple text and only 68
per cent of candidates for the Primary School Completion Certificate passing the
exam (8). Although teachers had received large salary increases in 2017, there remained problems around deployment, with a new system for rational allocation of
teaching staff facing 'many obstacles' (9). There were few opportunities for teacher
training, which were nearly entirely donor funded, unsustainable, and ad hoc; nor
were school directors adequately trained for their role.

Despite some gradually improving trends, the Guinean leadership appears to
have shown the least commitment and capability of all our case-study countries
to improving education outcomes. This is consistent with the predictions of our
model and our expert coding of Guinea as a narrow-dispersed settlement.

Political settlements and policy domains

This chapter has shown that although we can often see a fairly straightforward
read-through from political settlement type to actual outcomes, this is not always
so and in some cases we identify unexpected patterns of performance. We argue
that this reflects the ways in which specific policy domains are constituted and the
particular ways in which they are embedded within different political settlement
types. Four particular factors emerge as being significant here: the political salience
of a given policy domain to the ideas and incentives of the ruling coalition; the

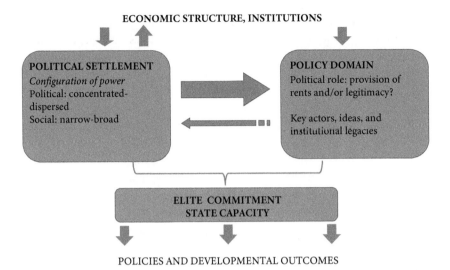

Fig. 6.11 Domains of power

Source: Authors' own

configuration of power between different actors within the domain, particularly in the form of coalitions; and the nature of the policy challenge of interest. We briefly reflect on each of these with reference to the foregoing material and also the wider body of ESID findings.

As Figure 6.11 illustrates, all policy domains necessarily exist in some form of relationship with the wider political settlement within which they are located. What matters from a developmental perspective, we argue, is the particular salience of the domain to the ruling coalition and broader settlement and the role it plays in sustaining both. This could involve the provision of rents or legitimacy, both of which are critical to political survival, but it could also involve the fulfilment of certain ideological objectives. To take Rwanda's surprisingly poor performance when it comes to promoting higher-quality learning in its schools, this can be traced to the dominant leader's modernist beliefs in transforming the country, which directly informed the overnight conversion of the language of instruction to English. We found something similar in Bangladesh, where education was seen primarily by governing elites in both main parties as a tool for generating governable citizens with political loyalty to a particular version of the country's political history, rather than a site of learning per se (Hossain et al. 2019). The problems in Rwanda were further compounded by the fact that education officials are used as the eyes and ears of the central government on the ground, often spending more time monitoring other aspects of local government and reporting upwards than focusing on improving the quality of learning (Williams 2019). This degree of central oversight seems to be a key element of Rwanda's relative success in some domains, as in health, whilst coming at a cost in another.

Looking beyond social sectors, domains that are critical to governing elites because they provide rents are particularly prone to being used in ways that tilt them away from what should be core developmental objectives. Our investigation of the political dynamics of growth (Pritchett et al. 2018) found that the economic domain could be divided into different types of rents-space, some of which involved firms having to compete for opportunities (e.g. manufacturers) whilst others were thick with rents (e.g. extractive industries). This mattered both in terms of the relative contribution to structural transformation but also in terms of other spillover effects; whereas manufacturers generally demanded higher-quality public goods (e.g. a healthier, better-educated workforce, roads), rentiers tended to demand private or club goods and to foster collusive forms of governance. In the rentier oil sectors of Africa's new producers, we found that whereas high degrees of dispersed power resulted in a free-for-all scramble for rents that could be termed 'resource factionalism' in countries like Kenya (Tyce 2020), and unregulated deals-making in Ghana, a mixture of more concentrated power arrangements and an ideological commitment to resource nationalism enabled Uganda to at least make deals with international oil companies that were aligned in the national interest (Hickey et al. 2020).

The second key feature of policy domains concerns their internal configuration of power, particularly in terms of the relative power of different actors with ideas and vested interests, and how this interacts with the wider political settlement.

In the economic domain this is already well understood, whether in terms of the relative bargaining power between capital and labour or between national governments and transnational actors such as oil companies. However, this is equally important in social policy domains such as education and gender equity. The reluctance of governing elites to prioritize learning over schooling flows most directly from the relative power and coherence of the coalitions lined up behind either agenda (Hickey and Hossain 2019). Those whose interests are served primarily by a focus on access include populist leaders with large and predominantly rural constituencies, local political leaders, and teachers' unions, all of whom benefit from the mixture of legitimacy and rents offered by an expansionary approach that values the quantity of visible provision over the less-tangible provision of quality. This coalition, which also received large-scale financial and ideological support from international development agencies during the 1990s in particular, has significantly higher levels of holding power than those actors with an interest in learning. This includes business owners who require a better-trained workforce to be internationally competitive, middle-class parents and, of late, some international development agencies. These actors are both individually and/or collectively weaker than their counterparts in most developing countries, where limited economic development means that domestic firms don't yet need educational upgrading to be competitive and middle classes have exited the public sector in favour of private provision. These factors help explain why the case of Cambodia, with its higher presence of firms competing in international markets and stronger moves towards structural transformation, seems poised to make greater progress in this area than many.

The configuration of power within the domain of women's interests, defined not in biological terms but in relation to the issues around which women in given contexts actually mobilize, directly shapes the progress that is possible around certain policy agendas. Our research into the passage of domestic violence legislation shows how women's movements need to build different types of coalition depended on the type of political settlement they were operating in (Nazneen et al. 2019). Where power was more concentrated, as in Rwanda and to a lesser extent Uganda, the key alignment had to be with the ideas and interests of the executive, whereas the dispersion of power in contexts such as Ghana made building alliances with political actors very difficult. The highly competitive political marketplace operating in such settings actually reduced the space for programmatic politics whilst also empowering interests actively opposed to gender equity, as with the Islamist party in Bangladesh. The key breakthrough here came when feminist activists were able to forge an alliance with senior bureaucrats in the Women's Ministry during a political hiatus in which partisan rule was suspended in order for elections to take place. The balance of power in this domain was further shifted in favour of the pro-women's rights coalition at this point because the Islamist party was temporarily prevented from mobilizing due to a separate legal challenge. Far from being fully 'settled', the configurations of power within both the overall settlement and a given domain, and how they interact, is a highly dynamic affair that needs to be continually tracked to identify windows of opportunity for progressive reform.

The final dimension of policy domains that we discuss here concerns the nature of the policy challenge that is at issue. One of the reasons that political settlements may not perform as expected might be because certain types of settlement are better suited to implementing some domain-level policy agendas than others because of the different types of state capability required to deliver on specific policy challenges (Andrews et al. 2017). For example, improving access to education can be seen as a largely 'logistical' policy challenge, requiring the provision of finance, building of schools, and hiring of teachers, whereas improving learning is an 'implementation-intensive' policy challenge as it requires changing the behaviour of multiple actors at multiple levels, and improving the quality of the thousands of interactions that occur between them on a daily basis (e.g. between supervisors and head teachers, head teachers and teachers, teachers and pupils) in which the exercise of local discretion and judgement seems important to success. This might explain why the concentrated settlement and top-down approach to governing education in Rwanda struggles to deal with local discretionary policy challenges that require multiple flows of information (Pritchett 2013).[17]

This distinction can also be extended to the economic domain. Our work on economic governance shows that countries in sub-Saharan Africa have been successful in building small 'pockets of effectiveness' that can deliver on logistical policy challenges like controlling inflation via highly trained experts in the ministry of finance and central bank. However, they have been much less successful at meeting the more transactional challenge of promoting structural transformation, a process that involves both working with and disciplining firms to align with national policy objectives (Hickey 2022). As ever, though, there is an important international dimension to this in that organizations like the World Bank and IMF have been far more supportive of building state capabilities that are aligned with a more minimalist and neo-liberal economic agenda than one that involves both structural transformation and a subsequently larger role for the state.

Conclusion

In this chapter we have chosen four archetypal cases to help corroborate and illustrate our main political settlement hypotheses. We found them to be largely confirmed, and, where they need to be qualified, this can be done by explaining how the political settlement interacts with a lower level of power relations: the policy domain. Specifically, that interaction is conditioned by the rents or legitimacy the domain provides to the political leadership, the bargaining power of actors specific to the domain, and the type of policy challenge involved.

In our final, concluding chapter, we discuss how an appreciation of the drivers of better and worse performance in specific policy domains provides some pointers to development partners and reformers for how best to work within or under particular types of political settlement. But before then, we seek to bolster the external validity of this chapter's findings by subjecting some of our hypotheses to large-n analysis.

---

[17] See also Andrews, Pritchett and Woolcock (2017: 107-110) and a series of 2014 videos by Lant Pritchett (accessible here: https://buildingstatecapability.com/2014/05/09/bsc-video-20-is-your-activity-locally-discretionary/).

7

Testing the Relations between Political Settlements, Conflict, and Development

A Large-*N* Analysis

In previous chapters we have discussed our political settlement concept, introduced a new typological theory and techniques for measurement, and illustrated and corroborated the theory first with reference to South Africa and then a four-country comparative study. As discussed in our opening chapters, this is by no means the first small-*N* comparative study on political settlements and development. In this chapter, we do something new. We bolster the external validity of our findings by subjecting them to large-*N* analysis, using the 2,718 country-years in our forty-two-country dataset. After looking at some initial descriptive statistics linking our concepts to major political economy outcomes, we run a regression analysis of our political settlement variables against economic growth, our proxy for economic development, and infant mortality reduction, our proxy for social development. This exercise helps us address some of the challenges to PSA outlined in Chapter 1, placing it more squarely within the social scientific mainstream.

Conflict, coups, and development: descriptive statistics

Before delving into our regression analysis, it is worth taking a short look at the basic hypothesis forwarded in this book and this chapter, namely that having a settlement is necessary for economic and social development. To capture the economic development of a country, we calculate the annual GDP per capita growth rate. GDP and population statistics required to calculate GDP per capita values are derived from the Penn World Tables (Feenstra et al. 2015). To calculate the annual GDP per capita growth, for each country-year we simply create a logged value of GDP per capita and subtract it from the variable's value in the previous year. To account for social development, we look at the annual growth (or rather decline) of the infant mortality rate (IMR) per 1,000 live births. The annual IMR status is taken from the World Development Indicators (World Bank 2020) and the growth variable constructed akin to the GDP per capita growth variable.

Political Settlements and Development. Tim Kelsall et al., Oxford University Press.
© Tim Kelsall et al., (2022). DOI: 10.1093/oso/9780192848932.003.0007

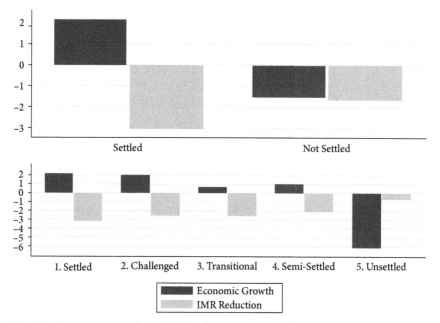

Fig. 7.1 Economic growth and IMR reduction across political-period types
Source: Authors' illustration using data from Schulz and Kelsall (2021b, 2021c)

In contrast to many social spending and other social development indicators, IMR measures have the double advantage that they (a) have a wide and consistent temporal coverage and (b) are measures of outcome rather than intent. Thus, they also endogenize the capacity to implement policies, which we theorize to be a mediating factor between political settlement types and development outcomes.

The descriptive statistics presented in Figure 7.1 support the hypothesis that having a settlement is necessary for economic and social development. On a more aggregated level, we find that periods that have witnessed a settlement have developed significantly faster both economically and socially than periods that were not settled. Specifically, whereas settled periods experience mean economic annual growth of over 2 per cent, periods that were not settled saw negative growth of around 1.6 per cent per annum. Perhaps surprisingly, periods without a settlement also saw a reduction in their infant mortality rate on average. However, this reduction was only half as fast as in settled periods.

These findings are also supported by the further disaggregation of political periods into the five period types described in Chapter 4: settled, challenged, transitional, semi-settled, and unsettled. Countries experiencing fully settled periods, on average, have been doing better on both development dimensions than all other types of period. Not surprisingly, unsettled periods (i.e. those experiencing a massive civil war) are characterized by extreme economic recession and stagnation in infant mortality rate reduction. These results thus provide clear evidence that having a political settlement matters for development.

We also conducted preliminary descriptive statistical analyses to see if some of Chapter 3's hypotheses about civil war[1] and coups[2] are borne out by the data. As Figure 7.2 demonstrates, narrow-dispersed settlements are, as we expected, significantly more prone to both coups and the onset of violent conflict, marking them out as the most fragile of our political settlement categories. Narrow-dispersed settlements also did worst on Government Effectiveness,[3] Impartial Bureaucracy[4] and second worst on Polity2 score[5] and Rule of Law.[6]

Broad-dispersed settlements tended to do better than broad-concentrated settlements on Polity2 score. However, both broad settlement types outperformed narrow settlements, showing that social foundation is a better predictor of democracy than power concentration (though it should be noted that since 'procedural democratic legitimation' is one of the components of the social foundation's co-optation score, this is partly true by design).

Broad-dispersed settlements are the least vulnerable to coups, but only slightly less so than narrow-concentrated ones. When it comes to Annual Conflict Propensity, there is, perhaps surprisingly, not a lot to choose between broad-concentrated, broad-dispersed, and narrow-concentrated types.

---

[1] Annual Conflict Onset Propensity (per cent) is defined as the likelihood that a certain country-year witnesses the onset of civil war. The data comes from the Uppsala Conflict Data Program/Peace Research Institute Oslo (UCDP/PRIO) Armed Conflict Dataset (Gleditsch et al. 2002; Pettersson and Öberg 2020). We re-coded the data so that the onset year of a civil war = 1; subsequent conflict years = missing; non-conflict years = 0. We then averaged/collapsed by our ESID-regime-type variable and multiplied the values by 100.

[2] Annual Coup Propensity (per cent) is defined as the likelihood that a certain country-year witnesses a coup attempt, with data coming from (Powell and Thyne 2011). We re-coded the data so that any coup attempt in a country-year = 1; and no coup attempt = 0. We then averaged/collapsed by our ESID-regime-type variable and multiplied the values by 100.

[3] The Government Effectiveness variable stems from the Worldwide Governance Indicators (Kaufmann and Kraay 2019). It combines into a single grouping responses on the quality of public service provision, the quality of the bureaucracy, the competence of civil servants, the independence of the civil service from political pressures, and the credibility of the government's commitment to policies. The main focus of this index is on 'inputs' required for the government to be able to produce and implement good policies and deliver public goods. The scale goes from −2.5 to 2.5, from low to high government effectiveness.

[4] Data from Varieties of Democracy (V-Dem) Variable is based on the VDEM 'Rigorous and impartial public administration (v2clrspct)' variable (Coppedge et al. 2020). It focuses on the extent to which public officials generally abide by the law and treat like cases alike, or conversely, the extent to which public administration is characterized by arbitrariness and biases (i.e. nepotism, cronyism, or discrimination). Scores should range from −5 (low impartiality) to 5 (high impartiality).

[5] Data from (Marshall et al. 2019). Scale goes from −10 to 10, from most autocratic to most democratic.

[6] Based on average VDEM Rule of Law Index Score (v2x_rule). The index is capturing the question 'To what extent are laws transparently, independently, predictably, impartially, and equally enforced, and to what extent do the actions of government officials comply with the law?' Scores should range from from low to high (0–1).

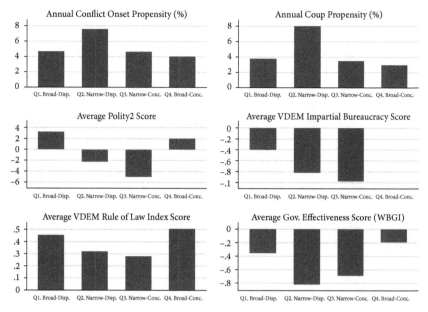

Fig. 7.2 Mapping the ESID typology against key political economy outcomes

Note: Bars are in order: Q1 broad-dispersed; Q2 narrow-dispersed; Q3 narrow-concentrated; and Q4 broad-concentrated.

Source: Authors' illustration using data from Schulz and Kelsall (2021b, 2021c)

Economic and social development: regression analysis

After finding preliminary support for the book's core hypotheses using both qualitative and descriptive analytical methods, we turn to regression analysis as a final method. Before discussing the model specification and core regression results, we first describe how we created two further key independent variables to test our empirical framework.

The ESID multiplicative and categorical indices

We have already described in Chapter 4 how we constructed our power concentration and social foundation indices. For the regression analyses in this chapter, we want to test the explanatory power of the two described variables in their own right, but also, as per our typology, as they unfold jointly. To do so, we create two further indices. First, the **PS multiplicative index (PS-MI)** is an efficient and straightforward measurement to capture the ESID typology.[7] To build it, we simply

---

[7] It corresponds to our *x_sfspc_add* variable in the dataset.

multiply a country-period's SFS (after being transformed to range from 0 to 1) and power concentration score. Through the multiplication, only countries with high scores on both sub-components have the high scores in the index. This index is also scaled to score from 0 to 1, hereby facilitating interpretation in the regression exercise.

The **PS categorical index (PS-CI)** is a more direct and intuitive representation of the ESID typology.[8] Here dimensions are joined to build a four-category-consisting variable corresponding to the four ESID political settlement types or quadrants. The dimensions' respective sample means serve as dimensional cut-off points, based on which cases are assigned to the different typological categories. This technique informed the mapping of political settlements illustrated in Figure 4.4 in Chapter 4. While this aggregation is more intuitive, it is limited by the fact that the variation within the respective types is lost through the aggregation process. By confining the substantial and continuous variation of the social foundation index (SFI) and PCI into four categories, the potential for significant covariation between the PS-CI and our development outcomes is constrained by construction. Hence, from an empirical perspective, we find the continuous multiplicative index more meaningful.

Model specifications and control variables

Overall, we calculate six main ordinary least squares (OLS) regression models, combining our two continuous outcomes with our three sets of independent variables. That is, Models 1 and 2 include the PCI and the SFS index separately within the same regression models. Models 3 and 4 concentrate on the PS-MI. And Models 5 and 6 regress the ESID categorical index against our two outcomes. The structure of the models is exemplified by the equation of Model 3:

$$y_{it+1} = \beta_0 + \beta_1 x_{it} + \beta_2 z_{it} + \delta_i + \lambda_t + e_{it} \tag{1}$$

where y_{it} is the annual growth in GDP per capita in country i in year $t + 1$; β_0 is the regression constant; x_{it} is the country-year specific PS-MI value; z_{it} is a vector of country-year specific control variables; δ_c are country fixed effects; λ_t are year fixed effects; and e_{it} is the country-year-specific error term.

All outcomes are forward-led by one year (which is identical to lagging all independent variables) as a measure to address potential reverse causality between dependent and independent variables. The simple logic is that the independent

---

[8] It corresponds to our *x_esidettlementype* variable in the dataset in terms of construction logic, though the numeration of the quadrants was adapted to our numeration in Figure 3.2 in Chapter 3.

Table 7.1 Summary statistics of regression variables

Variables	N	mean	sd	min	max
Dependent variables					
AnEcGr (t+1)	2,358	1.821	5.134	−62.17	30.20
AnIMRGr (t+1)	2,256	−2.952	2.457	−39.10	35.20
Explanatory variables					
Power concentration	2,418	0.520	0.201	0	1
Social foundation	2,418	33.98	13.35	5.271	80.63
PS multiplicative index	2,418	0.274	0.161	0	1
PS categorical index	2,418	2.705	1.194	1	4
Control variables					
GDP pc (ln)	2,398	7.923	0.797	5.745	10.52
IMR status ln	2,298	4.133	0.756	0.993	5.633
Polity2	2,692	−1.186	6.165	−10	10
Fuel income	2,158	59.79	144.2	0	1,285
ODA	2,010	5.143	7.697	−0.643	94.95

Source: Schulz and Kelsall (2021c)

variable at time *t-1* is less likely to be caused by the dependent variable at time *t*. As shown in Appendix F, the main models (3 and 4) are robust to using longer temporal leads.

Moreover, as indicated by Equation 1, all models include country- and year-fixed effects. Thus, potential omitted variable bias from time-invariant variables (e.g. geography, colonial history, or culture) as well as cross-country temporal shocks (such as the oil crisis) are accounted for. Each model also controls for logged GDP per capita (Feenstra et al. 2015) or the logged IMR (World Bank 2020) to account for convergence effects, Polity2 (Marshall et al. 2019), income from oil/gas/coal per capita (Haber and Menaldo 2011), and the net ODA received as a share of gross national income (GNI) (World Bank 2020), as all of these might affect both the political settlement *and* the outcomes simultaneously. Lastly, standard errors are clustered at the country level to account for heteroskedasticity and serial autocorrelation in the panel data. Table 7.1 presents the key summary statistics for all variables included in the six main models calculated.

Lastly, transforming our dataset's country-periods to the country-year level generates a total of 2,418 country-year observations on our core explanatory variables. Given missing values on the outcome and control variables, the actual number of observations in our regression models lie between 1,337 and 1,339 observations.

Results

Table 7.2 presents the respective results from the regression analysis. Model 1 regresses both the SFS and the PCI against annual GDP per capita growth.

Table 7.2 Results from the survey data regression analyses

	(1) AnEcGr (t+1)	(2) AnIMRGr (t+1)	(3) AnEcGr (t+1)	(4) AnIMRGr (t+1)	(5) AnEcGr (t+1)	(6) AnIMRGr (t+1)
Power concentration	3.55*** (1.10)	−1.62** (0.76)				
Social foundation	0.04* (0.02)	−0.05** (0.02)				
GDP pc (ln)	−0.85 (0.57)		−0.84 (0.56)		−0.69 (0.61)	−0.07** (0.03)
Polity2	0.00 (0.04)	−0.05* (0.03)	−0.00 (0.04)	−0.06** (0.03)	0.04 (0.05)	0.00 (0.00)
Fuel income	−0.00 (0.00)	0.00 (0.00)	−0.00 (0.00)	0.00 (0.00)	−0.00 (0.00)	0.00 (0.00)
ODA	0.12*** (0.04)	−0.01 (0.02)	0.12*** (0.04)	−0.01 (0.02)	0.13*** (0.04)	−0.01 (0.02)
IMR status (ln)		−0.92* (0.48)		−0.88 (0.54)		−0.96* (0.52)
PS multiplicative index			5.02*** (1.40)	−3.02** (1.26)		
Q1. broad-dispersed					0.00 (.)	0.00 (.)
Q2. narrow-dispersed					−0.12 (0.55)	0.60 (0.36)
Q3. narrow-concentrated					1.07** (0.53)	0.16 (0.41)
Q4. broad-concentrated					0.44 (0.53)	−0.08 (0.47)
Constant	4.53 (4.32)	4.55 (2.72)	6.42 (4.30)	2.75 (2.68)	6.57 (4.65)	1.91 (2.67)
Observations	1337	1339	1337	1339	1337	1339

Notes: * $p < 0.10$, ** $p < 0.05$, *** $p < 0.01$. P-values in parentheses. Two-way fixed effects and additional controls included. Standard errors clustered at the country level.
Source: Schulz and Kelsall (2021c)

The two regression coefficients clearly support the book's theoretical argument. First, always holding all other variables constant, we find that the PCI is positively and highly significantly associated with economic growth. Specifically, going from the lowest observed PCI value in our dataset to the highest is associated with a 3.55 percentage point increase in annual GDP per capita growth. Though only significant at the 10 per cent-level of significance, a higher SFS is also associated with faster economic growth. Specifically, a one percentage point increase in the SFS is associated with a 0.04 percentage point increase in economic growth. Though this appears as a fairly small coefficient size at the percentage level, multiplying it by the difference between the lowest and the highest level of SFS (75 per cent, see also Table 7.1), we find a 3-percentage point difference in annual economic growth. Over time, these differences imply vastly diverging economic fortunes.

Model 2 reproduces Model 1, only that it employs IMR growth/reduction as the outcome (negative values implying the desirable reduction) and substituting the state of GDP per capita with that of IMR to control for convergence effects. Again, both the SFS and PCI are significantly and now (as expected) negatively associated with IMR growth. Although note that whereas the effect size and significance of PCI has decreased to −1.62 and the 5 per cent-level of significance, that for the SFS has 'increased' to −0.05 and the 5 per cent-level of significance. As such, it appears that, holding all other variables constant, PCI per se might be more important in explaining economic development, whereas SFS on its own is equally relevant in explaining social development. This is consistent with our predictions in Chapter 3.

In Models 3 and 4 we regress the Political Settlement Multiplicative Index, that is, the index representing both our SFS and PCI in one, against our two outcomes. As suggested by the previous results, the PS-MI is highly significantly related with improvements in our economic and social development proxies, at the 1 per cent- and 5 per cent-levels of significance respectively. Specifically, moving from the lowest to the highest level of the EMI is associated with a 5.02 percentage point faster annual growth in GDP per capita and a 3.02 percentage point faster reduction in the IMR. This provides the strongest and empirically most rigorous evidence for our theoretical expectation that countries with high values in both PCI and SFS are most likely to do well both with regard to their economic and social development. As presented in Appendix F, note also that these two main models are robust to longer time leads of the dependent variable as well as to excluding Rwanda, Ethiopia, Zambia, South Africa, and Uganda, which were included despite not fitting the core selection criteria, but being of interest to ESID more generally.

Lastly, in Models 5 and 6 we run our Political Settlement Categorical Index (PS-CI) against our outcomes. Note here that the broad-dispersed settlement category serves as the base category to all other categories (and is therefore denoted by '0.00' in the regression table). Positive coefficient signs on the other three settlement categories therefore would mean that they are associated with faster economic growth (Model 5) than a broad-dispersed settlement in the context; whereas negative signs would indicate a better performance with regard to IMR reduction (Model 6). From the respective coefficient sizes and signs we can then infer a ranking between the categories on how strongly they are associated with positive development outcomes. One first finding that might stand out to readers is that only one of the categorical coefficients in Models 5 and 6 are significant at standard levels of significance. As elaborated earlier, this should not come as a big surprise. By confining the substantial and continuous variation of the SFI and PCI into four categories, the potential for significant covariation between the PS-CI and our development outcomes is constrained by construction. Nevertheless, and having to be careful not to overstate these findings, we think that observing a ranking between the four categories can be a useful and intuitive method to analyse and present the data (while Models 3 and 4 are clearly preferable from a statistical standpoint).

Looking first at Model 5, that is, economic growth, we find interesting patterns. As expected, both concentrated settlements grow considerably faster than the two dispersed settlement types. Specifically, broad-concentrated settlements grow 0.44 percentage points faster than broad-dispersed settlements; and narrow-concentrated settlements even 1.07 percentage points faster, a coefficient significant at the 5 per cent-level of significance. The finding that narrow-concentrated settlements grow faster than broad-concentrated ones also fits with our assumptions that in regard to economic development, the power concentration component of our typology appears to do more of the heavy lifting than the SFS.

With regard to our social development outcome, IMR reduction (Model 6), this picture shifts slightly. Here broad-concentrated settlements perform best, closely followed by broad-dispersed (0.08 percentage points difference between the two) and narrow-concentrated settlements (0.16 percentage point slower reduction than the base category). Reducing IMR 0.60 percentage points more slowly than broad-dispersed settlements, narrow-dispersed settlements trail the pack. While needing to highlight that none of these differences is significant in a formal statistical sense, they do complement the picture painted by the previous more robust models that whereas the PCI is somewhat more relevant for economic growth, the SFS component appears more relevant in regard to social development.

Conclusion

To conclude, the regression analyses support the key hypotheses generated by the book's theoretical framework. Both higher levels of power concentration and social foundation size are associated significantly with faster economic and social development. In doing so, power concentration seems to be particularly relevant for economic development and the social foundation size for social development. Aggregating the two dimensions into joined indices that more directly capture the hypothesized interactive impact of the typology further substantiates these findings. Holding a vector of relevant control variables constant, including both country- and year-fixed effects, having both higher levels of SFS and PCI is on average associated with better social and economic development.

Perhaps one final observation on one of our control variables, Polity2. As discussed in previous chapters, regime type has often been pitched against PSA in both debates among academics and practitioners. Our results indicate clearly that political settlements matter even when controlling for regime type. Moreover, at least in this specification, looking at the low coefficient sizes and significance levels of the Polity2 covariates, one might argue that our political settlement variables outperform regime type in explaining development patterns (particularly with regard to economic development).[9] This does not mean, in our view, that regime type does not matter. Indeed, we think that the institutional structures of the polity are a part of what we perceive as a political settlement and stand in significant correlation with a settlement's power configuration and social foundation size. Yet what we believe we have shown with this quantitative exercise, is that even when holding the regime type constant, political settlements' power configurations and social foundation size matter substantially for development.

---

[9] Looking at Model 3, whereas a one standard deviation change in our PS multiplicative index is associated with a 0.81 per cent *faster* annual economic growth, a one standard deviation change in the Polity2 variable is associated with a 0.03 per cent *reduction* in annual economic growth.

PART III

IMPLICATIONS

In Part Three we revisit the argument and discuss some of the implications for policymakers and reformers.

8

Summary, Policy Implications, and Future Research

The argument revisited

We began this book with the argument that despite the high degree of interest in and funding for PSA in both conflict and development studies and in policy circles, not all was well in the field. Conflict and development analysts understood the term 'political settlement' in different ways, there was a lack of conceptual clarity, and no clear grounds for measurement. Lack of an agreed basis for measurement, in particular, posed an obstacle to PSA's admission into the mainstream social scientific community. This book has attempted to address these problems, and to put the future of PSA on a firmer conceptual and scientific footing. It has also generated a new set of hypotheses and tests around a new typology of political settlements which can help explain the variation we find in development outcomes in real-world polities. We have also introduced a lower-level concept, the 'policy domain', which can explain variation at a more granular level. Combining the two concepts can provide useful pointers for policymakers. In this Conclusion we retrace the steps in our argument and our main findings, before discussing policy implications and future directions for political settlements research.

Conceptual clarification

In Chapters 1 and 2 we traced the roots of PSA to diverse strands in conflict and peacebuilding, political science, historical sociology, and development studies. We situated the growing popularity of the term within a 'post-institutional' turn in political studies, arguing that PSA had much in common with these developments yet promised something additional. After further scrutinizing the ordinary language roots of the term in Chapter 2, we argued that a political settlement should be thought of as an ongoing agreement or common understanding among a society's most powerful groups over a set of political and economic institutions expected to generate for them a minimally acceptable level of benefits, and which thereby ends or prevents generalized civil war and/or political and economic disorder.

Political Settlements and Development. Tim Kelsall et al., Oxford University Press.
© Tim Kelsall et al., (2022). DOI: 10.1093/oso/9780192848932.003.0008

Using the analogy of a marriage, we have argued that there is no contradiction in seeing a settlement as both a one-off agreement, such as a peace agreement, and an ongoing and evolving relationship more akin to a political order. At the same time, we have stressed that formal agreements are not necessary, that agreements or understandings may be tacit or imposed, and we have made a distinction between a political settlement and cognate political science terms such as political system, order, or social contract. We have, however, rejected the idea that a political settlement is compatible with a mere balance of power in the midst of very high levels of competitive violence, as that seems to us to contradict everyday understandings of the term, even if those levels of violence are ostensibly sustainable.

We have stressed that our definition is an expansive one, and is compatible with the study of peace agreements, political institutions, the sociological basis of the groups that have and lack power, and their configuration. We have admitted that behind political settlements or at the very least entangled with them, are ideas (although we have not included ideas as a discrete item in our definition). Most excitingly, however, we have argued that political settlements analysis (PSA) opens up the possibility of analysing the relationship among these different elements and outcomes in the areas of politics, conflict, and development.

A new typological theory

In the line of enquiry developed in this book, we have chosen to develop the theory around how the demographic and sociological composition of powerful groups, and their political configuration, can help explain elite commitment to and state capacity for development. In this respect we have drawn heavily on the previous work of Mushtaq Khan and Brian Levy, while integrating insights from comparative politics, sociology, and collective-action theory. In Chapter 3, we argued for a typological classification of political settlements with two new dimensions. The 'social foundation', which refers to those powerful groups which represent the settlement's 'insiders' by virtue of being co-opted by the top political leadership. And the 'configuration of power', which tracks the relative strength of different powerful groups and their arrangement in respect of one another.

If the social foundation is about the sociology and demography of power, the political configuration is about its geometry. We hypothesize that the social foundation is strongly related to the political elite's commitment to development, and, in particular, how inclusive it is. Other things being equal, where the social foundation is broad and deep, we hypothesize that there will be a stronger elite commitment to providing broad-based development benefits. Conversely, where the social foundation is narrow or shallow, there will be less of an incentive to distribute development benefits broadly.

When it comes to the geometry of power, we hypothesize that the political configuration is strongly related to the political leadership's ability to implement policies, and to create state capacity for development more generally. Other things being equal, we hypothesize that where power is concentrated—*that is, where collective-action problems among political elites are effectively addressed, resulting in a coherent allocation of decision-making procedures and authority among insiders*—the potential for effective implementation is greater, and where it is dispersed, it is weaker. We need to emphasize, however, that it is not impossible to implement policy effectively in dispersed power contexts, though it is generally more difficult. Moreover, we must stress that the ability to implement policy effectively does not guarantee that policy or its outcomes will be good. Power concentration can be both a blessing and a curse. And to add a little nuance to the picture, there are reasons to think that for some developmental tasks, such as delivering quality education, dispersed power may be an advantage.

Taking these two dimensions together yields a four-quadrant typology, in which political settlements can be broad-dispersed, narrow-dispersed, narrow-concentrated, and finally broad-concentrated. Each quadrant comes with its own collective-action and political development challenges, and a set of hypothesized relationships to elite commitment, state capability, and likely development outcomes.

Put simply, broad-dispersed settlements will display relatively strong elite commitment to delivering broad-based benefits, but rather weak capacity to do so. There is likely to be more of an emphasis on short-term or populist policy measures, and a greater reliance on clientelistic benefit distribution. There may also be a stronger emphasis on social as opposed to economic development, as the former is likely to require fewer short-term sacrifices of the sort that a dispersed power configuration would find difficult to impose.

Narrow-dispersed settlements are likely to face similar problems when it comes to implementing policy for broad-based development. However, unlike in the case of broad-dispersed settlements, political elites will have less incentive even to try. With either an organizationally weak or successfully repressed political opposition, the leadership will feel little pressure to distribute benefits beyond a relatively narrow circle. At the same time, the internal fractiousness of the elite is likely to make the polity inherently unstable, and weaken its ability for any type of long-term development.

Governing elites in narrow-concentrated settlements face similarly weak incentives to distribute benefits broadly, but greater capacity to implement policies that serve long-term elite interests. In particular, such settlements are particularly well placed to be able to implement long-term economic growth policies, engaging in primitive accumulation and/or imposing consumption sacrifices on the majority of the population as they invest in infrastructure and capital stock. They are also more likely to be able to design an industrial policy that is insulated from political competition for unproductive rents. In time, such growth policies may deliver more widespread benefits through trickle-down effects and trigger new cycles of expanded political inclusion, though this is not guaranteed. Moreover, mindful of the contribution of human capital to economic growth, elites in narrow-concentrated settlements may invest in education and health and have relatively strong capacity to implement such policies effectively. Again, however, one would expect educational and health gains to be tilted disproportionately towards the elite.

Broad-concentrated political settlements are on the face of things most likely to deliver inclusive development. With a broad swathe of the population endowed with disruptive power, elites will feel impelled to deliver broad-based benefits for their own political, and in some cases, physical, survival. In addition, power concentration in and around the top leadership makes it easier to plan for the long term and to implement policy through an effective state administration, and/or to build state capacity for effective implementation. Like broad-dispersed settlements, broad-concentrated ones may place a higher emphasis on social than economic development. However, they typically have greater capacity to nurture forms of economic growth that will provide a financial basis for these policies.

Complicating matters slightly, however, we hypothesize that on the right side of Chapter 3's typology, that is, the 'concentrated' power configurations, each quadrant contains two distinct pathways that condition how serious elites are about building state capability and pursuing long-term development, inclusive or otherwise. These are related to the availability of point resources and elite threat perceptions, and help to explain some of the 'within-quadrant' variation we find in the real world.

Measurement and testing

To be able to test our new theory we needed to be able to code and classify political settlements. To do this, we employed an expert survey of forty-two countries in the Global South, from independence or 1960 to 2018. We began by dividing each country's political history into distinct periods, each of which, according to our definition, marked a change or evolution in the political settlement. We then asked twenty-eight questions of each country for each political period. The bulk of the questions revolved around the composition, size, and relative strength of three conceptual blocs: the leader's bloc (LB), the contingently loyal bloc (CLB) (which jointly make up the ruling coalition) and the opposition bloc (OB). Inspired by Mushtaq Khan, this three-bloc structure is a novel way of thinking about the power configuration of political settlements and is not found in other political science databases. As such, it represents one of PSA's most distinctive contributions to political science and development studies. Other questions traced the modes by which these blocs were incorporated into or under the settlement, others intervening variables such as decision-making and implementation power, and others additional variables of interest such as systemic threats, the political power of indigenous capitalists, and elite commitment to social and economic development policy.

Out of the answers to these questions we constructed our two main typological variables, the social foundation and the configuration of power, and we then mapped the journey of our forty-two countries across political settlement types over time.

In Chapter 5 we described this journey in some detail for South Africa, a country that, since 1960, has experienced all four types of settlement. The emphasis was on showing how empirical developments in that country were reflected in the country codings, but also how the concepts provide a helpful language for explaining what we observe. On the one hand, we have a broad story of South Africa transitioning between settlement types, and on the other, by lifting the hood and examining the construction of these variables, we arrive at a more precise and fine-grained analytical narrative than more conventional accounts.

In Chapter 6 we turned to small-n comparative analysis. Here we picked four countries: Ghana, Guinea, Cambodia, and Rwanda, which, over the past two decades, have represented broad-dispersed, narrow-dispersed, narrow-concentrated, and broad-concentrated settlements respectively. To a large degree, our hypotheses were borne out. Narrow-concentrated Cambodia experienced the fastest growth, which, as we might expect, was of a rather rapacious kind, followed by a slightly slower but less exclusionary growth experience in Rwanda. Ghana was next, demonstrating, as expected, a disappointing capacity for industrial policy, followed by Guinea, where per capita income had actually fallen. On social development, Rwanda and Ghana, as expected, topped the bill when it came to government spending, though with much more impressive results, especially on maternal health, in Rwanda. Cambodia, despite comparatively low spending, outperformed Ghana on maternal mortality, a phenomenon perhaps only partly explained by its concentrated-power configuration. Guinea performed poorly on social indicators, despite recent and somewhat unexplained increases in health spending. Overall, and as predicted, Rwanda demonstrated the strongest commitment to building state capability for development (see also Yanguas 2017), even though, as acknowledged earlier, this did not always lead to positive outcomes, as in the case of educational quality.

In sum, we found a strong read-through from our political settlement types to both intervening causal mechanisms—elite commitment and state capacity—and development outcomes. However, the picture was not uniform. In four of our twelve cases we found that political settlement type only partially explained our findings. Here, we invoked the idea of the policy domain, a meso-level field of interests, ideas, and power relations nested within political settlements, to explain puzzles such as better-than-expected maternal health performance in Cambodia, and worse-than-expected education performance in Rwanda. We also pointed to several examples from other ESID work of where the idea of a policy domain was an essential complement to that of the political settlement. We return to this question later.

The results of Chapters 5 and 6 can be treated as illustrative of the method and explanatory potential of PSA. They were not designed to provide a rigorous test of the theory. That is provided to a greater degree by Chapter 7, in which we subject the relationship between social foundation, power configuration, economic and social development to a regression analysis. Using growth in per capita income as our proxy for economic development, and employing lagged variables, country fixed effects, and a variety of controls, we find a strong positive relationship between power concentration and economic development. Taking infant mortality reduction as our proxy for social development, we find a strong positive relationship with the size of the social foundation and social development. We also find, via the ESID multiplicative index, that power concentration and breadth of social foundation reinforce each other when it comes to driving economic and social development. Although not as statistically significant—for reasons we explain—we also find some support for our typological categorical variables. To wit, narrow-concentrated settlements tend to grow the fastest, followed by broad-concentrated, then broad-dispersed and narrow-dispersed political settlements. With regard to our social development outcome, broad-concentrated settlements perform best, closely followed by broad-dispersed and narrow-concentrated settlements, with narrow-dispersed settlements trailing the pack.

Advice for policymakers

As we saw in our Introduction, some political settlements theorists have argued that PSA is more suited to policy advice than mid-range hypothesizing and prediction. Our view is that if you are to advise policymakers using a portable model, the model ought ideally to be validated by reference to empirical results across space and time. We have constructed a new typological theory and model, and we have validated it across forty-two countries in the Global South. That does not mean that it will hold without exception; it simply means that on average it is likely to hold, and is therefore a good place for policymakers to start.

The advice we give should be treated as a set of 'first bets', or 'compass bearings' for policymakers, especially development partners, who are seeking to advance the cause of inclusive development. The findings might also be of interest for other inclusive development champions, whether in civil society or governments of the Global South.[1]

So, what is our advice? In broad-concentrated settlements, especially those facing resource scarcity, governing elites are already likely to be committed to broad-based development and to have created, or be in the process of creating, the state capacity to deliver it. Development partners can therefore assist the government with finances, or technical advice. In a sense, much standard bilateral and multilateral support already takes this form, although it is only in this type of settlement that it is likely to work well. Even here, however, the government may have some policy blind spots, and, although the settlement is broad, specific minority groups may still be politically marginalized. Development partners can play an advisory function or help marginalized groups to lobby the government, if the context allows.

In narrow-concentrated settlements, development partners will need to be more imaginative. Governing elites are unlikely to be committed to broad-based development, so development partners will want to either try and shift their incentives, or substitute for them. In more predatory settlements, based most likely on point-source resource exploitation, development partners might support global initiatives that make such industries less exclusionary. Where the government is resource poor and perhaps committed to more dynamic forms of economic development, they might try to leverage inclusive spillovers, as with the Better Factories initiative in Cambodia.

Another option is to impress upon the elite the human capital aspect of economic development, thereby generating increased interest in the social sectors. Indeed, political elites in narrow-concentrated settlements may be content to outsource a large measure of responsibility to development partners here. Donors can work with champions in government and civil society to develop and test social policy solutions, which might be scaled if and when the government comes to grasp their political advantages. Note that development partners should not be in too much of a hurry to move from parallel programmes to 'systems strengthening'. The latter is only likely to work when the government is genuinely motivated to deliver broad-based benefits. If permitted, development partners can also try and encourage societal voice, a prelude to social-foundation broadening. However, the degree to which this voice is confrontational or constructive will need to be tailored to context, with backlash a distinct possibility.

---

[1] Some of the advice might conceivably translate to Northern country contexts, though given that the theory was developed for the Global South and we have not surveyed Northern countries, we make no claims here.

In broad-dispersed settlements, the political elite will probably recognize the importance of delivering broad-based development benefits, especially on the social front, yet the government's capacity to plan and implement effective long-term development policy is likely to be weak. Developmental initiatives will probably take the form of populist gestures or patronage handouts. Top-down, system-wide reform efforts are unlikely to work well in these contexts, governing elites not having the strength or breathing space to implement them. Our data suggest that the best chance of nurturing progress is by building pockets of effectiveness in the administration and/or nurturing multi-stakeholder coalitions around particular issues or problem areas (even if, sadly, pockets of effectiveness are harder to sustain in dispersed power settings) (Hickey 2021). By definition, power in broad-dispersed societies is de facto more decentralized, and development partners should build on that, leveraging the nascent developmental coalitions that can sometimes be found in civil society, the private sector, traditional leaders, or religious organizations. Work at sub-national level may be particularly fruitful. Either way, the trick is to build capability and keep up momentum around a set of policy reforms across administrations and above (or below) the melee of patronage politics. Again, development partners may have to temper their ambitions around system-wide strengthening. This is likely to take longer than in concentrated settlements, and to be built from the bottom up or the middle outwards, as islands of effectiveness are joined to form archipelagos and then continental land masses.

Narrow-dispersed settlements represent the biggest challenge for development partners and other reformers. Development partners can try a combination of the strategies we suggested for narrow-concentrated and broad-dispersed settlements. Elites in narrow-dispersed settlements often rely on point-source resource exploitation or criminal activities, and trying to reform the international system within which such goods are traded or activities take place may help shift elite attention into economic sectors with more positive spillovers. Where such sectors, such as export manufacturing, small business, and smallholder agriculture, can be identified, development partners can provide assistance. Government is also likely to be comparatively disinterested in social development and have little capability to deliver it. Again, development partners may have to invest seriously in parallel or non-state solutions, until such time as governing elites feel genuinely motivated, probably through a broadening of the settlement, or perhaps for ideological reasons, to provide such benefits themselves.

But there are no easy answers here, and many narrow-dispersed settlements teeter permanently on the brink of conflict. Such conflicts are often a legacy of the way state boundaries were drawn at the close of the colonial period, together with the incentives created by the manner of these states' incorporation into the global states system. Doubtless, state-building and development are highly transnationalized processes in the Global South and we are aware that the positioning of countries within their broader historical and global political economy context is not the result of their PS type. A long-term solution may require a more radical re-imagining of the global system than our largely country-based exercise has considered. To be sure, weak regulation at a global level enables a whole range of global 'bads' around finance, taxation, arms, drugs, etc., that directly undermine governance and embed predatory elites.

Before moving on, it is essential to add a very important caveat. We have produced a typology of political settlements, we have illustrated how the typological dimensions have developmental effects by choosing four archetypal cases, and have demonstrated a general association between variables and outcomes across cases using regression analysis. However, when we map political settlements typologically we find that they are scattered, apparently randomly, across our four quadrants, and while the differences between a Rwanda and a Guinea may be easy to discern, those between a Senegal and a Dominican Republic, sitting just either side of our typological cut-offs, are likely to be much more difficult.

Another way of putting this is to say that countries do not cross the threshold between political settlement types and suddenly start behaving radically differently, in the way that H_2O behaves radically differently when it crosses the 0 degrees Celcius threshold. Thus, for countries that lie close to the cross-hairs of our political settlements typology (and it is a significant proportion) our advice to policymakers needs to be taken with an even bigger grain of salt. The read-through from political settlement type to policy commitment is likely to be weaker here.

In this way we believe our coding exercise points to both the strengths and limitations of PSA. In archetypal cases, and comparing statistically both ends of the spectrum, we find large effects, but countries closer together will differ less radically. One of the pitfalls of using a qualitative typology as an interpretive model, is that there is a great temptation to fit a country into one box or another and then succumb to confirmation bias when predicting for policymakers the likely political settlement effects. Our comparative coding exercise invites us to consider many, non-archetypal cases on their own terms. A plausible hypothesis is that in non-archetypal settlements, the explanatory significance of policy domain politics will rise, though that remains to be rigorously tested.

Generally speaking, however, we believe the general advice of the ESID Programme to policymakers remains sound. When devising inclusive development strategies, policymakers should focus on context, that is the political settlement (though with a caveat about political settlement type); capacity, that is, whether the state can deliver; and coalitions, which can help catalyse reform even in unpropitious contexts.[2]

---

[2] www.effective-states.org/the-three-cs-of-inclusive-development-context-capacity-and-coalitions/.
  See also https://www.effective-states.org/how-to-work-politically-for-inclusive-development-four-principles-for-action/#principle-one.

Another important point to flag is the finding that political settlements cross-cut regime types, and exercise their influence at least partly independently of regime type. Too much of the debate in the politics of development has focused on the relative advantages of democracy and authoritarianism. Although there is an association between power concentration and authoritarianism it is not a strong one. Moreover, we have shown that power concentration alone is a better predictor of development outcomes than regime type, and, normative issues aside, we hope this will contribute to a process of transcending the democracy–authoritarianism debate in relation to development outcomes.

Future research

The creation of our dataset and the testing of our hypotheses has answered, or at least shed light on, a few important questions in the study of politics and development. However, it opens the door to many more. In the following pages, we list a few of the areas of research that the dataset could be used for.

Small-N research

To date, comparative political settlements research programmes have had to pick case studies largely on the basis of intuition, or a vague idea that one country is 'dominant' and another 'competitive'. Our comparative codings make a much more informed process of case selection, both synchronic and diachronic, possible. The foundations have been laid for qualitatively rich yet rigorously selected small-N studies to flourish.

Further, although we have only surveyed forty-two countries, our survey is available to be applied to other countries, so that adventurous scholars can extend PSA into new terrain.

One area into which we would like to see PSA extend is multi-level analysis. What is the relationship between national political settlements and sub-national political units such as states, regions, or cities? What is the relationship between national political settlements and transnational factors? Or between political settlements and the political power and technical capability of domestic capitalist classes? Our dataset and survey provide some of the building blocks for such an analysis.

Large-N research

Thus far, we have only tested our theory against a couple of development outcomes. We have not even tested all of our own hypotheses. For example, a more elaborate set of hypotheses than appear in Chapter 3, especially as related to the coup/civil war trap, is provided in Ferguson (2020). We have demonstrated that narrow-dispersed settlements are the least developmental and most fragile, but we have not begun to explore whether there are any 'best-bet' pathways from this type to other, more developmental and/or democratic ones. Indeed, it is possible to imagine our dataset being combined with others, for example, on peace agreements, to explore relationships between peace agreements, the political settlements they found, political stability, and development. A whole field of exploration is imaginable here.

Another debate in the field concerns the difference between inclusive development outcomes and inclusive development processes, which might be described as the difference between substantive and procedural accountability. By generating some initial data on the relationship between political settlement type and democracy, and the relationship of both to development outcomes of different sorts, our study has begun to shed light on that, and deeper exploration might permit more informed judgements about potential trade-offs.

It is also possible to envisage using the dataset to test the relationship between political settlements and a whole host of other downstream development indicators: economic complexity, universal health coverage, aid effectiveness, domestic revenue mobilization, Covid-19 response, 'gross national happiness', to name but a few. A very important area that we have not even begun to explore is gender outcomes. Yet our survey explicitly codes powerful and powerless groups by gender, so there is much useful work that could be done here.

Upstream variables could also be explored. For example, what difference does colonial heritage, ethnic diversity, resource abundance, capitalist development, or internal and external threat perception make to the emergence and sustainability of broad-concentrated political settlements? In what circumstances do broad-concentrated settlements emerge under conditions of political democracy? In what circumstances do dispersed settlements overperform?

We have also not gone very far in exploring interaction effects. How does resource abundance affect the way narrow-concentrated settlements behave? How do ideas, for example, socialist legacies, affect how effectively different political settlement types promote social policy? Exploration of these different factors might lead ultimately to the creation of more sub-types, and thus more fine-tuned advice for policymakers.

We have stressed throughout that one of the advantages of PSA is to transcend the 'democracy–autocracy' debate. Another recent book that attempts to do this is Acemoglu and Robinson's *The Narrow Corridor* (Acemoglu and Robinson 2019). The authors speak about the historical rarity of what they call, 'shackled leviathans', that is, powerful centralized states with the power to protect their people and deliver social goods, yet which are accountable to a society to whom they are in bondage. Shackled leviathans exist and develop in a 'narrow corridor' between despotism and either anarchy or the 'cage' of traditional norms.

Shackled leviathans are not synonymous with democracies, since there are many democracies that have very weak states, and there are some pre-modern shackled leviathans that were not democracies. For us, there is an elective affinity between shackled leviathans and at least some variants of broad-concentrated settlements—especially those where the breadth of the social foundation is based on the reality of societal power rather than just a perception. By tracing the processes by which broad-concentrated settlements emerge, PSA and the dataset we have produced can thus shed more light on the pathways by which societies get into, or turn out of, 'the corridor'.[3]

Typological refinement

There may also be considerable scope for refining our indices and categories. For example, currently our cut-off points for deciding when a country crosses from one political settlement type to another are given by the survey means. Scrutiny of the dataset might, however, reveal more meaningful cut-off points, connoting more 'freezing-point' type transitions. Further, when it comes to variable construction, we did not play around to any great extent with the weighting of our variables' different component parts. We chose a weighting that seemed epistemically plausible and stuck to it. However, by experimenting with different weightings, researchers might discover a mapping that makes the joints of reality more visible and delivers even stronger results, injecting more statistical significance into our categorical variable analysis.

Also, and as Chapters 5 and 6 illustrated, our main variables are composites. As such, they secrete quite a lot of potentially interesting variation. For example, Guinea was discussed as a 'narrow-dispersed' settlement, but it is interesting that the OB in Guinea is quite large and powerful, with the 'narrowness' of that country's coding driven by the level of government repression. There may be other 'narrow-dispersed' settlements, however, where the opposition is small and weak, with the 'narrowness' of the coding driven not by government repression, but by the majority of the population's lack of disruptive potential. It would be interesting to know whether these different variants of 'narrowness' have different developmental effects. The construction of our dataset makes that possible.

Readers will be conscious that our typology, by collapsing the Khanian variables onto a single axis, squashes some of the variation we find there. Some countries, for example, Ghana and Uganda, that one would expect to appear in different quadrants in his typology and were coded as such in the original ESID work, are in the same quadrant in ours. Because our data is publicly available and our methods

---

[3] Note that Acemoglu and Robinson also stress the importance of coalitions in bringing about far-reaching changes in governance.

transparent, researchers can discover precisely why that is the case.[4] However, it may be interesting to explore exactly how much explanatory power has been gained and how much has been lost by our method.

Improving and extending the data

Political settlements are not easy things to pin down; coders have limited knowledge and do not always agree on their codings. As discussed in Chapter 4, we have taken a variety of measures to weight the data to ensure intra-country coder reliability, yet we fully admit that the results are not perfect. In the future, there may be scope to improve the data by drawing on a wider pool of experts and developing more sophisticated methods for inter-coder reliability. There may also be ways of providing better inter-country benchmarks, further improving comparability. We have no doubt that country experts and comparativists will be able to quibble with the precise positioning of some of our settlements. Eyeballing the charts, we ourselves feel there are still some countries that are positioned not quite correctly. For example, although our Kenyan coders were all quite unified, and we thus saw little reason to challenge them, we wonder whether the political settlement there is really as broad as they imply. Fortunately, our initial reading of anomalies such as these suggests to us that a recalibration, rather than weakening our results, would strengthen them still further. And if country experts and political settlement analysts continue to disagree with our codings, we invite them to specify in detail why, an exercise that we hope will elevate the quality of political settlements research.

Finally, the coding exercise could be extended to many more countries. We cannot say whether this would strengthen or weaken our conclusions, but the politics and development community deserves to find out.

In conclusion: thanks to the questions we have answered and the ones that remain to be addressed, and despite the imperfections and limitations of our data, we believe this book has succeeded in putting PSA on a much sounder conceptual and scientific footing than hitherto, demonstrating—as our opening chapter title suggests—its considerable promise for the understanding and practice of development.

---

[4] The PolSett dataset can be accessed through the Political Settlements page on the ESID website: https://www.effective-states.org/political-settlements/

The Khan and Levy Approaches

In this appendix we take the opportunity to highlight some differences between our own approach and that of the two approaches that have inspired us most: those of Mushtaq Khan and Brian Levy.

Khan's argument, in a nutshell, is the following: politics in developing countries is fundamentally different from politics in capitalist countries. Since developing countries have a small formal sector, the incomes these sectors generate, unlike in capitalist countries, cannot be the main determinant of political power. Rather, political power is largely shaped by informal economic sectors. These sectors generate informal political organizations, notably patron–client networks or factions, that is, pyramidal aggregations of individuals and groups beneath a leader. These factions form the building blocks of politics in all developing countries, and they frequently mobilize politically to secure policies and institutions that will deliver benefits to them. Whatever their ideological, religious, or ethnic complexion, they are mainly about seeking rents or other economic benefits. If political and economic institutions are not delivering rents in line with these factions' expectations, factions will mobilize to try and change the institutions. Considerable political instability and perhaps violence are likely to result. However, when institutions deliver a distribution of benefits that is compatible with the distribution of factional power in society, we have what is called a political settlement, that is, a reproducible macro-social order.

Naturally, not all political settlements are the same, and a useful way of distinguishing them, according to Khan, is by reference to the 'holding power' of the 'ruling coalition' vis-à-vis excluded factions and its own, lower-level factions, the ruling coalition being defined as 'the factions that control political authority and state power in different societies' and 'holding power' as, 'the capability of an individual or group to engage and survive in conflicts' (Khan 2010: 6). As illustrated in Figure A.1, in political settlements where the ruling coalition is weak vis-à-vis excluded factions, it is likely to feel politically vulnerable and have a short time-horizon. By contrast, when it is weak vis-à-vis its own lower-level factions, it is likely to find it difficult to enforce policies or institutions that those factions oppose. These two variables generate four different types of political settlement, with differing implications for institutional reform.

Despite its intuitive appeal, we find there to be a problem with the hypothetical relations specified by Khan's matrix. For example, if the ruling coalition is essentially a pyramidal structure, and lower-level factions are strong, then surely the individual at the apex of that structure is vulnerable to being displaced by competitors lower down. *Ipso facto*, that individual should also have a short time-horizon (cf. Whitfield et al. 2015: 24). Further, an authoritarian coalition that faces strong opposition from excluded factions might also find it difficult to implement its policies, insofar as those factions can mobilize to protest against them. Thus, the enforcement/time-horizon distinction seems to collapse under scrutiny. Arguably, a more precise definition of the ruling coalition and where to draw the line between the leadership and lower-level factions, as we hope to have supplied in Chapter 4, would help correct this.

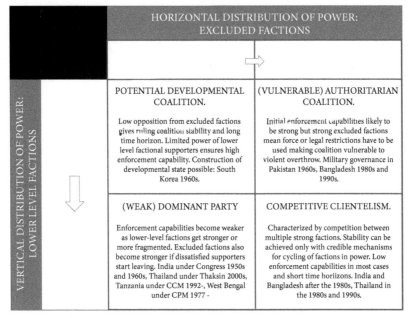

	HORIZONTAL DISTRIBUTION OF POWER: EXCLUDED FACTIONS	
	POTENTIAL DEVELOPMENTAL COALITION. Low opposition from excluded factions gives ruling coalition stability and long time horizon. Limited power of lower level factional supporters ensures high enforcement capability. Construction of developmental state possible: South Korea 1960s.	(VULNERABLE) AUTHORITARIAN COALITION. Initial enforcement capabilities likely to be strong but strong excluded factions mean force or legal restrictions have to be used making coalition vulnerable to violent overthrow. Military governance in Pakistan 1960s, Bangladesh 1980s and 1990s.
	(WEAK) DOMINANT PARTY Enforcement capabilities become weaker as lower-level factions get stronger or more fragmented. Excluded factions also become stronger if dissatisfied supporters start leaving. India under Congress 1950s and 1960s, Thailand under Thaksin 2000s, Tanzania under CCM 1992-, West Bengal under CPM 1977 -	COMPETITIVE CLIENTELISM. Characterized by competition between multiple strong factions. Stability can be achieved only with credible mechanisms for cycling of factions in power. Low enforcement capabilities in most cases and short time horizons. India and Bangladesh after the 1980s, Thailand in the 1980s and 1990s.

(Left vertical axis label: VERTICAL DISTRIBUTION OF POWER: LOWER LEVEL FACTIONS)

Fig. A.1 Mushtaq Khan's typology of political settlements in clientelist societies
Source: Adapted from Khan (2010).

Another ambiguity in Khan's approach is an equivocation over whether the political settlement is a macro-sociopolitical order or whether it is simply the balance of coalitional power around some proposed institutional change or other. If it is the former, we should be able to observe some kind of general relationship between political settlement types and overall patterns of social and economic development. If it is the latter, it can only be used to analyse outcomes on very specific policy or institutional issues. And, if this is the case, it is not clear that PSA has any great advantage over other forms of political economy analysis, which employ a less reductive approach to actors, institutions, and power.

As we explain in Chapter 6, we follow ESID in addressing this issue by preserving the term 'political settlement' for the former, and adding an additional concept, the 'policy domain' for the latter. This provides greater purchase over another observable puzzle in development studies, namely why states' ability to implement progressive reforms seems to be uneven not only between states, but *between different branches of the same state.*

This brings us to a related point about holding power. Holding power is the ability of factions to engage in and survive in conflicts. The first problem with this is that it relies on a very zero sum understanding of power. Granted some development policies have winners and losers, but there may be others, especially those which address coordination problems, that are better thought of as positive sum games, a point we discuss at greater length in Chapter 3. Moreover, the power of a ruling coalition will be partly dependent on its ability to present its policy choices as win-win situations: to get both its own internal and perhaps external factions to support it. But there seems little room for ideology, persuasion, or manipulation in Khan's worldview, or at least if there is, they play second fiddle to hard-nosed calculations about resources. Further, even where conflict is important, different policies will engender different levels of conflict, and if factions are as fluid and instrumental as

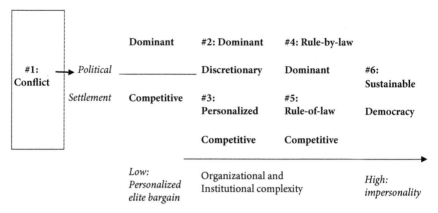

Fig. A.2 Brian Levy's 'Development Typology'
Source: Levy (2014)

Khan thinks, different factional alignments can be expected for different policy choices. Thus the holding power of a ruling coalition is never fixed: it varies issue by issue. But if holding power varies issue by issue, how can we create a generalized typology of political settlements?

We now move to Brian Levy's work (see Fig. A.2). Like Khan, Levy provides a typology of political settlements, but whereas Khan differentiates between the strength of the ruling coalition vis-à-vis excluded factions and its own internal factions, Levy collapses these into a single dimension of elite power. In his schema, the basic distinction between political settlement types is based on violence potential: where the disparity in the violence potential of the rulers and their opponents is large, the settlement is classed as 'dominant', and where it is small, it is 'competitive'. Slightly differently, where 'the rulers' grip on power is strong in the sense that it would take an extraordinary level of commitment by the opponents to mount a credible challenge to the status quo', the settlement is 'dominant', and where the reverse is true, it is 'competitive' (Levy 2014: Loc 732).

When it comes to operationalizing this definition, however, Levy (2014) uses a re-weighted version of the Polity IV dataset's (Marshall et al. 2019) composite measure of 'democracy'. Yet one of the purported strengths of political settlements analysis is its ability to unpack the democracy–authoritarianism distinction and identify states with similar attributes yet different regime types (Kelsall 2016). Put differently, the problem with using authoritarianism and democracy as proxies for more and less dominant political settlements is that they fail adequately to capture the empirical phenomenon of dominance and its posited attributes, namely long time-horizon and strong enforcement capacity. As we know, there are authoritarian regimes that appear to have very short time-horizons (Daniel arap Moi's Kenya, for instance) and weak enforcement capacity (Yoweri Museveni's Uganda) and democratic regimes that have the reverse (Botswana under Seretse Khama). Thus, we need a better way of measuring political settlements and their dimensions.[1]

---

[1] A recent book that also attempts to some degree to transcend the autocracy–democracy dichotomy is Daron Acemoglu and James Robinson's, *The Narrow Corridor* (2019). We pick up a discussion of this in Chapter 8.

Levy's horizontal dimension, meanwhile, depicting the institutional and organizational complexity of a country, attempts to capture North et al's (2009, 2012) transition from so-called 'limited access orders' (LAOs) to 'open access orders' (OAOs). As we have seen, for North et al., LAOs prevail in those countries where powerful elites create 'personalized elite bargains' to solve the problem of violence. Specifically, in LAOs the elite bargain is held together through highly personalized and often informal institutions that distribute privileged access to sources of power and wealth only to certain elites. OAOs by contrast—which prevail only in the most advanced industrial countries—are bound together not via particularistic and often off-budget wealth distribution, but via impersonal, impartial, formal, and politically open institutions.

Levy suggests measuring (im)personalization using a combination of three elements of the Worldwide Governance Indicators (WGIs), namely Government Effectiveness, Rule of Law, and Control of Corruption. While Levy himself (2014) acknowledges that the WGIs and other governance indicators are notoriously imprecise (cf Arndt and Oman 2006), his attempt to create an institutional/political settlement typology that is relatively consistent and comparable across countries and time is laudable and important. Unfortunately, using 'Government Effectiveness' as a proxy, and maybe even 'Control of Corruption' for institutional complexity very much risks identifying the independent variable with its outcome.

We believe our approach overcomes these conceptual ambiguities and measurement problems.

A Few Simple Game Models of Collective-action Problems Related to Political Settlements

In terms of methodology, game theory, flexibly applied, offers a broad array of systematic approaches to analysing both collective-action problems and multiple distinguishable social environments. Game theory, actually, is not a theory; it is a methodological toolbox for understanding strategic behaviour. Strategic behaviour permeates human societies, occurring whenever one person's or one group's actions affect others. Game-theoretic reasoning fits Nobel Prize economist Thomas Schelling's (2006) concept of vicarious problem-solving. Analysts (or strategic players) attribute goals to individuals, organizations, or groups, along with possible actions they might take and various obstacles and constraints. On this basis, they can infer (roughly predict) the likely behaviour of others. People engage in such inference repeatedly. A teenager might ponder: Dare I ask my friend out on a date? A parent might anticipate a child's reaction to a specific demand, request, reward, show of affection, and so forth. Note that game-theoretic modelling permits both social and material goals (status, power, health, consumption, approval, revenge, affection, money, etc.). Game-theoretic reasoning requires only an assumption that humans seek goals. Hence its breadth of application.

As such, game theory offers a series of approaches to institutional and political settlement analysis. In this regard, economic historian Douglass North defines institutions as 'the rules of the game in a society' (North 1990: 3), a notion that invites game-theoretic analysis of institutions, which can also apply to PSA. Now consider how game theorists specify the 'rules' of a game. The rules of a game specify six conditions that affect strategic interactions:

1. Who plays: which parties participate and, by extension, who cannot
2. The specific actions (moves) each player might take
3. The sequencing of moves—or lack thereof
4. What each player knows or does not know at each stage of the game. For example, does player A know the moves available to B? Does A understand B's goals?
5. All possible outcomes, meaning all possible final combinations of moves
6. The payoffs to each player at each possible outcome, where *payoff* signifies *everything* the player cares about, including money, time, health, status, outcomes for others, fairness, etc.[1]

---

[1] Simple games often focus only on material payoffs (e.g. money), but nothing about game theory requires sole focus on material payoffs (and for this reason, unfortunately, the term *payoff* may suggest limitations to game-theoretic analysis that simply do not exist).

Table B.1 Prisoners' dilemma game

		Group B Negotiate	Fight
Group A	Negotiate	2, 2	0, 3
	Fight	3, 0	1, 1*

Institutions prescribe many such specifics. A few examples: Who can vote? Who can apply for certain jobs? Who can attend certain committee meetings? Who receives what information? Who chairs meetings? Can a meeting chair set the agenda? What information does the chair have concerning the preferences or possible actions of committee members, and vice versa? Game-theoretic models can specify such conditions and, perhaps more importantly, force analysts to consider such context-relevant specifics in detail, along with many ensuing strategic implications.

With this background, consider how a few simple models might illustrate key elements of collective-action problems that accompany establishing a political settlement.[2] Table B.1 shows a prisoners' dilemma game that can illustrate the first-order problem of limiting violence. Groups A and B each simultaneously decide (i.e. without observing what the other does before making its own decision) whether to *negotiate* (N) or *fight* (F). If both choose N, both do better than if both choose F, but if one chooses F and the other chooses N, the fighter seizes the immediate benefits and the negotiator loses all.[3]

Both players have a dominant strategy of F (since 4 > 3 and 2 > 1). The (Nash) equilibrium occurs at combination FF, where each receives 1, even though both would receive 2 at NN. Absent some mechanism that would alter either the strategies or the payoffs, the collective-action problem of limiting violence remains unresolved. This same logic can apply to much larger groups (a variation on Figure 4).

With slight modification, Table B.1 can also represent the associated second-order collective-action problem of rendering potential agreements to limit violence credible. Simply rename the strategies *Honour* for full adherence to an agreement to limit violence and *Cheat* for reneging on part or all of the agreement. In cases where cheating generates higher material or social payoffs, the same prisoners' dilemma exists; moreover, this second-order problem can undermine any motivation to negotiate at all. By again relabelling the strategies, now to the more general terms *Cooperate* and *Defect*, Table B.1 can represent any first-order collective-action problem of free riding. Here Defect may signify failing to contribute to a public good, to limit one's use of a common resource, or to limit activities that lead to (or produce) negative externalities. For related second-order collective-action problems, strategies Honour and Cheat still apply.

A second simple game, chicken, can more decisively represent inter-group conflict as a first-order collective-action problem. Again, the players, here Authorities and Opposition, possess strategies F and N, but now the worst possible outcome for each arises when both choose F.

---

[2] The remaining argument in this Appendix offers only a thumbnail sketch of applying game-theoretic logic to PSA. For detail on applying game-theoretic logic to collective-action problems in general, see Ferguson (2013).

[3] Group A chooses N or F up and down the rows; B chooses across the columns. Each 'payoff' represents a player's net gains (or losses) at a specific combination of strategies (NN, NF, FN, FF). The first (second) number shows A's (B's) payoff. Rankings are ordinal, implying only that 3 > 2 > 1 > 0.

Table B.2 Game of chicken

		Authorities Negotiate	Fight
Opposition	Negotiate	2, 2	0, 4*
	Fight	4, 0*	−4, −4

Table B.3 Game of battle

		Team A Plan A	Plan B
Team B	Plan A	2, 1*	0, 0
	Plan B	0, 0	1, 2*

Table B.2 shows two Nash equilibria at NF and FN (since 4 > 2 and 0 > −4). Hence, the diagram does not offer a single prediction. At either equilibrium, both players would not unilaterally alter their strategy, since any deviation would lower their payoffs. Moreover, each prefers the equilibrium in which it fights and the other party negotiates. If both stick to their guns (perhaps literally) the worst possible outcome (FF) remains a distinct possibility. This simple diagram can also represent, perhaps higher-stakes, first-order collective-action problems of attempting to forge a political settlement. More generally, any of the following types of conflicts (among others) can fit its logic: wars, ethnic strife, high-stakes bargaining (e.g. budget negotiations in the US Congress; negotiations over Brexit; strikes), family arguments, etc. Associated second-order collective-action problems related to honouring or cheating could also take on either a prisoners' dilemma or a chicken dynamic.

Note further, that in the case of chicken, if one player can move first (and stick to its move) it can achieve its preferred equilibrium—that is, it can realize a first-mover advantage. If the authorities can start with F and credibly signal that they will stick with F no matter what, the opposition does best by choosing N, and vice versa.[4]

A third simple game (Table B.3), battle (more commonly battle of the sexes), can represent conflicts that involve transparent gains from cooperation, but different preferences over how to cooperate. Teams A and B would benefit each if both chose the same plan (a manner of cooperating), but A prefers plan A and B prefers plan B. Again, the logic could apply to either achieving a political settlement or interacting within a given settlement.

Two Nash equilibria arise, this time occurring where both choose the same plan and again with no single predicted outcome. If both teams insist on their preferred plan, each receives nothing (combination AB). Likewise, if each yields to the other, they again receive nothing (combination BA). In a dynamic framework, insistence on one's own plan could convert to a game of chicken. Note further, that second-order collective-action problems might also reflect this logic if the two parties interpret 'honour' differently and each prefers its own interpretation.

A more detailed strategic representation can involve variable instead of numerical payoffs. In Table B.1, for example, we could replace numbers 0, 1, 2, 3 with

---

[4] A sequential game-tree diagram, similar to that shown in Figure 3B.1 but with moves and payoffs adjusted, can represent this case.

variables q, x, y, z, possibly with subscripts A and B to denote distinct payoffs for each player. Each variable can depend on (become a function of) specific conditions in the political/economic environment that additional variables could represent. For example, if Group A consists of rainforest farmers, A's expected returns to excess land-clearing (a type of defection in a case where deforestation represents depletion of a common resource) may depend on the expected revenue from selling crops (R), average family size (F), etc. More generally, each payoff could represent a combination (e.g. a weighted average) of items the player cares about such as money, time, health, status, outcomes for friends, outcomes for enemies, each of which may respond to specific contextual variables. For example, social norms can influence the degree to which certain players care about outcomes for others or the degree to which they might feel guilt for defecting. Social norms could resolve Table B.1's prisoner's dilemma by augmenting payoffs to cooperation and lowering payoffs to defection or, for second-order collective-action problems, increasing the payoffs for Honouring agreements and reducing those for Cheating. Formal institutions can do the same, sometimes by adding direct rewards and/or punishments.

Survey Countries' Periodic Movement in the Political Settlement Space

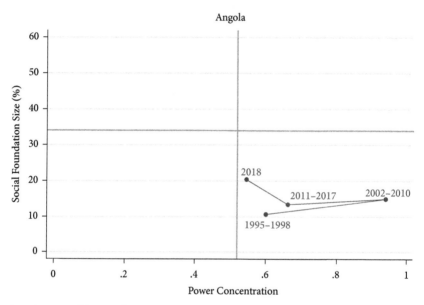

Fig. C.1 Angola's periodic movement in the political settlement space
Source: Schulz and Kelsall (2021c)

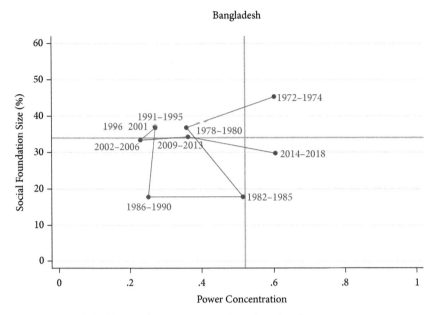

Fig. C.2 Bangladesh's periodic movement in the political settlement space
Source: Schulz and Kelsall (2021c)

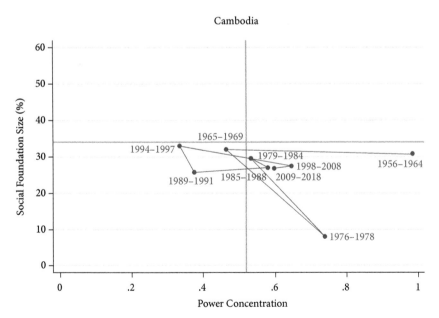

Fig. C.3 Cambodia's periodic movement in the political settlement space
Source: Schulz and Kelsall (2021c)

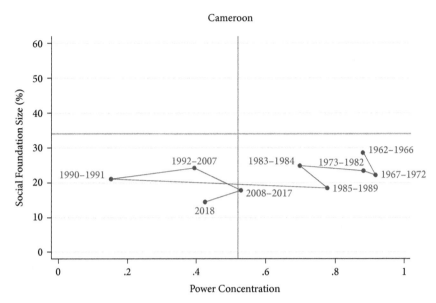

Fig. C.4 Cameroon's periodic movement in the political settlement space
Source: Schulz and Kelsall (2021c)

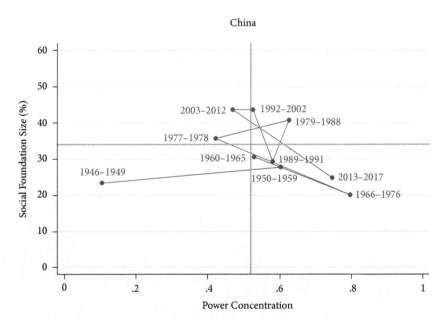

Fig. C.5 China's periodic movement in the political settlement space
Source: Schulz and Kelsall (2021c)

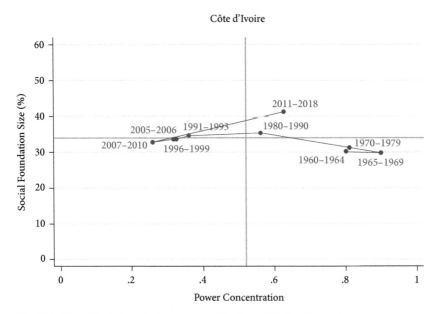

Fig. C.6 Côte d'Ivoire's periodic movement in the political settlement space
Source: Schulz and Kelsall (2021c)

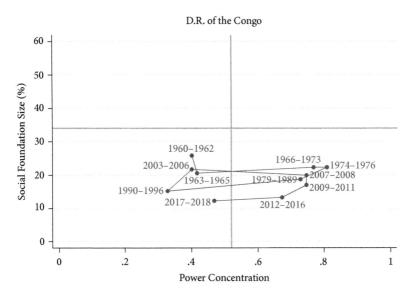

Fig. C.7 Democratic Republic of the Congo's periodic movement in the political settlement space
Source: Schulz and Kelsall (2021c)

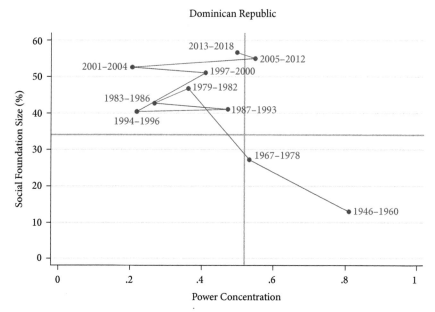

Fig. C.8 Dominican Republic's periodic movement in the political settlement space
Source: Schulz and Kelsall (2021c)

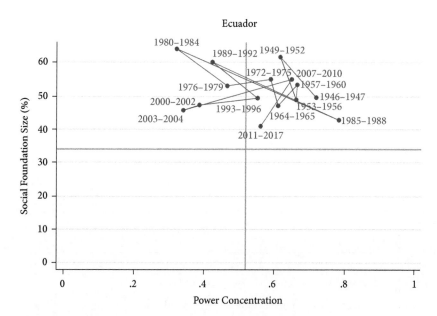

Fig. C.9 Ecuador's periodic movement in the political settlement space
Source: Schulz and Kelsall (2021c)

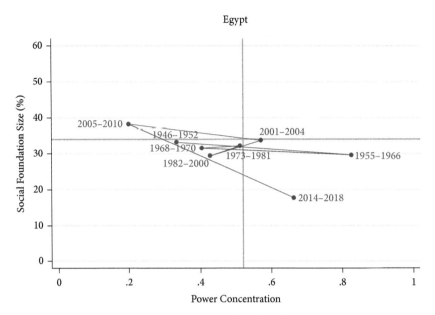

Fig. C.10 Egypt's periodic movement in the political settlement space
Source: Schulz and Kelsall (2021c)

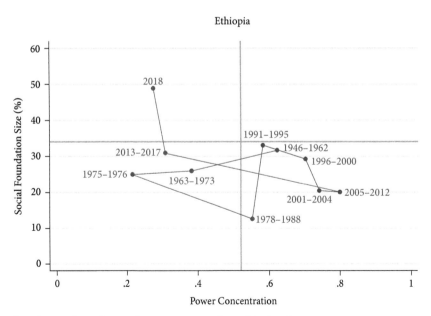

Fig. C.11 Ethiopia's periodic movement in the political settlement space
Source: Schulz and Kelsall (2021c)

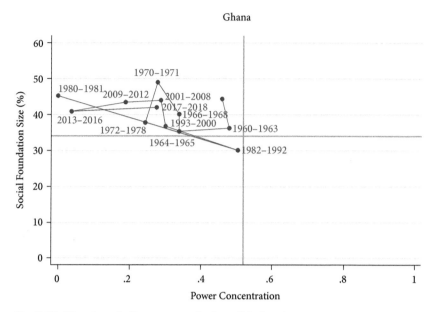

Fig. C.12 Ghana's periodic movement in the political settlement space
Source: Schulz and Kelsall (2021c)

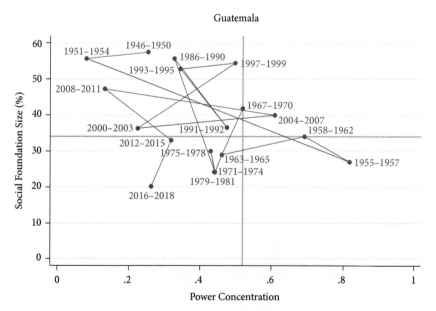

Fig. C.13 Guatemala's periodic movement in the political settlement space
Source: Schulz and Kelsall (2021c)

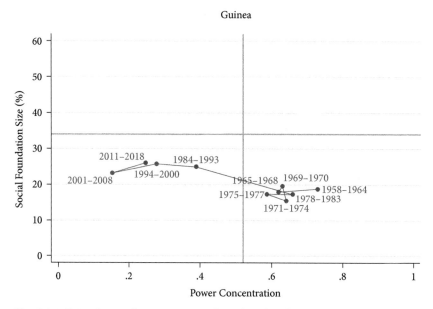

Fig. C.14 Guinea's periodic movement in the political settlement space
Source: Schulz and Kelsall (2021c)

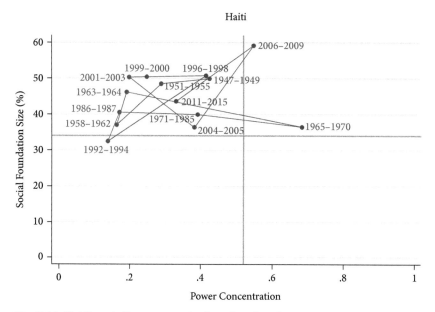

Fig. C.15 Haiti's periodic movement in the political settlement space
Source: Schulz and Kelsall (2021c)

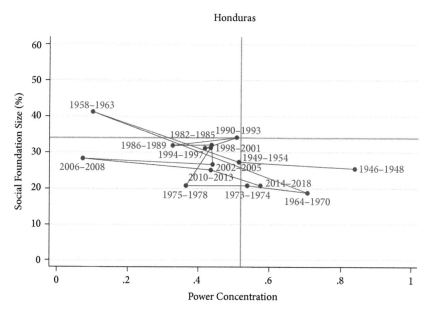

Fig. C.16 Honduras's periodic movement in the political settlement space
Source: Schulz and Kelsall (2021c)

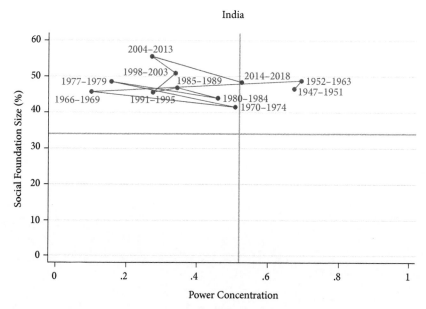

Fig. C.17 India's periodic movement in the political settlement space
Source: Schulz and Kelsall (2021c)

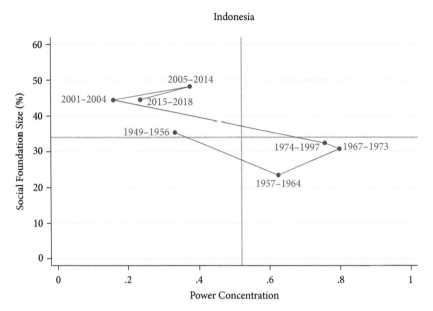

Fig. C.18 Indonesia's periodic movement in the political settlement space
Source: Schulz and Kelsall (2021c)

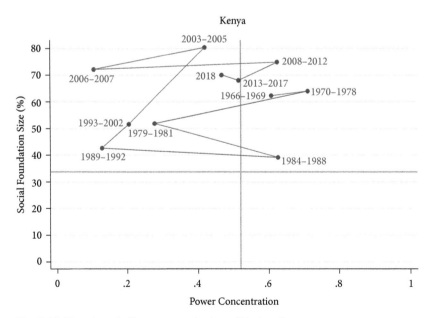

Fig. C.19 Kenya's periodic movement in the political settlement space
Source: Schulz and Kelsall (2021c)

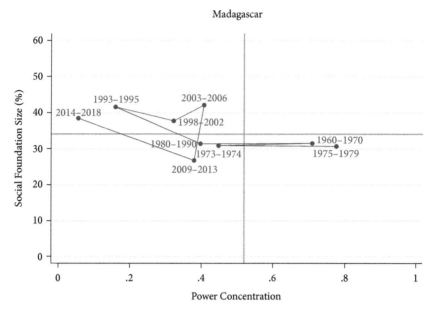

Fig. C.20 Madagascar's periodic movement in the political settlement space
Source: Schulz and Kelsall (2021c)

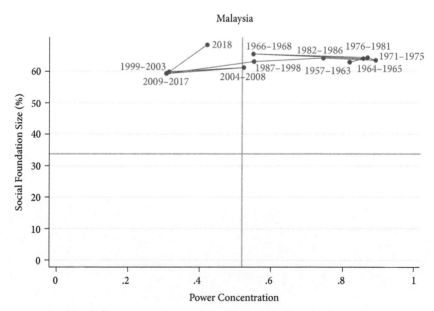

Fig. C.21 Malaysia's periodic movement in the political settlement space
Source: Schulz and Kelsall (2021c)

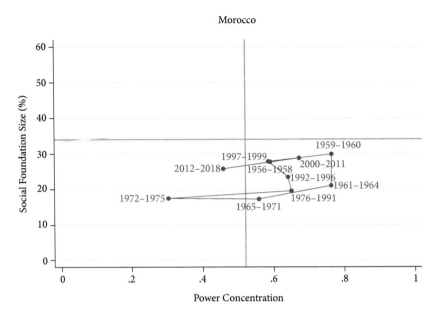

Fig. C.22 Morocco's periodic movement in the political settlement space
Source: Schulz and Kelsall (2021c)

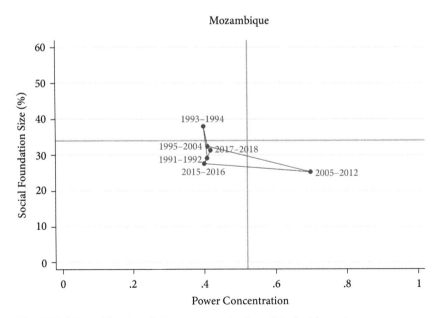

Fig. C.23 Mozambique's periodic movement in the political settlement space
Source: Schulz and Kelsall (2021c)

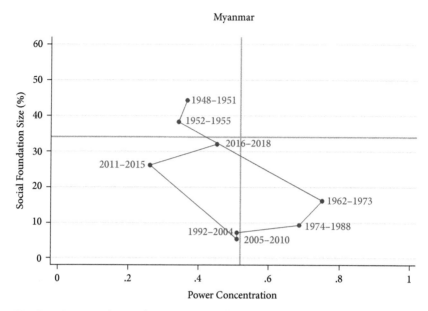

Fig. C.24 Myanmar's periodic movement in the political settlement space
Source: Schulz and Kelsall (2021c)

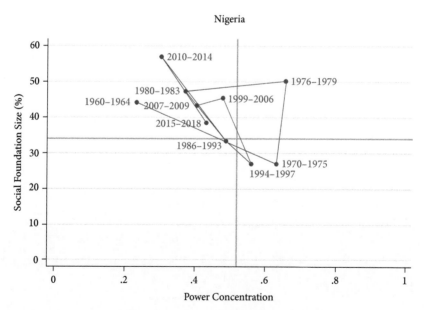

Fig. C.25 Nigeria's periodic movement in the political settlement space
Source: Schulz and Kelsall (2021c)

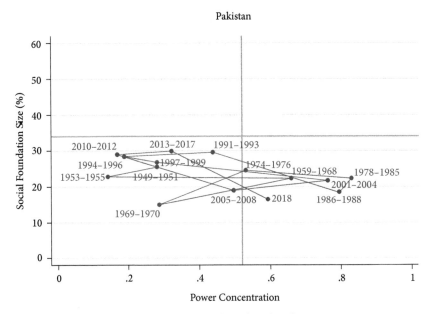

Fig. C.26 Pakistan's periodic movement in the political settlement space
Source: Schulz and Kelsall (2021c)

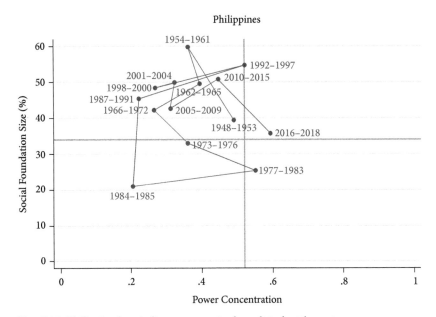

Fig. C.27 Philippines' periodic movement in the political settlement space
Source: Schulz and Kelsall (2021c)

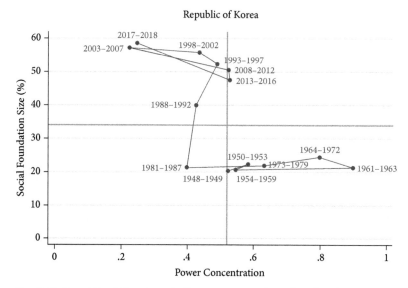

Fig. C.28 Republic of Korea's periodic movement in the political settlement space
Source: Schulz and Kelsall (2021c)

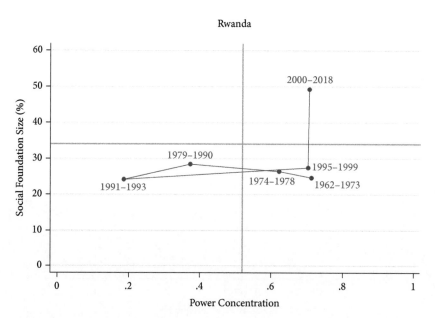

Fig. C.29 Rwanda's periodic movement in the political settlement space
Source: Schulz and Kelsall (2021c)

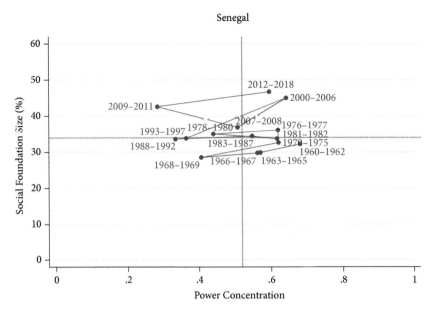

Fig. C.30 Senegal's periodic movement in the political settlement space
Source: Schulz and Kelsall (2021c)

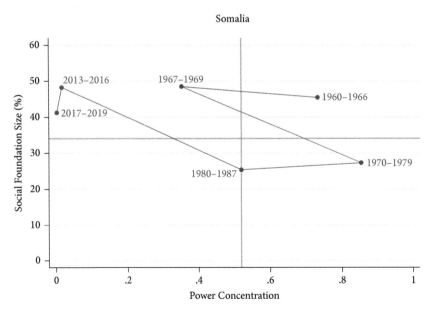

Fig. C.31 Somalia's periodic movement in the political settlement space
Source: Schulz and Kelsall (2021c)

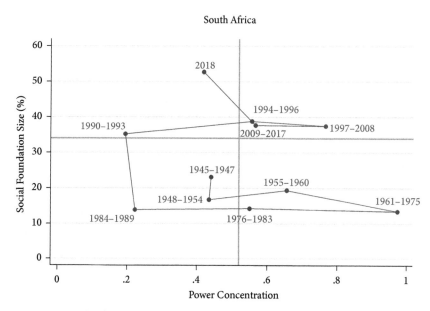

Fig. C.32 South Africa's periodic movement in the political settlement space
Source: Schulz and Kelsall (2021c)

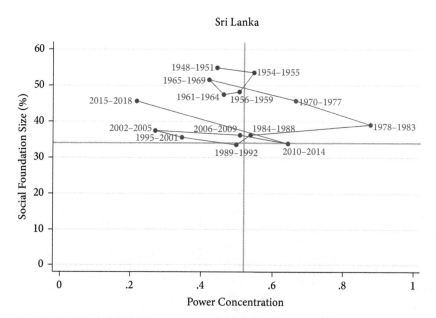

Fig. C.33 Sri Lanka's periodic movement in the political settlement space
Source: Schulz and Kelsall (2021c)

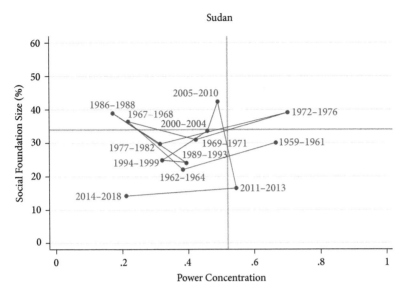

Fig. C.34 Sudan's periodic movement in the political settlement space
Source: Schulz and Kelsall (2021c)

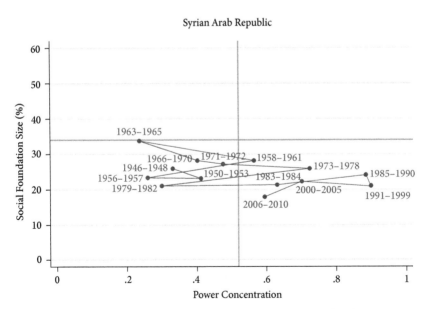

Fig. C.35 Syrian Arab Republic's periodic movement in the political settlement space
Source: Schulz and Kelsall (2021c)

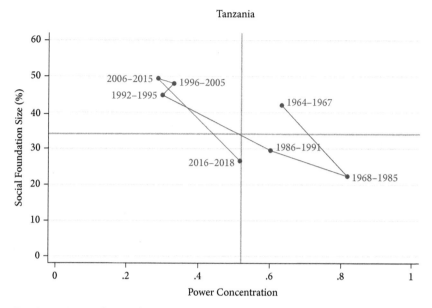

Fig. C.36 Tanzania's periodic movement in the political settlement space
Source: Schulz and Kelsall (2021c)

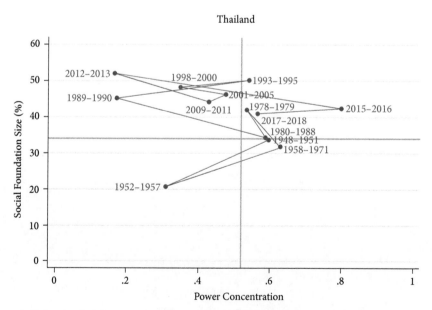

Fig. C.37 Thailand's periodic movement in the political settlement space
Source: Schulz and Kelsall (2021c)

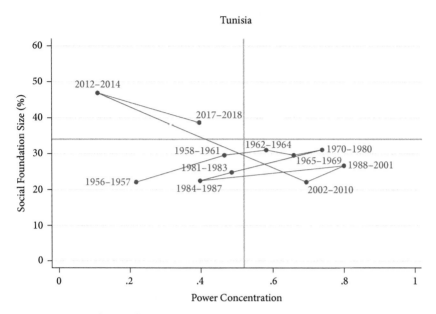

Fig. C.38 Tunisia's periodic movement in the political settlement space
Source: Schulz and Kelsall (2021c)

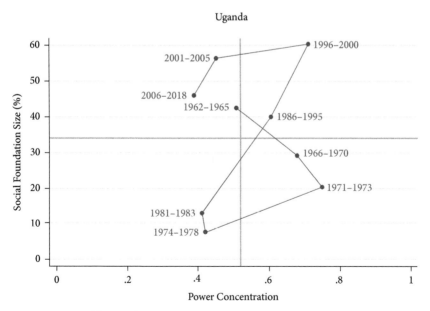

Fig. C.39 Uganda's periodic movement in the political settlement space
Source: Schulz and Kelsall (2021c)

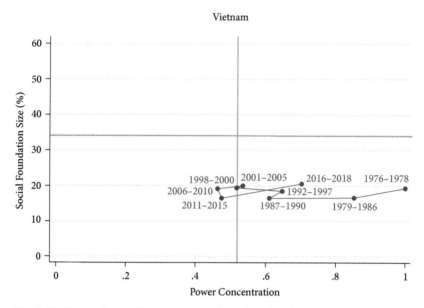

Fig. C.40 Vietnam's periodic movement in the political settlement space
Source: Schulz and Kelsall (2021c)

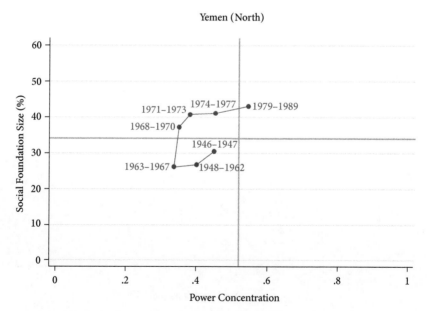

Fig. C.41 North Yemen's periodic movement in the political settlement space
Source: Schulz and Kelsall (2021c)

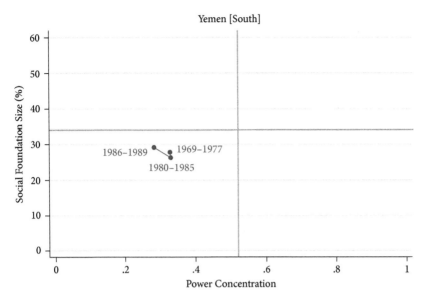

Fig. C.42 South Yemen's periodic movement in the political settlement space
Source: Schulz and Kelsall (2021c)

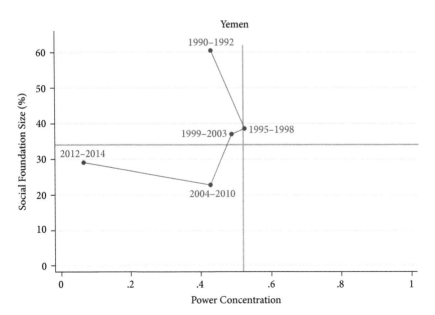

Fig. C.43 Yemen's periodic movement in the political settlement space
Source: Schulz and Kelsall (2021c)

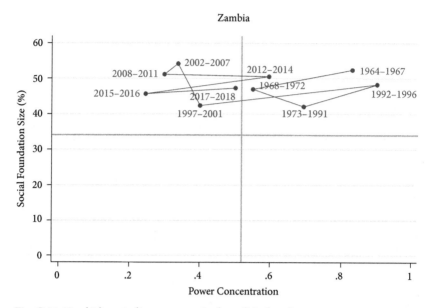

Fig. C.44 Zambia's periodic movement in the political settlement space
Source: Schulz and Kelsall (2021c)

A List of Archetypal Political Settlements

Note that political settlements can evolve or change even under the same leader, and the Leader suffix '1', '2', etc. in the final column refers to the 1st, 2nd, etc. iteration of that Leader's settlement.

Table D.1 Archetypal political settlement periods

Country	Period	Leader	ESID_type_typical_Name
Rwanda	2000–2018	Paul Kagame 3	Broad-Concentrated
Kenya	1970–1978	Jomo Kenyatta 3	Broad-Concentrated
Ecuador	1946–1947	Velasco Ibarra 1	Broad-Concentrated
Uganda	1996–2000	Museveni 2	Broad-Concentrated
Malaysia	1982–1986	Mahathir Mohamad 1	Broad-Concentrated
Malaysia	1957–1963	Tunku Abdul Rahman 1	Broad-Concentrated
Zambia	1964–1967	Kaunda 1	Broad-Concentrated
Malaysia	1964–1965	Tunku Abdul Rahman 2	Broad-Concentrated
Malaysia	1976–1981	Hussein Onn Jaafar	Broad-Concentrated
Malaysia	1971–1975	Abdul Razak Hussein 2	Broad-Concentrated
Zambia	1992–1996	Chiluba 1	Broad-Concentrated
Somalia	2013–2016	Hassan Sheikh Mohamud 1	Broad-Dispersed
Kenya	2006–2007	Mwai Kibaki 2	Broad-Dispersed
Tunisia	2012–2014	Marzouki 1	Broad-Dispersed
India	1977–1979	Desai 1	Broad-Dispersed
Thailand	2012–2013	Yingluck Shinawatra 1	Broad-Dispersed
Haiti	1958–1962	Duvalier, Francois 1	Broad-Dispersed
Kenya	1993–2002	Moi 5	Broad-Dispersed
Tanzania	2006–2015	Kikwete	Broad-Dispersed
Dominican Republic	2001–2004	Hipólito Mejía 1	Broad-Dispersed
Korea	2003–2007	Roh Moo Hyun 1	Broad-Dispersed
Haiti	1986–1987	Namphy 1	Broad-Dispersed
Korea	2017–2018	Moon Jae-in 1	Broad-Dispersed
Philippines	1998–2000	Estrada 1	Broad-Dispersed
Haiti	1951–1955	Magloire 2	Broad-Dispersed
Kenya	1979–1981	Moi 1	Broad-Dispersed
India	2004–2013	Singh, Manmohan 1	Broad-Dispersed
Ethiopia	2018	Abiy Ahmed 1	Broad-Dispersed
Ghana	1970–1971	Busia	Broad-Dispersed
Zambia	2008–2011	Banda	Broad-Dispersed

Continued

Table D.1 *Continued*

Country	Period	Leader	ESID_type_typical_Name
Haiti	2011–2015	Martelly 1	Broad-Dispersed
Malaysia	2009–2017	Najib Abdul Razak	Broad-Dispersed
Malaysia	1999–2003	Mahathir Mohamad 3	Broad-Dispersed
Ecuador	1980–1984	Aquilers and Larrea 1	Broad-Dispersed
Philippines	2001–2004	Gloria Macapagal—Arroyo 1	Broad-Dispersed
Haiti	2001–2003	Aristide 3	Broad-Dispersed
Guatemala	1986–1990	Cerezo 1	Broad-Dispersed
Honduras	1964–1970	Lopez Arellano 1	Narrow-Concentrated
DRC	1979–1989	Mobutu 4	Narrow-Concentrated
Guinea	1958–1964	Touré 1	Narrow-Concentrated
Ethiopia	2001–2004	Meles Zenawi 3	Narrow-Concentrated
Uganda	1971–1973	Amin 1	Narrow-Concentrated
DRC	2007–2008	Joseph Kabila 3	Narrow-Concentrated
DRC	2009–2011	Joseph Kabila 4	Narrow-Concentrated
Myanmar	1962–1973	Ne Win 2	Narrow-Concentrated
Pakistan	2001–2004	Pervez Musharraf 2	Narrow-Concentrated
Morocco	1961–1964	Hassan II 1	Narrow-Concentrated
DRC	1966–1973	Mobutu 1	Narrow-Concentrated
Cameroon	1985–1989	Biya 2	Narrow-Concentrated
China	1966–1976	Mao Zedong 3	Narrow-Concentrated
Pakistan	1986–1988	Muhammad Zia-ul-Haq 2	Narrow-Concentrated
Ethiopia	2005–2012	Meles Zenawi 4	Narrow-Concentrated
Dominican Republic	1946–1960	Rafael Trujillo 1	Narrow-Concentrated
DRC	1974–1976	Mobutu 2	Narrow-Concentrated
Tanzania	1968–1985	Nyerere 2	Narrow-Concentrated
Pakistan	1978–1985	Muhammad Zia-ul-Haq 1	Narrow-Concentrated
Korea	1961–1963	Park Chung Hee 1	Narrow-Concentrated
Cameroon	1967–1972	Ahidjo 3	Narrow-Concentrated
Angola	2002–2010	Dos Santos 6	Narrow-Concentrated
South Africa	1961–1975	Verwoerd 2, Vorster 1	Narrow-Concentrated
Guatemala	2016–2018	Jimmy Morales	Narrow-Dispersed
Cameroon	1990–1991	Biya 3	Narrow-Dispersed
Philippines	1984–1985	Marcos 4	Narrow-Dispersed
Sudan	2014–2018	Al-Bashir 6	Narrow-Dispersed
Tunisia	1956–1957	Muhammad al-Amin 1	Narrow-Dispersed
South Africa	1984–1989	Botha 2	Narrow-Dispersed
Bangladesh	1986–1990	Ershad 2	Narrow-Dispersed
Pakistan	1969–1970	Yahya Khan 1	Narrow-Dispersed
Thailand	1952–1957	Plaek Pibulsongkram 2	Narrow-Dispersed
Morocco	1972–1975	Hassan II 3	Narrow-Dispersed
Cambodia	1994–1997	Ranariddh	Narrow-Dispersed
DRC	1990–1996	Mobutu 5	Narrow-Dispersed

Source: Schulz and Kelsall (2021c)

Unbundling the Social Foundation over Time in Democratic-era South Africa

Table E.1 Unbundling the social foundation over time in democratic era South Africa

	ESID all data average	Mandela (1994– 1996)	Mbeki (1997– 2007)	Zuma (2009– 2017)	Ramaphosa (2018–)
Social foundation (% population)	34.0%	38.7%	37.3%	37.6%	52.6%
Leadership bloc					
Size	35.8%	65%	48%	41%	44%
o/w powerful	20.7	30.1	19.3	19.0	21.3
Powerful/size	*0.58*	*0.46*	*0.40*	*0.46*	*0.48*
Co-optation score	0.72	0.90	0.87	0.81	0.88
Contingently loyal bloc					
Size	27.3%	14%	20%	21%	27.5%
o/w powerful	14.9	7.2	14.6	11.3	22.1
Powerful/size	*0.55*	*0.51*	*0.73*	*0.54*	*0.80*
Co-optation score	0.67	0.89	0.87	0.81	0.87
Opposition bloc					
Size	36.9%	21%	32%	38%	28.5%
o/w powerful	19.0	6.3	9.4	18.6	17.8
Powerful/size	*0.51*	*0.3*	*0.29*	*0.49*	*0.62*
Co-optation score	0.46	0.80	0.82	0.71	0.82

Source: Schulz and Kelsall (2021c)

Alternative Regression Analysis Results

Table F.1 Regression analysis results replacing social foundation size with total powerful population share (TPPS)

	(7) AnEcGr (t+1)	(8) AnIMRGr (t+1)	(9) AnEcGr (t+1)	(10) AnIMRGr (t+1)	(11) AnEcGr (t+1)	(12) AnIMRGr (t+1)
Power concentration	**3.41*****	**−1.51***				
	(1.06)	(0.76)				
Total powerful population share	**0.04***	**−0.05***				
	(0.02)	(0.03)				
GDP pc (ln)	−0.86		−0.92		−0.74	
	(0.55)		(0.57)		(0.65)	
Polity2	0.03	−0.08***	0.02	−0.08***	0.04	−0.08***
	(0.04)	(0.02)	(0.04)	(0.02)	(0.04)	(0.02)
Fuel Income	−0.00	0.00	−0.00	0.00	−0.00	0.00
	(0.00)	(0.00)	(0.00)	(0.00)	(0.00)	(0.00)
ODA	0.11**	−0.01	0.11***	−0.00	0.12***	−0.01
	(0.04)	(0.02)	(0.04)	(0.02)	(0.04)	(0.02)
IMR Status ln		−0.86*		−0.93*		−0.97*
		(0.45)		(0.53)		(0.55)
PS Multi. Index (TPPS)			**4.65*****	**−3.05****		
			(1.16)	(1.41)		
1. Broad-Concentrated					**0.00**	**0.00**
					(.)	(.)
2. Broad-Dispersed					**−0.80**	**0.35**
					(0.62)	(0.54)
3. Narrow-Dispersed					**−0.52**	**0.43**
					(0.57)	(0.48)
4. Narrow-Concentrated					**0.42**	**0.13**
					(0.54)	(0.57)
Constant	3.64	5.38**	6.40	3.17	**6.86**	**1.92**
	(4.40)	(2.58)	(4.43)	(2.64)	(5.16)	(2.85)
Observations	1,297	1,299	1,297	1,299	1,297	1,299

Note: * p < 0.10, ** p < 0.05, *** p < 0.01. P-values in parentheses. Two-way fixed effects and additional controls included. Standard errors clustered at the country-level.
Source: Authors' own calculations using data from Schulz and Kelsall (2021c) and Marshall (2019)

Table F.2 Main regression models (3 and 4) re-run using two- and three-year leads as well as excluding the four ESID countries

	Leads			No ESID Countries		
	(13) AnEcGr (t+2)	(14) AnIMRGr (t+2)	(15) AnEcGr (t+3)	(16) AnIMRGr (t+3)	(17) AnEcGr (t+1)	(18) AnIMRGr (t+1)
PS Multi. Index	3.92***	−2.99**	3.16**	−2.90**	3.63**	−2.14***
	(1.35)	(1.23)	(1.24)	(1.15)	(1.44)	(0.65)
GDP pc (ln)	−1.89***		−2.20***		−0.75	
	(0.62)		(0.67)		(0.60)	
Polity2	−0.07**	−0.06**	−0.08***	−0.05*	−0.03	−0.06**
	(0.03)	(0.03)	(0.02)	(0.02)	(0.05)	(0.02)
Fuel Income	−0.00	0.00	−0.00	0.00	−0.00	0.00
	(0.00)	(0.00)	(0.00)	(0.00)	(0.00)	(0.00)
ODA	0.07**	0.00	0.04	−0.00	0.13**	0.01
	(0.03)	(0.02)	(0.03)	(0.02)	(0.05)	(0.03)
IMR Status (ln)		−1.68**		−2.40***		−0.47
		(0.63)		(0.70)		(0.54)
Constant	15.13***	6.71**	18.27***	10.30***	6.58	0.08
	(5.15)	(3.26)	(5.28)	(3.61)	(4.49)	(2.73)
Observations	1,337	1,339	1,337	1,339	1,171	1,173

Note: * $p < 0.10$, ** $p < 0.05$, *** $p < 0.01$. P-values in parentheses. Two-way fixed effects and additional controls included. Standard errors clustered at the country-level.
Source: Authors' own calculations using data from Schulz and Kelsall (2021c) and Marshall (2019)

Political Settlement Survey Instrument and Coder Notes

A General Introduction to Political Settlements

In recent years, political settlements analysis has become an increasingly influential approach in conflict and development studies—but most of its concept formation and theory-building has been based on a small number of case studies. Using expert opinion, this survey attempts for the first time to systematically collect data that will allow us to code political settlements and their evolution, across countries and across time.

We define a political settlement as *an ongoing agreement (or acquiescence) among a society's most powerful groups to a set of political and economic institutions expected to generate for them a minimally acceptable level of benefits, and which thereby ends or prevents generalized civil war and/or political and economic disorder.*

Put simply, our assumption is that groups stop fighting or refrain from fighting or other forms of serious disorder, either when they are forced to or when they can see some benefit from it. However, benefits do not fall from the sky: their distribution is mediated by institutions. Conflicting actors (e.g. political parties, militias, social movements) and the groups that support them agree on a set of political and economic institutions that they believe will provide opportunities for them to secure an acceptable distribution of benefits (even if the benefit is simply to not risk being killed). If the institutions do not yield the expected benefits, they are likely to start fighting again.

In more detail, every political settlement implies:

1. **A reduction or prevention of violent conflict**. Political settlements end, or prevent the outbreak of, high-intensity, society-wide civil war or social and economic disorder. They may be compatible, however, with intense sub-regional conflict, high

levels of violent repression, vigorous levels of institutionalized political competition, or temporary outbreaks of regime-threatening protest or disorder. To say that a country has a political settlement is not to say that its governing institutions are popular or even that they have broad legitimacy; it is to say that they are having a certain amount of success in controlling competitive violence and disorder;

2. **An agreement.** An agreement may be formal, as in the case of a peace-treaty; informal, as in the case of verbal, private agreements among powerful groups; or even tacit, in the sense of a set of mutually understood expectations. Different types of actors or groups may be involved in different types or levels of agreement, e.g. party leaders may be involved in making formal peace-treaties, while their followers merely acquire a set of expectations about what the agreement implies. Agreement can be entered into voluntarily by two or more groups of roughly equal standing, or it may be imposed by a stronger group on a weaker group. In the latter case, agreement shades into forced acquiescence. Here, the weaker group nevertheless calculates that it is better to accept the institutions and expected benefits on offer, at least for the time being, than incur the costs associated with further fighting;

3. **A configuration of powerful groups.** Every polity is made up of a myriad of groups, some of which have the organizational power, acting alone or jointly, to make, unmake, or reproduce settlements. The power of these groups is not static and can be expected to change over time. However, large changes in the relative power of these groups are often associated with changes in the political settlement. As we explain below, our approach draws on existing political settlements theory to divide society into three main blocs and then a range of more and less powerful sub-groups, based on those groups' ability to engage in struggles that shape the settlement. Obviously, there are other ways of understanding power in society, but we ask you to bear with us;

4. **Political and economic institutions.** For us, an institution is, 'a combination of mutually understood and self-enforcing beliefs, conventions, social norms, social rules, or formal rules that jointly indicate or prescribe behavioural regularities in specific or varied social contexts'.[1]

   For our purposes we build on yet also move beyond the well-established distinction between formal and informal institutions[2] and differentiate between de jure and de facto institutions. Specifically, in identifying changes in political settlements we care about actual applied (de facto) changes in institutions, rather than merely formal though not applied (de jure) changes in institutions.

   By political and economic institutions we mean the monitored and enforced meta-institutions that create or shape behavioural regularities around the basic rules of the national political and economic game. These meta-institutions govern such things as who makes the rules, how they make them, and who, broadly, is expected to benefit. A change in any, or all these institutions, formal or informal, may be sufficient to warrant talk of there being an evolution or change in a political settlement. As such we ask you to pay attention not only to phenomena such as constitutions, party, and electoral systems, but also to informal institutions, such as patron–client relations,

---

[1] Ferguson, William D. (2013), *Collective Action and Exchange: A Game-theoretic Approach to Contemporary Political Economy* (Stanford, CA: Stanford University Press), p. 152.

[2] Helmke, Gretchen and Levitsky, Steven (2003), 'Informal institutions and comparative politics: a research agenda. Working paper #307', (Kellogg Institute, accessible at http://kellogg.nd.edu/sites/default/files/old_files/documents/307_0.pdf), p. 9.

gender norms, and so on. The test is whether the change is de facto, whether it is *major*, and whether there is some evidence that it is taken with a view to ending or forestalling war or other forms of system-threatening disorder, even if this disorder is visible only on the distant horizon or merely hypothesized by a country's leaders.

5. **An acceptable distribution of benefits.** Here we refer to the sum total of material and non-material benefits generated by political and economic institutions. When there is a political settlement, the expectations of the country's most powerful groups are being met, at least in the minimal sense that they calculate there is more to lose from violently opposing the current institutions than in acquiescing to them.

Phase 1: Creation and Classification of Political Periods

The first step in our survey is to create a basic periodization by identifying the most obvious potential 'break or evolution points' in a country's political history since 1945 or independence. We have created an initial periodization which we are asking our experts to corroborate or interrogate.

It is important to highlight that the key goal of this exercise is to create a periodization that closely tracks variation in major de facto changes in the political rules of the game and the configuration of power, many of which will proxy for evolution or change in the political settlement.

As mentioned earlier, at a macro level we divide society into three main blocs. In more detail, these are: (1) the leader's bloc: that is, the segment of the population whose political loyalty the current de facto leader perceives s/he can be reasonably assured of, at least in the short term; (2) The contingently loyal bloc: The segment of the population that is currently aligned with the de facto leader (evidenced by either some meaningful representation in the highest levels of government or a formal or informal agreement/pact to conditionally support the leader's bloc) but whose political loyalty s/he cannot be assured of; and (3) The opposition bloc: the segment of the population that is not currently aligned with either of the above (compare also the more detailed description in Phase 2 below).

Using this method, changes of leader are a good proxy for changes in the configuration of powerful groups. Using the Archigos database of (de facto) political leaders, each change in the leadership of a country was consequently identified as a basic break point. (Note that if multiple leaders ruled in a calendar year, only the one that ruled longest in that year is coded). However, leadership change is only a proxy.

If you feel that a leadership change did not connote a major change in the configuration of power, for example because the existing leader was replaced by someone from the same group with similar ideas and a similar degree of authority, please strike out that change.

In addition, we used additional databases and web resources to identify other potential break points which *might* signify major change or evolution in the de facto rules of the game and/or the configuration of power, namely:

1. the composition and power of the ruling coalition;
2. formal political institutions;
3. the degree of violent contestation and/or the propensity of the government losing a war;
4. the economic and social ideology of the head of government; and/or
5. the degree to which the state can conduct domestic policy autonomously of foreign states or organizations.

Please note that this list is not exhaustive. *There might be other criteria you think are relevant for tracking changes in the configuration of power (e.g. changes in informal institutions, movements of very powerful sub-groups from one bloc to another) and if so, we would like you to tell us about them. Also, if de jure changes we have suggested are not major de facto changes, they should be overruled by you.*

Finally, we make a judgement as to whether the country was best described as 'unsettled', 'challenged', 'settled', 'semi-settled' or 'transitional'.

- a. **Unsettled:** This category is intended to capture those periods in which civil war was so all-encompassing and the possibility of the government losing militarily so serious and tangible, that all it could really engage in was consolidating authority and securing its imminent military survival (rather than also engaging in economic or social policy, etc.). That is, a period similar to that in Syria from 2012–2017, or Libya in 2011. Such all-encompassing warfare is, by our definition, incompatible with there being a political settlement. This is indicated for us by two criteria: 1) a threshold of 'substantial or prolonged warfare' (i.e. ≥5) according to the Major Episodes of Political Violence dataset (MEPV) (Marshall 2017);[3] and 2) an intrastate war having caused 1,000 *battle-related* deaths per year according to the Uppsala Armed Conflict Dataset (i.e. deaths that were not the result of *one-sided* violence by the government or by a formally organized group against civilians). If both of these hold, we provisionally code a period as unsettled, subject to the caveats below;
- b. **Challenged:** We use this category to capture periods where there are serious and prolonged *violent or disorderly* challenges to the regime but in which it is not under tangible threat of being militarily overthrown by oppositional groups. For us, this is indicated **EITHER** by a period in which there was *substantial and prolonged* warfare [see above] but in which the violence *was geographically limited* to a particular region with a relatively small population e.g. <25% of the country **OR** a period in which there was serious political violence or warfare but *at a lower intensity* than in the above case [i.e. MEPV 3–4 or MEPV ≥5, but with less than 1,000 battle-related deaths per year] **OR** alternatively, a period where there were very regular and very large protests or demonstrations against the ruling group or the political system itself;
- c. **Settled:** We use this category to capture periods lasting at least two years where there appears to be a substantial agreement or truce among *the most* powerful groups around the basic rules of the political game, even though there may be extensive repression of less powerful groups, minor insurgencies or sporadic violence and disorder. Coding a period as 'settled' does not imply that it was peaceful, without repression, or democratic. It only means that we did not find the period to meet the 'challenged' or 'unsettled' thresholds set out above. Do please indicate, however, if you think it did;
- d. **Semi-Settled:** We use this category to capture short periods in which there is a lack of agreement among the most powerful groups over the basic rules of the political game and/or the general composition of the ruling coalition, even if this is not manifested as substantial or prolonged warfare or disorder. For us, this is indicated by a situation in which there was no serious political violence (MEPV <3) but a significant change in leadership, power, or institutions occurs after less than two years;
- e. **Transitional:** We use this category to capture periods in which there is a planned transition from war to peace, autocracy to democracy, or to organize elections.

---

[3] Please compare the MEPV codebook for more detail (particularly pages 9 to 11).

This is indicated by a period in which there was no substantial or prolonged warfare [i.e. MEPV <5] and there was an officially designated transitional period.

Please note that:

1. If you think that our codings do not capture the spirit of our concepts—for example, we have coded a period as 'challenged' when actually, notwithstanding the indicators, the ruling coalition was under tangible threat of being militarily overthrown—please inform us;

2. The periods identified are in many cases identical to what we would term 'political settlement periods'—but not always, which is why we simply call them 'periods' or 'political periods';

3. If multiple periods occur in a calendar year, it is coded according to the one that occupies the greatest duration. For example, a calendar year controlled by the same leader, which was first settled for 3 months, then unsettled for 5 months, and finally settled again for the remaining 4 months would be classified as 'unsettled'. If the 'unsettled' period had lasted only for three months, however, the calendar year would be coded as 'settled'.

4. In Phase 2 we will ask coders only to code periods that were 'settled' as well as 'challenged' and 'transitional' periods that lasted longer than two years;

5. Please note that if you have chosen to amalgamate some of our periods because the breaks do not denote major de facto changes, this may lead us to change our classification of the period/s affected from 'semi-settled' to 'settled'.

Phase 2:   Main Survey Questionnaire

Section I: The Settlement's Configuration of Power

Notes: Political settlements analysis is based on the idea that peace reigns when there is a basic agreement or equilibrium among the most powerful groups in society around political institutions and the distribution of benefits they are expected to yield. Thus, our survey attempts to capture those powerful groups, their internal relations, and their relations with each other. We do so by dividing society into three basic political groups or population blocs:

(A) The leader's bloc (LB). That is, the segment of the population whose political loyalty the current de facto leader is likely to believe s/he can count on, at least in the short term. In other words, the leader is likely to feel that this segment will continue to support him/her, even in the event of a moderate or temporary fall in his/her repressive or distributional capabilities. (By political loyalty, we mean a determination to defend the leader against challenges and/or to not defect from or make serious political trouble for him/her, where serious political trouble refers to deliberate actions that might directly or indirectly threaten the leader's political survival);

(B) The contingently loyal bloc (CLB). The segment of the population that is currently aligned with the de facto leader (evidenced by either some meaningful representation in the highest levels of government or a formal or informal agreement/pact to conditionally support the leader's bloc) but whose political loyalty s/he cannot be assured of (in other words, the leader is likely to believe there is a realistic possibility that it could defect and/or make serious political trouble for him/her should the opportunity arise—e.g. a temporary or moderate fall in the leader's repressive or distributional capabilities, an election, etc.);

(C) The opposition bloc (OB). The segment of the population that is not currently aligned with the LB or the CLB and does not feel represented by government. Note that this will include

both members of the official and outlawed political opposition, including those in exile. For convenience, it is also where we place individuals who have no political alignment, no interest in politics, and no prospect of being mobilized into national politics.

1. **For each political period please estimate roughly which percentage of the total adult-aged population each bloc represented (***Note that the percentages should add up to 100%***).**

   Obviously, this requires some educated guesswork on the part of coders. Firstly, because affiliations are not entirely transparent and secondly because allegiances shift over time. On the first problem, we ask coders to make rough guesstimates based on such evidence as internal party, leadership, and general elections; putsches, coups, and attempted coups; reports of purges, political factionalism, and infighting; the breadth and depth of political repression, etc. On the second problem, and because it would be too cumbersome to ask for data month by month or year by year, we ask coders to make a judgement about the average or 'typical' alignment of the population with these blocs for each period. For example, if the leader was tremendously popular in his first year in office, but then extremely unpopular for the remainder of a ten-year period, we would expect coders to enter a low percentage for the LB.

2. **Given the repressive capabilities of the leader's bloc, please estimate how powerful each bloc would likely have appeared to the leader to be.**

   Note we ask about perceptions because one of the things we will test is the relationship between leadership perceptions and policy commitment. As such, power that was not perceptible to the leader or that was only perceived ex post is not of interest to us. Granted, this creates some methodological difficulties as the perceptions of the leader are not entirely transparent. However, we ask you to consider as evidence speeches, statements, or policy documents by the leader/ruling coalition; commentaries by contemporary observers identifying the relative size and strength of the blocs; convincing historical accounts of the leader/ruling coalition's mindset; etc.

   a. **Extremely powerful:** it could single-handedly change the settlement or prevent it from being changed by others.

   b. **Quite powerful:** it could not single-handedly change the settlement or prevent it from being changed, but would likely make a big difference in struggles over the settlement.

   c. **Somewhat powerful:** it could not single-handedly change the settlement or prevent it from being changed, but would likely make a significant difference in struggles over the settlement.

   d. **Somewhat powerless**: it would likely make only a small difference in struggles over the settlement.

   e. **Powerless:** it would likely make virtually no difference in struggles over the settlement.

3. **How high was the (perceptible) likelihood that the CLB (or a majority of it) would split or withdraw support from the LB?**

   Where withdrawing support could, for example, play out as the CLB not backing the leader in an internal party election, or not defending the leader in the event of a violent or other challenge from the OB.

   a. **Low:** there was a possibility that the CLB would split or withdraw support from the LB but only a low one;

   b. **Medium:** there was a moderate likelihood that the CLB would split or withdraw support from the LB;

    c. **High:** there was a high likelihood that the CLB would split or withdraw support from the LB.

4. **How high was the (perceptible) likelihood that the OB (or a majority of it) would join the LB in the ruling coalition?**

    a. **None:** there was virtually no possibility that the OB would join the LB in the ruling coalition;

    b. **Low:** there was a possibility that the OB would join the LB in the ruling coalition, but a low one;

    c. **Medium:** there was a moderate likelihood that the OB would join the LB in the ruling coalition;

    d. **High:** there was a high likelihood that the OB would join the LB in the ruling coalition.

5. **For each period, please list each bloc's *most powerful* political sub-groups and indicate whether they were 'extremely powerful', 'quite powerful', or only 'somewhat powerful' (as per the options in Question 2 above).**

By a politically powerful sub-group we mean an organizationally distinct, somewhat politically self-conscious group within the bloc—it could be a political party (which may act as an umbrella), an ideological, personalistic, or ethnic faction, a pressure group, an economic, class, or occupational group, a section of the military, a militia or terrorist group, a foreign backer, a demographic category, or fractions of any of the above. The threshold for inclusion is whether it could, without too big a stretch of the imagination, make a significant difference to power struggles either within or between blocs (where by 'too big a stretch of the imagination' means this could only be imagined as the outcome of a highly improbable sequence of events, and by 'political struggles' we mean struggles over the key issues that determine the cohesion of the bloc and or relations between blocs). Here, we ask coders to make educated guesstimates based on such phenomena as ideological or sociological affinities between the blocs and different groups in society, the blocs' political messaging, evidence of voting behaviour (where it exists), evidence of direct or indirect political action on the part of certain groups, evidence of internal party, leadership, and general elections, putsches, coups, and attempted coups, reports of purges, political factionalism, and infighting, etc. On this definition the number of groups that could be included is potentially very large, so we ask coders to list a maximum of twenty per bloc, thus perhaps aggregating certain groups where necessary and sensible. Again, we are looking for the 'typical' affiliation for the period—so if ethnic group A was aligned with the leader's bloc for six of the seven years of a period before drifting away from it, it should be coded with the leader. Alternatively, if a group's loyalty was genuinely split and it seems inappropriate to code it one way or another, coders can make a note of this. And as before, we expect these power attributes to have been perceptible or foreseeable to the leader. To be more specific, sometimes leaders are brought down by unexpected and uncoordinated acts of individual passive resistance or the unexpected emergence of a social or political movement that appears out of nowhere. We are not interested in such phenomena in this question.

Apart from indicating the power of each sub-group, please also indicate how power within the sub-group was balanced between genders, choosing from M (male-dominated), F (female-dominated), and N (power was balanced between the genders). For example, if trade unions were an 'extremely powerful' sub-group with power balanced between the two genders, you would write 'trade unions (EP N)'. If traditional leaders, for example, were 'quite powerful' and male-dominated, you would write 'traditional leaders (QP M)'. And if teachers, for example, were 'somewhat powerful' and female-dominated, you would write 'teachers (SP F)'.

6. **For each period and bloc, please list any** *relatively powerless* **groups.**

   Examples of such groups might be women, youth, poor people, specific ethnic minorities, or other political, economic, or sociological categories which may be noteworthy on account of their marginalization; such groups need not be either organized or self-conscious. The threshold for inclusion is that it would require a big stretch to imagine the group making a significant difference in political struggles both within or between blocs. To provide an example, coders may feel that under the LB are a certain percentage of poor women, but that, without the benefit of hindsight, it would be hard to imagine this group making a significant difference in struggles both within the bloc or between the bloc and others. As such, 'poor women' should be listed as a group under 'LB'. Again, we ask coders to list a maximum of twenty groups per bloc. And as before, we expect these power attributes to have been perceptible to bloc leaders.

   As in the previous question, please code these sub-groups according to gender, e.g. 'Poor Women (F)'.

7. **For each period and bloc, please estimate** *what percentage of the bloc* **falls into this 'relatively powerless' category.**

   Following the example above, poor women, when added to other relatively powerless groups in the bloc, might constitute 50% of the LB. As such, coders should enter '50' under 'LB'.

8. **For each period and bloc, please state, on average, how powerful high-level leaders were vis-à-vis intermediate-level leaders and ordinary members/ followers.**

   Note, to be **powerful** *here implies an ability to dictate terms to other actors, thanks to the unlikelihood of being removed, abandoned, or otherwise sanctioned by other actors. Note further that* **high-level leaders** *are likely, as individuals, to have a national, or in federal states, state-level sphere of influence by virtue of their official or unofficial positions in the bloc's most powerful sub-groups.* **Intermediate-level leaders** *are likely as individuals, to have a regional or sub-regional sphere of influence by virtue of their official or unofficial positions in the bloc's most powerful sub-groups, or perhaps a national sphere of influence but only in the bloc's less powerful sub-groups.* **Ordinary members or followers** *do not occupy disproportionately influential official or unofficial positions in the bloc's sub-groups and are not disproportionately influential as individuals.*

   a. De facto power rested with **high-level leaders**
   b. De facto power was shared by **high-level leaders and intermediate-level leaders**
   c. De facto power rested with **intermediate-level leaders**
   d. De facto power rested with **intermediate-level leaders and ordinary members/followers**
   e. De facto power was shared relatively equally across **leaders and ordinary members/followers.**
   f. De facto power rested with **ordinary members/followers**

9. **For each period and bloc, please state how cohesive/fragmented the bloc was.**
   a. The bloc was **very cohesive** and had no major competing factions.
   b. The bloc was **fairly cohesive:** it had different factions or fractions, which were moderately competitive.
   c. The bloc was **fairly incohesive:** it had different factions or fractions, which were very competitive.

d. The bloc was **very incohesive**, with extreme competition among different factions or fractions.

Section II: Blocs' Relationship to the Settlement

10. **For each period and bloc, please estimate, on average, how important the following methods were as a strategy for incorporating the bloc's *leaders* <u>into or under</u> the settlement, on a scale of 1–4, where 1 = not important, 2 = slightly important, 3 = fairly important, and 4 = very important (irrespective of whether the strategy was ultimately successful).**

   a. **Violent repression:** This refers to the containment of challenges to the settlement by means such as: murders, disappearances, political arrests, public intimidation and incarceration, deliberate impoverishment, destruction of property, forced relocation, violent dispersion of public events and demonstrations, etc.;

   b. **Non-violent repression:** This refers to the containment of challenges to the settlement by means such as: legal confinement, surveillance, infiltration, tax audits, interference in the ability to gain employment or business, restrictions on fund raising, negative propaganda or scapegoating, censorship, restrictions on access to the media, outlawing assembly, etc.;

   c. **Clientelistic material cooptation:** This refers to the creation of support for or acquiescence to the settlement through the targeted provision of private (e.g. money, jobs, rents) or club (e.g. schools, roads) goods to individuals or communities as a *conditional exchange for* political support or loyalty;

   d. **Clientelistic non-material cooptation:** This refers to the creation of support for or acquiescence to the settlement through the targeted provision of political or status goods such as leadership positions (in either higher- or lower-level political organs) or symbolic benefits (e.g. language recognition, special group status) to individuals or communities, as a *conditional exchange for* political support or loyalty; *note that in situations where leadership positions are valued solely for the access to income/rents they provide, we would expect you, other things being equal, to code a higher value for c. clientelistic material cooptation than d. clientelistic non-material cooptation;*

   e. **Programmatic material legitimation:** This refers to the creation of support for or acquiescence to the settlement through the provision of club or public goods (e.g. universal health care, a sound investment climate) to individuals or communities, irrespective of their political loyalty or support;

   f. **Universalistic ideological legitimation:** This refers to the creation of support for or acquiescence to the settlement through the inculcation or articulation of ideological beliefs such as socialism, liberalism, nationalism, or national or world religions, in or for individuals or communities, irrespective of political loyalty or support;

   g. **Procedurally democratic legitimation:** This refers to the creation of support for or acquiescence to the settlement through the provision of opportunities to individuals or communities to vote and/or stand in formally free elections to form a government.

11. **For each period and bloc, please estimate how important, on average, the following methods were as a strategy for incorporating the bloc's *followers/ordinary members* <u>into or under</u> the settlement, on a scale of 1–4, where**

1 = not important, 2 = slightly important, 3 = fairly important, and 4 = very important (irrespective of whether the strategy was ultimately successful).

   a. Violent repression
   b. Non-violent repression
   c. Clientelistic material cooptation
   d. Clientelistic non-material cooptation
   e. Programmatic material legitimation
   f. Universalistic ideological legitimation
   g. Procedurally democratic legitimation

12. **For each bloc, please provide an opinion on the scale, on average, of any settlement-generated material benefits (e.g. salaries, rents, public spending) it received relative to its size:**
   a. **Very High:** It received a level of material benefits very disproportionately high relative to its size;
   b. **High:** It received a level of material benefits disproportionately high relative to its size;
   c. **Proportionate:** It received a level of material benefits about proportionate to its size;
   d. **Low:** It received a level of material benefits disproportionately low relative to its size.
   e. **Very Low**: It received a level of material benefits very disproportionately low relative to its size.

13. **For each bloc, please provide an opinion on how any settlement-generated material benefits (e.g. salaries, rents, public spending) enjoyed by this bloc were, on average, distributed between leaders and followers (where Mobutu's Zaire might be an example of a 'massively inegalitarian distribution' and contemporary Denmark an 'egalitarian' distribution):**
   a. **Massively inegalitarian:** Leaders captured a massively disproportionate share of material benefits.
   b. **Highly inegalitarian**: Leaders captured a highly disproportionate share of material benefits.
   c. **Moderately inegalitarian:** Leaders captured a moderately disproportionate share of material benefits.
   d. **Slightly inegalitarian:** Leaders captured a slightly disproportionate share of material benefits.
   e. **Egalitarian:** Leaders and followers received a more or less proportionate share of material benefits.

Section III: Decision-making and Implementing Power of the Leadership

Note: Extant political settlements theory has hypothesized certain relationships between the balance or configuration of power in society and the capabilities of the political leadership, and these questions are intended to help us explore these.

14. **To what extent was power concentrated in the de facto leader of the country, in the sense that s/he could *make* major policy decisions, e.g. on economic policy, fiscal policy, social policy, national security?**

By 'make' a policy decision, we mean formulate an authoritative course of policy action and present it to lower-level political organs, if appropriate, for successful ratification. Thus, a settlement with a Prime Minister who was able, after consultation with Cabinet, to formulate major bills which were then passed smoothly into legislation by Parliament with minimal dilution of the bills' original intentions, would have a moderate degree of decision-making power concentration. By contrast, a settlement which had a Prime Minister whose major bills were routinely pulled apart and changed very significantly by Parliament, would have moderately dispersed power.

    a. Power was **highly concentrated** in the leader, in the sense that s/he could make major policy decisions with minimal consultation or bargaining with other powerful actors;

    b. Power was **moderately concentrated** in the leader, in the sense that s/he could make major policy decisions but only after meaningful consultation or bargaining with other powerful actors;

    c. Power was **moderately dispersed**, in the sense that the leader could make major policy decisions but only after extensive consultation or bargaining with other powerful actors;

    d. Power was **highly dispersed**, in the sense that the leader struggled to make major policy decisions, even after extensive consultation or bargaining.

15. **To what extent was *implementing power* concentrated in the political leadership, in the sense that its major de facto policy decisions were *implemented* without intentional resistance or dilution?**

    For this question, political leadership refers to the political individual, group, or organ that has ratified a policy decision and passed it to the bureaucracy or non-governmental partner for implementation. Note that with this question we are interested in implementation problems that stem from political resistance or subversion; we are not interested in implementation problems that may stem from shortages in financial or human resources, nor in the ultimate wisdom or success of policy decisions.

    a. Implementing power was **highly concentrated** in the political leadership, in the sense that its major policy decisions were implemented with minimal resistance or dilution;

    b. Implementing power was **moderately concentrated** in the political leadership, in the sense that its major policy decisions were implemented but with some resistance or dilution;

    c. Implementing power was **moderately dispersed**, in the sense that the leadership's policy decisions were implemented, but only with significant resistance or dilution;

    d. Implementing power was **highly dispersed,** in the sense that the political leadership's policy decisions were subject to extensive resistance or dilution.

Section IV: Foreign Influence and Internal and External Threats

16. **For each period, how important to the maintenance of the settlement was military support by a foreign power?**

    a. **Not important:** The government could maintain the settlement wholly through its own military means.

b. **Marginally important:** The government received some foreign military support which was helpful; however, the government would probably have managed to maintain the settlement without it.

c. **Important:** Without foreign military support, the settlement would probably have collapsed sooner.

d. **Very important:** Without foreign military support, the settlement would almost certainly have collapsed much sooner.

17. **For each period, how important to the maintenance of the settlement was financial or technical assistance by a foreign power?**

a. **Not important:** The government could maintain the settlement wholly through its own financial and technical means.

b. **Marginally important:** The government received some foreign financial and technical support which was helpful; however, the government would probably have managed to maintain the settlement without it.

c. **Important:** Without foreign financial and technical support, the settlement would probably have collapsed sooner.

d. **Very important:** Without foreign financial and technical support, the settlement would almost certainly have collapsed much sooner.

18. **For each period, was there a (perceptible) threat to the *political survival* of high-level LB leaders from one or more of the following domestic or international groups, where political survival refers to the ability to stay in office, and 'perceptible threat' means 'perceptible to those leaders'? For each group code from 1–4 where '1' = No threat; '2' = Low threat; '3' = Moderate threat; and '4' = High threat.**

a. Rural subordinate classes

b. Rural dominant classes

c. Urban subordinate classes

d. Urban dominant classes

e. Ethnic, regional, or religious groups

f. An opposition group in exile

g. The military

h. A neighbouring country

i. A non-neighbouring country

19. **For each period, was there a (perceptible) threat to the *physical survival* of high- or intermediate-level LB leaders from one or more of the following domestic or international groups, where physical survival refers to the ability to live without fear of being killed, imprisoned, or driven into exile? For each group code from 1–4 where '1' = No threat; '2' = Low threat; '3' = Moderate threat; and '4' = High threat.**

a. Rural subordinate classes

b. Rural dominant classes

c. Urban subordinate classes

d. Urban dominant classes

e. Ethnic, regional, or religious groups

f. An opposition group in exile

g. The military

h. A neighbouring country

i. A non-neighbouring country

Section V: Economic Organizations

Notes: In addition to the configuration of the political settlement, a prominent strand of political settlements theory treats manufacturing firms' economic capabilities and political power as an important additional variable in explaining state capacity and development outcomes. Our aim is to generate data that will allow us to test hypotheses associated with this position.

20. **By developing country standards and for each period, please specify the average level of technological and entrepreneurial capabilities of domestically owned firms in the formal manufacturing sector.**
    a. **Low:** On average, firms could successfully adopt only simple technologies.
    b. **Medium:** On average, firms could successfully adopt moderately complex technologies.
    c. **High:** On average, firms could successfully adopt complex technologies.
21. **Please specify the average level of political power of domestically owned firms in the formal manufacturing sector.**
    a. **Low:** The government found it easy to dictate terms to firms.
    b. **Medium:** The government found it neither easy nor hard to dictate terms to firms.
    c. **High:** The government found it hard to dictate terms to firms.

Section VI: Economic and Social Policy

Notes: In this section we ask experts to describe the character of key economic policies in the country. We do so with a view to exploring relationships between political settlements, policies, and development outcomes.

22. **Please describe the government's industrialization strategy for each period. Choose from the options below.**
    a. A strong emphasis on import-substituting industrialization.
    b. A similar emphasis on import-substituting and export-oriented industrialization.
    c. A strong emphasis on export-oriented industrialization.
    d. The state had no industrialization strategy.
23. Please specify how the government treated Foreign Direct Investment (FDI).
    a. The government discouraged the inflow of FDI;
    b. The government permitted FDI, but placed strong conditions on it and/or provided little support;
    c. The government encouraged FDI, placing moderate conditions on it and/or providing moderate support;
    d. The government strongly encouraged FDI, placing few conditions on it and/or providing a high level of support;
    e. The government did not have an FDI strategy
24. **Please specify how vigorously the state intervened in the economy.**
    a. **Strong:** The state controlled most industries and heavily regulated and coordinated private companies, or at least it attempted to.
    b. **Medium:** The state controlled only a few key industries, yet strongly regulated and coordinated private companies, or at least it attempted to.

   c. **Light:** The state controlled only a few key industries if any, and otherwise did not intervene strongly in the business of private enterprises.

25. **Please specify whether de facto state policy prioritized the agricultural over the industrial sector.**
   a. Agriculture was strongly prioritized over the industrial sector.
   b. Agriculture was prioritized over the industrial sector.
   c. Agriculture and industry were treated equally.
   d. Industry was prioritized over agriculture.
   e. Industry was strongly prioritized over agriculture.

26. **Was economic development a priority for the top leadership, beyond their statements? Please code on a scale from 1–5, where**
   a. Very low priority
   b. Low priority
   c. Medium priority
   d. High priority
   e. Very high priority

27. **Was social development, for example, spending on education, health, potable water, social insurance, etc., a priority for the top leadership, beyond their statements? Please code on a scale from 1–5, where**
   a. Very low priority
   b. Low priority
   c. Medium priority
   d. High priority
   e. Very high priority

Bibliography

Abdulai, Abdul-Gafaru. 2018. 'The Political Economy of Maternal Healthcare in Ghana.' ESID Working Paper No. 107. Manchester: Effective States and Inclusive Development Research Centre, The University of Manchester. http://dx.doi.org/10.2139/ssrn.3272848.

Abdulai, Abdul-Gafaru, and Giles Mohan. 2019. 'The Politics of Bureaucratic 'Pockets of Effectiveness': Insights from Ghana's Ministry of Finance.' ESID Working Paper No. 119. Manchester: Effective States and Inclusive Development Research Centre, The University of Manchester. http://dx.doi.org/10.2139/ssrn.3430440.

Acemoglu, Daron, Simon Johnson, and James Robinson. 2004. 'Institutions as the Fundamental Cause of Long-run Growth.' NBER Working Paper Series, Working Paper No. 10481. Cambridge, MA: National Bureau of Economic Research (NBER).

Acemoglu, Daron, Simon Johnson, and James Robinson. 2005. 'Rise of Europe, Atlantic Trade, Institutional Change, and Economic Growth.' *American Economic Review* 95, no. 3 (June): 546–79.

Acemoglu, Daron, and James Robinson. 2008. 'Persistence of Power, Elites, and Institutions.' *American Economic Review* 98, no. 1 (March): 267–93.

Acemoglu, Daron, and James Robinson. 2019. *The Narrow Corridor: States, Societies and the Fate of Liberty*. London: Penguin Books.

Adida, Claire. 2015. 'Do African Voters Favour Coethnics: Evidence from a Survey Experiment in Benin.' *Journal of Experimental Political Science*, no. 1 (Spring): 1–11.

Akerlof, George A. 1970. 'The Market for Lemons: Quality Uncertainty and the Market Mechanism.' *Quarterly Journal of Economics* 84(2) 488–500.

Albertus, Michael, and Victor Menaldo. 2014. 'Gaming Democracy: Elite Dominance during Transition and the Prospects for Redistribution.' *British Journal of Political Science* 44, no. 3 (July): 575–603.

Ampratwum, Edward, Mohammed Awul, and Franklin Oduro. 2019. 'Decentralization and teacher accountability: The political settlement and sub-national governance in Ghana's education sector.' In *The Politics of Education in Developing Countries: From Schooling to Learning*, edited by Sam Hickey and Naomi Hossain, 44–63. Oxford: Oxford University Press.

Andrews, Matt, Lant Pritchett, and Michael J. V. Woolcock. 2017. *Building State Capability: Evidence, Analysis, Action*. Oxford: Oxford University Press.

Annear, Peter L., and Shakil Ahmed. 2012. 'Institutional and Operational Barriers to Strengthening Universal Coverage in Cambodia: Options for Policy Development.' Working Paper Series. Melbourne: Nossal Institute for Public Health.

Anonymous. 2012. 'Using Political Economy Analysis to Improve EU Development Effectiveness.' A DevCo background note. Draft, January 2012.

AusAid. 2011. 'Framework for Working in Fragile and Conflict-affected States: Guidance for Staff.' Canberra: AusAid.

Balint-Kurti, Daniel. 2017. 'Guinea's Bribery Saga Reaches New Peaks.' *Global Witness*. https://www.globalwitness.org/en/blog/guineas-bribery-saga-reaches-new-peaks/

Bardhan, Pranab and Mookherjee, Dilip. 2020. "Clientelistic Politics and Economic Development: An Overview". *The Handbook of Economic Development and Institutions*, edited by Jean-Marie Baland, François Bourguignon, Jean-Philippe Platteau and Thierry Verdier, 84–102. Princeton, NJ: Princeton University Press. https://doi.org/10.1515/9780691192017-004

Barry, Abdourahmane. 2010. 'Understanding the Guinean Education System: Evolution and Some Performance Indicators.' *The African Symposium* 10, no. 1 (June): 91–103.

Basu, Kaushik. 2000. *Prelude to Political Economy: A Study of the Social and Political Foundations of Economics.* Oxford: Oxford University Press.

Bebbington, Anthony, Abdul-Gafaru Abdulai, Denise Humphreys Bebbington, Marja Hinfelaar, and Cynthia A. Sanborn. 2018. *Governing Extractive Industries: Politics, Histories, Ideas.* Oxford: Oxford University Press.

Behuria, Pritish. 2019. 'Twenty-first Century Industrial Policy in a Small Developing Country: The Challenges of Reviving Manufacturing in Rwanda.' *Development and Change* 50, no. 4 (July): 1033–62.

Behuria, Pritish, Lars Buur, and Hazel Gray. 2017. 'Studying Political Settlements in Africa.' *African Affairs* 116, no. 464 (July): 508–25.

Behuria, Pritish, and Tom Goodfellow. 2017. 'The disorder of 'miracle growth' in Rwanda. Understanding the limits of transitions to Open Ordered Development.' In *Deals and Development: The Political Dynamics of Growth Episodes*, edited by Lant Pritchett, Eric Werker, and Kunal Sen, 217–49. Oxford: Oxford University Press.

Behuria, Pritish, and Tom Goodfellow. 2019. 'Leapfrogging Manufacturing? Rwanda's Attempt to Build a Services-led "Developmental State".' *European Journal of Development Research* 31: 581–603.

Bell, Christine. 2015. "What we talk about when we talk about political settlements. Towards inclusive and open political settlements in an era of disillusionment." Political Settlements Working Papers No 1. Edinburgh, UK: Political Settlements Research Programme, The University of Edinburgh. https://www.pure.ed.ac.uk/ws/portalfiles/portal/23462146/20150901_PSRP_Concepts_Working_Paper_1_1.pdf

Bell, Christine, and Jan Pospisil. 2017. 'Navigating Inclusion in Transition from Conflict: The Formalised Political Unsettlement.' *Journal of International Development* 29, no. 5 (July): 576–93.

Besley, Timothy and Torsten Persson. 2011. *Pillars of Prosperity: The Political Economics of Development Clusters.* Princeton, NJ: Princeton University Press.

Booth, David and Frederick Golooba-Mutebi. 2012. 'Developmental Patrimonialism? The Case of Rwanda.' *African Affairs* 111, no. 444 (July): 379–403. https://doi.org/10.1093/afraf/ads026.

Booth, David, and Frederick Golooba-Mutebi. 2014. 'Policy for Agriculture and Horticulture in Rwanda: A Different Political Economy?' *Development Policy Review* 32, no. s2 (November): s173–s198. http://dx.doi.org/10.1111/dpr.12081.

Booysen, Susan. 2011. *The ANC and the Regeneration of Power.* Johannesburg: Wits University Press.

Booysen, Susan. 2015. *Dominance and Decline: The ANC in the Time of Zuma.* Johannesburg: Wits University Press.

Bowles, Samuel. 1985. 'The Production Process in a Competitive Economy: Walrasian, Neo-Hobbesian, and Marxian Models.' *American Economic Review* 75, no. 1 (March): 16–36.

Bowles, Samuel, and Herbert Gintis. 1992. 'Power and Wealth in a Competitive Capitalist Economy.' *Philosophy and Public Affairs* 21, no. 4 (Autumn): 324–53.

Bowles, Samuel, Steven N. Durlauf, and Karla Hoff, eds. 2006. *Poverty Traps.* Princeton, NJ: Princeton University Press.

Branch, Daniel. 2011. *Kenya: Between Hope and Despair, 1963–2011* New Haven and London: Yale University Press.

Brenner, Robert. 1993. *Merchants and Revolution: Commercial Change, Political Conflict, and London's Overseas Traders 1550–1653.* Princeton, NJ: Princeton University Press.

Burton, Michael G., and John Higley. 1987. 'Elite Settlements.' *American Sociological Review* 52, no. 3: 295–307.

Bussolo, Maurizio, María E. Dávalos, Vito Peragine, and Ramya Sundaram. 2018. *Toward a New Social Contract: Taking on Distributional Tensions in Europe and Central Asia. Europe and Central Asia Studies.* Washington, DC: World Bank. DOI:10.1596/978-1-4648-1353-5.

Buur, Lars and Lindsay Whitfield. 2011. 'Engaging in Productive Sector Development: Comparisons between Mozambique and Ghana.' Danish Institute for International Studies (DIIS) Working Paper, No. 22, vol. 2011. Copenhagen: Institut for Internationale Studier/Dansk Center for Internationale Studier og Menneskerettigheder.

Cameron, David. 2012. "Combating poverty at its roots." *Wall Street Journal,* 1 November 2012. https://www.wsj.com/articles/SB10001424052970204712904578090571423009066

CAMFEBA n.d. 'Government-Private Sector Forum.' Phnom Penh: Cambodian Federation of Employers and Business Associations (CAMFEBA).

Cederman, Lars-Erik, Andreas Wimmer, and Brian Min. 2010. 'Why Do Ethnic Groups Rebel? New Data and Analysis.' *World Politics* 62, no. 1 (January): 87–119.

CEIC *Data*. 2014. 'Guinea Education Statistics.' *Using World Bank data,* accessed 24 July 2020. https://www.ceicdata.com/en/guinea/education-statistics.

Centeno, Miguel Angel. 2002. *Blood and Debt: War and the Nation-State in Latin America.* University Park, PA: Penn State University Press.

Chambers, Vikki. 2012. 'Improving Maternal Health When Resources Are Limited: Safe Motherhood in Rural Rwanda.' Policy Brief 05. London: Africa Power and Politics.

Chambers, Vikki, and Frederick Golooba-Mutebi. 2012. 'Is the Bride Too Beautiful? Safe Motherhood in Rural Rwanda.' Research Report No. 04. London: Africa Power and Politics Programme.

Chege, Michael. 2008. 'Kenya: Back from the Brink?' *Journal of Democracy* 19, no. 4 (October): 125–39. doi:10.1353/jod.0.0026.

Chemouni, Benjamin. 2017. 'The Politics of Core Public Sector Reform in Rwanda.' ESID Working Paper No. 88. Manchester: Effective States and Inclusive Development Research Centre, The University of Manchester.

Cheng, Christine, Jonathan Goodhand, and Patrick Meehan. 2018. 'Elite Bargains and Political Deals Project: Synthesis Paper—Securing and Sustaining Elite Bargains that Reduce Violent Conflict.' Unpublished draft: Stabilisation Unit, UK Government (Home Office).

Connell, Sarah Elizabeth. 2011. 'Maternal Mortality in Cambodia: Efforts to Meet the Millennium Development Goal for Maternal Health.' Thesis, Georgia State University. https://scholarworks.gsu.edu/iph_theses/198.

Coppedge, Michael, John, Gerring, Carl, Henrik, Knutsen et al. 2019. 'The Methodology of "Varieties of Democracy" (V-Dem)1.' *Bulletin of Sociological Methodology/Bulletin de Méthodologie Sociologique* 143, no. 1: 107–33. doi:10.1177/0759106319854989.

Coppedge, Michael, John, Gerring, Carl, Henrik, Knutsen, Staffan I. Lindberg, Jan Teorell, David, Altman, Michael. Bernhard, et al. 2020. *V-Dem [Country-Year/Country-Date] Dataset v10: Varieties of Democracy (V-Dem) Project.*

De Waal, Alex. 2019. 'Sudan: A Political Marketplace Framework Analysis.' Occasional Paper No. 19. Medford, MA: World Peace Foundation Conflict Research Programme, The Fletcher School, Tufts University.

DFID. 2010. 'Building Peaceful States and Societies. A DFID Practice Paper.' London: DFID.

Di John, John, and James, Putzel. 2009. 'Political Settlements: Issues Paper.' Birmingham: Governance and Social Development Resource Centre, University of Birmingham.

Diallo, Mamadou S. 2019. 'Basic Education Reforms in Guinea: Context and Concerns.' *West East Journal of Social Sciences* 8, no. 3: 283–96.

Dingle, Antonia, Timothy Powell-Jackson, and Catherine Goodman. 2013. 'A Decade of Improvements in Equity of Access to Reproductive and Maternal Health Services in Cambodia, 2000–2010.' *International Journal for Equity in Health* 12, no. 1 (July): 51.

Doner, Richard F., Bryan K. Ritchie, and Dan Slater. 2005. 'Systemic Vulnerability and the Origins of Developmental States: Northeast and Southeast Asia in Comparative Perspective.' *International Organization* 59, no. 2 (Spring): 327–61.

Doumbouya, Mohamed Lamine. 2008. 'Accessibilité des services de santé en Afrique de l'Ouest: le cas de la Guinée.' HAL.

Downing, Brian. 1992. *The Military Revolution and Political Change: Origins of Democracy and Autocracy in Early Modern Europe.* Princeton, NJ: Princeton University Press.

Ear, Sophal. 2011. 'Growth in the rice and garments sectors.' In *Cambodia's Economic Transformation*, edited by Caroline Hughes and Kheang Un, 70–93. Uppsala: Nordic Institute of Asian Studies Press.

Easterly, William, Jozef Ritzan, and Michael Woolcock. 2006. 'Social Cohesion, Institutions, and Growth.' Working Paper No. 94. Washington, DC: Center for Global Development.

Eichengreen, B, D Park and K Shin. 2013. "Growth slowdowns redux: New evidence on the middle-income trap", National Bureau of Economic Research (NBER) Working Paper 18673.

Easton, David. 1965. *A Framework for Political Analysis.* Englewood Cliffs: Prentice-Hall.

Ertman, Thomas. 1997. *Birth of the Leviathan: Building State and Regimes in Medieval and Early Modern Europe.* Princeton, NJ: Princeton University Press.

Feenstra, Robert. C., Robert Inklaar, and Marcel P. Timmer. 2015. 'The Next Generation of the Penn World Table.' *American Economic Review* 105, no. 10 (October): 3150–82.

Ferguson, William D. 2013. *Collective Action and Exchange: A Game-theoretic Approach to Political Economy.* Palo Alto, CA: Stanford University Press.

Ferguson, William D. 2020. *Collective Action, Inequality, and Development: A Political Economy Approach.* Palo Alto, CA: Stanford University Press.

Foucher, Vincent. 2015. 'Ebola en Guinée: une épidémie "politique"?' https://www.crisisgroup.org/fr/africa/west-africa/guinea/ebola-en-guinee-une-epidemie-politique.

France24. 2016. 'Audio Recordings Drag Guinea President into Mine Bribery Scandal.' https://www.france24.com/en/20161201-exclusive-audio-recordings-guinea-president-conde-simandou-mine-bribery-rio-tinto.

Franck, Raphael, and Ilia Ranier. 2012. 'Does the Leader's Ethnicity Matter? Ethnic Favoritism, Education, and Health in Sub-Saharan Africa.' *American Political Science Review* 106, no. 2 (May): 294–325.

Fritz, Verena, and Alina Rocha Menocal. 2007. 'Understanding State-building from a Political Economy Perspective.' London: ODI.

Fukuyama, Francis. 2014. *Political Order and Political Decay: From the Industrial Revolution to the Globalization of Democracy.* New York: Farrar, Straus and Giroux.

Gerring, John. 2011. *Social Science Methodology: A Unified Framework*. Cambridge: Cambridge University Press.

Giliomee, Herman. 2016. *Historian Herman Giliomee: An Autobiography*. Cape Town: Tafelberg Publishers.

Gleditsch, Nils Petter, Peter Wallensteen, Mikael Eriksson, Margareta Sollenberg, and Håvard Strand. 2002. 'Armed Conflict 1946–2001: A New Dataset.' *Journal of Peace Research* 39, no. 5 (September): 615–37.

Global Times. 2013. 'Lack of Skilled Labor, Quality Human Capital Major Concerns for Cambodia: Survey.' 12 March 2013.

Goemans, Henk E., Kristian Skrede Gleditsch, and Giacomo Chiozza. 2009. Introducing Archigos: A Dataset of Political Leaders. *Journal of Peace Research* 46, no. 2 (March): 269–83.

Goertz, Gary. 2006. *Social Science Concepts: A User's Guide*. Princeton and Oxford: Princeton University Press.

Goldman Sachs, *Two Decades of Freedom—A Twenty-Year Review of South Africa*, 2013. Available at http://www.goldmansachs.com/our-thinking/outlook/colin-coleman-south-africa/20-yrs-of-freedom.pdf

Golooba-Mutebi, Frederick, and Yvonne Habiyonizeye. 2018. 'Delivering Maternal Health Services in Rwanda: The Role of Politics.' ESID Working Paper No. 18. Manchester: Effective States and Inclusive Development Research Centre. The University of Manchester.

Gottesman, Evan. 2004. *Cambodia after the Khmer Rouge: Inside the Politics of Nation Building*. Chiang-Mai: Silkworm Books.

Gray, Hazel. 2012. 'Tanzania and Vietnam: A Comparative Economy in Political Transition.' PhD thesis. School of Oriental and African Studies, University of London.

Gray, Hazel. 2018. *Turbulence and Order in Economic Development: Institutions and Economic Transformation in Tanzania and Vietnam*. Oxford: Oxford University Press.

Great Britain. Northern Ireland Department. 1972. 'Political Settlement. Statements issued on Friday 24 March 1972 by the Prime Minister and the Government. Presented to Parliament by Command of His Excellency the Governor of Northern Ireland, March 1972.' Belfast and London: Her Majesty's Stationery Office.

Greif, Avner. 2006. *Institutions and the Path to the Modern Economy: Lessons from Medieval Trade*. Cambridge: Cambridge University Press.

Gyimah-Boadi, E., and Theo Yakah. 2012. 'Ghana: The Limits of External Democracy Assistance.' Working Paper No. 2012/40. Helsinki: United Nations University World Institute for Development Economics Research (UNU-WIDER).

Haber, Stephen, and Victor Menaldo. 2011. 'Do Natural Resources Fuel Authoritarianism? A Reappraisal of the Resource Curse.' *American Political Science Review* 105, no. 1 (February): 1–26.

Haggard, Stephen, and Robert Kaufman. 2008. *Development, Democracy and Welfare States: Latin America, East Asia, and Eastern Europe*. Princeton, NJ: Princeton University Press.

Harbers, Imke, and Abbey Steele. 2020. "The Subnational State: A Typology for Cross-National Comparison." *Latin American Politics and Society* 62, no. 3 (Fall): 1–18. doi:10.1017/lap.2020.4.

Hausmann, Ricardo, Cesar A. Hidalgo, Sebastian, Bustos, Michele Coscia, Sarah, Chung, Juan, Jimenez, Alexander, Simoes, and Muhammed A. Yildirim, n.d. 'The Atlas of Economic Complexity: Mapping Paths to Prosperity.' Cambridge, MA: Center for International Development, Harvard University.

Hausmann, Ricardo, Dani Rodrik, and Andres Velasco. 2008. 'Growth Diagnostics.' In *The Washington Consensus Reconsidered: Towards a New Global Governance*, edited by Narcís Serra, Joseph E. Stiglitz, 324–357. Oxford, UK: Oxford University Press.

Havel, Vaclav. 1985. *The Power of the Powerless*. New York: M.E. Sharpe.

Helmke, Gretchen, and Steven Levitsky. 2003. 'Informal institutions and comparative politics: a research agenda.' Working paper #307. Kellogg Institute. Accessed 17 January 2021. http://kellogg.nd.edu/sites/default/files/old_files/documents/307_0.pdf

Hickey, Sam. 2011. 'The Politics of Social Protection: What Do We Get from a "Social Contract" Approach?' *Canadian Journal of Development Studies/Revue canadienne d'études du développement* 32, no. 4: 426–38. https://doi.org/10.1080/02255189.2011.647447.

Hickey, Sam. 2013. 'Thinking about the Politics of Development: Towards a Relational Approach.' ESID Working Paper No. 1. Manchester: Centre for Effective States and Inclusive Development, The University of Manchester.

Hickey, Sam. 2019. 'The Politics of State Capacity and Development in Africa: Reframing and Researching "Pockets of Effectiveness".' Pockets of Effectiveness Working Paper No. 1. Manchester: The University of Manchester. http://dx.doi.org/10.2139/ssrn.3467520.

Hickey Sam, ed. 2022. *Pockets of Effectiveness and the Politics of State-building in sub-Saharan Africa*. (Oxford: OUP).

Hickey, Sam, Abdul-Gafaru Abdulai, Angelo Izama, and Giles Mohan. 2015. 'The Politics of Governing Oil Effectively: A Comparative Study of Two New Oil-rich States in Africa.' ESID Working Paper No. 54. Manchester: Effective States and Inclusive Development Research Centre, The University of Manchester.

Hickey, S., A-G. Abdulai, A. Izama, and G. Mohan. 2020. 'Responding to the commodity boom with varieties of resource nationalism: a political economy explanation for the different routes taken by Africa's new oil producers', *The Extractive Industries and Society*, 7(4): 1246–1256.

Hickey, Sam, and Naomi Hossain, eds. 2019. *The Politics of Education in Developing Countries: From Schooling to Learning*. Oxford: Oxford University Press.

Hirsch, Alan, and Brian Levy. 2018. 'Elaborate scaffolding, weak foundations: Business–government relations and economic reform in democratic South Africa.' ESID Working Paper No. 105. Manchester: Effective States and Inclusive Development Research Centre, The University of Manchester. https://papers.ssrn.com/sol3/papers.cfm?abstract_id=3272796

Hobsbawm, Eric. 1990. *Nations and Nationalism since 1780: Programme, Myth, Reality*. New York: Cambridge University Press.

Holland, Alisha C. 2017. *Forbearance as Redistribution: The Politics of Informal Welfare in Latin America*. New York. Cambridge University Press.

Hossain, Naomi, Mirza M. Hassan, Muhammad Ashikur Rahman, Khondoker Shakhawat Ali, and Md. Sajidul Islam. 2019. 'The politics of learning reforms in Bangladesh.' In *The Politics of Education in Developing Countries: From Schooling to Learning*, edited by Sam Hickey and Naomi Hossain, 64–85. Oxford: Oxford University Press.

Huber, Evelyne, and John D. Stephens. 2012. *Democracy and the Left: Social Policy and Inequality in Latin America*. Chicago, IL: University of Chicago Press.

Hudson, David, Heather Marquette, and Sam Waldock. 2016. 'Everyday Political Analysis.' Developmental Leadership Program. https://www.dlprog.org/publications/research-papers/everyday-political-analysis

Hughes, Caroline, and Tim Conway. 2003. 'Understanding Pro-poor Political Change: The Policy Process—-Cambodia.' Second draft, August 2003. London: Overseas Development Institute.

Hughes, Caroline, and Kheang Un. 2011. 'Cambodia's economic transformation: Historical and theoretical frameworks.' In *Cambodia's Economic Transformation*, edited by Caroline Hughes and Kheang Un, 1–26. Uppsala: Nordic Institute of Asian Studies Press

Hui, Victoria Tin-bur. 2005. *War and State Formation in Ancient China and Early Modern Europe*. New York: Cambridge University Press.

Huntington, Samuel. 1968. *Political Order in Changing Societies*. New Haven, CT: Yale University Press.

Ingram, Sue. 2014. "Political settlements: the history of an idea in policy and theory." SSGM Discussion Paper 2014/5. Canberra: State Society and Governance in Melanesia Program, Australian National University.

Jones, Bruce, Molly Elgin-Cossart, and Jane Esberg. 2012. 'Pathways out of Fragility: The Case for a Research Agenda on Inclusive Political Settlements in Fragile States.' New York: Centre for International Cooperation.

Kaufmann, Daniel, and Aart Kraay. 2019. 'Worldwide Governance Indicators.' http://www.govindicators.org. Accessed 30 September 2020.

Kelsall, Tim. 2013. *Business, Politics and the State in Africa: Challenging the Orthodoxies on Growth and Transformation*. London: Zed Books.

Kelsall, Tim. 2016. 'Thinking and Working with Political Settlements.' Briefing. London: Overseas Development Institute.

Kelsall, Tim. 2018a. 'Towards a Universal Political Settlement Concept: A Response to Mushtaq Khan.' *African Affairs* 117, no. 469 (October): 656–69.

Kelsall, Tim. 2018b. 'Political Settlements or Power Configurations? A Response to Mushtaq Khan's "Power, Pacts, and Political Settlements".' *African Affairs* Comment. https://academic.oup.com/afraf/article-abstract/117/469/670/4998804?redirectedFrom=fulltext and *ResearchGate* http://dx.doi.org/10.13140/RG.2.2.15813.76005.

Kelsall, Tim. 2020. 'Political Settlements and Maternal Health in the Developing World: A Comparative Case Study of Rwanda, Ghana, Uganda and Bangladesh.' ESID Working Paper No. 137. Manchester: Effective States and Inclusive Development Research Centre, The University of Manchester. https://www.effective-states.org/wp-content/uploads/working_papers/final-pdfs/esid_wp_137_kelsall.pdf

Kelsall, Tim, Tom Hart, and Ed Laws. 2016. 'Political Settlements and Pathways to Universal Health Coverage.' Working Paper No. 432. London: Overseas Development Institute.

Kelsall, Tim and Matthias vom Hau. 2020. 'Beyond Institutions: A Political Settlements Approach to Development.' IBEI Working Papers, 2020/56. Barcelona: Institut Barcelona d'Estudis Internacionals (IBEI). https://www.jstor.org/stable/resrep28791

Kelsall, Tim, and Seiha Heng. 2014a. 'The Political Settlement and Economic Growth in Cambodia.' ESID Working Paper No 37. Manchester: Effective States and Inclusive Development Research Centre, The University of Manchester. http://dx.doi.org/10.2139/ssrn.2503368.

Kelsall, Tim, and Seiha Heng. 2014b. 'The Political Economy of Inclusive Healthcare in Cambodia.' ESID Working Paper No. 43. Manchester: Effective States and Inclusive Development Research Centre, The University of Manchester. http://dx.doi.org/10.2139/ssrn.2539172.

Kelsall, Tim and Seiha Heng. 2018. 'Not minding the gap: Unbalanced growth and the hybrid political settlement in Cambodia.' In *Deals and Development: The Political Dynamics of Growth Episodes*, edited by Lant Pritchett, Eric Werker and Kunal Sen, 129–58. Oxford: Oxford University Press.

Kelsall, Tim, Sothy Khieng, Chuong Chantha, and Tieng Muy. 2016. 'The Political Economy of Primary Education Reform in Cambodia.' ESID Working Paper No. 58. Manchester: Effective States and Inclusive Development Research Centre, The University of Manchester. http://dx.doi.org/10.2139/ssrn.2894172.

Keohane, Robert O. 1982. 'The Demand for International Regimes.' *International Organization* 36, no. 2 (Spring): 325–55.

Keovathanak, K. and Annear, P. L. 2011. 'The transition to semi-autonomous management of district health services in Cambodia: Assessing purchasing arrangements, transition costs and operational efficiencies of Special Operating Agencies.' In *Improving Health Sector Performance: Institutions, Motivations and Incentives* edited by Hossien Jalilian and Vicheth Sen, 45–75. Singapore: ISEAS.

Khan, Mushtaq. 1995. 'State failure in weak states: a critique of New Institutional Economics.' In *The New Institutional Economics and Third World Development*, edited by John Harris, Janet Hunter, and Colin Lewis, 71–86. London: Routledge.

Khan, Mushtaq. 2000. 'Rent-seeking as process.' In *Rents, Rent-Seeking and Economic Development: Theory and Evidence in Asia*, edited by Mushtaq Khan and K. S. Jomo, 70–144. Cambridge: Cambridge University Press.

Khan, Mushtaq. 2009. 'Governance Capabilities and the Property Rights Transition in Developing Countries.' Draft Paper. In Research Paper Series on 'Growth-Enhancing Governance'. London: School of Oriental & African Studies (SOAS), University of London. http://mercury.soas.ac.uk/users/mk17/Docs/Others.htm.

Khan, Mushtaq. 2010. 'Political Settlements and the Governance of Growth-enhancing Institutions.' Draft Paper. In Research Paper Series on 'Growth-Enhancing Governance'. London: School of Oriental & African Studies (SOAS), University of London.

Khan, Mushtaq. 2018a. 'Political Settlements and the Analysis of Institutions.' *African Affairs* 117, no. 469 (October): 636–655.

Khan, Mushtaq. 2018b. 'Power, Pacts and Political Settlements: A Reply to Tim Kelsall.' *African Affairs* 117, no. 469 (October): 670–94.

Kohli, Atul. 2004. *State-directed Development: Political Power and Industrialization in the Global Periphery*. Cambridge: Cambridge University Press.

Korpi, Walter, and Joakin Palme. 1998. 'The Paradox of Redistribution and Strategies of Equality: Welfare State Institutions, Inequality and Poverty in the Western Countries.' *American Sociological Review* 63, no. 5 (October): 661–87.

Kotoski, Kali. 2015. 'CAMFEBA on Industrial Relations and the Cambodian Economy.' *Phnom Penh Post*, 8 April 2015.

Lasswell, Harold D. 1936. *Politics: Who Gets What, When and How*. New York: Whittlesey House.

Lavers, Tom. 2018. 'Taking Ideas Seriously within Political Settlements Analysis.' ESID Working Paper No. 95. Manchester: Effective States and Inclusive Development Research Centre, The University of Manchester.

Lavers, Tom, and Sam Hickey. 2015. 'Investigating the Political Economy of Social Protection Expansion in Africa: At the Intersection of Transnational Ideas and Domestic Politics.' ESID Working Paper No. 47. Manchester: Effective States and Inclusive Development Research Centre, The University of Manchester.

Laws, Edward. 2010. 'The "Revolutionary Settlement" in 17th Century England: Deploying a Political Settlements Analysis.' Departmental Leadership Program (DLP) Background Paper No. 08. Birmingham: University of Birmingham.

Laws, Edward. 2012. 'Political Settlements, Elite Pacts, and Governments of National Unity.' Background Paper No. 10. Birmingham: Developmental Leadership Program.

Laws, Edward, and Adrian Leftwich. 2014. 'Political Settlements.' Departmental Leadership Program (DLP) Concept Brief No. 01. Birmingham: University of Birmingham. https://www.dlprog.org/publications/research-papers/political-settlements

Leftwich, Adrian, ed. 2004. *What Is Politics? The Activity and its Study*. Cambridge: Polity Press.

Lessnoff, Michael, ed. 1990. *Social Contract Theory*. Oxford: Basil Blackwell.

Levy, Brian. 2010. 'Development Trajectories: An Evolutionary Approach to Integrating Governance and Growth.' Economic Premise 15. Washington, DC: World Bank. https://openknowledge.worldbank.org/handle/10986/10188.

Levy, Brian. 2014. *Working with the Grain: Integrating Governance and Growth in Development Strategies*. Kindle Edition. New York: Oxford University Press.

Levy, Brian, Robert Cameron, Vinothan Naidoo, and Ursula Hoadley, eds. 2018. *The Politics and Governance of Basic Education: A Tale of Two South African Provinces*. Oxford: Oxford University Press.

Levy, Brian, Alan Hirsch, and Ingrid Woolard. 2015. 'Governance and Inequality: Benchmarking and Interpreting South Africa's Evolving Political Settlement.' ESID Working Paper No. 51. Manchester: Effective States and Inclusive Development Research Centre, The University of Manchester.

Levy, Brian, Alan Hirsch, Vinothan Naidoo and Musa Nxele. 2021. 'South Africa: When Strong Institutions and Massive Inequality Collide.' Paper. Carnegie Endowment for International Peace (Washington DC: March, 2021) https://carnegieendowment.org/files/202103-Levy_etal_SouthAfrica.pdf

Levy, Brian, and Michael Walton. 2013. 'Institutions, Incentives and Service Provision: Bringing Politics Back in.' ESID Working Paper No. 18. Manchester: Effective States and Inclusive Development Research Centre, The University of Manchester.

Liljestrand, Jerker, Mean Reatanak Sambath. 2012. 'Socio-economic Improvements and Health System Strengthening of Maternity Care Are Contributing to Maternal Mortality Reduction in Cambodia.' *Reproductive Health Matters* 20, 39: 62–72.

Lindemann, Stefan. E. 2010. 'Exclusionary Elite Bargains and Civil War Onset: The Case of Uganda.' Working Paper No. 76. London: Crisis States Research Programme, London School of Economics.

Lindert, Peter H. 1994. 'The Rise of Social Spending, 1880–1930.' *Explorations in Economic History* 31, no. 1 (January): 1–37. ISSN 0014–4983, https://doi.org/10.1006/exeh.1994.1001.

Lodge, Tom. 2003. *Politics in South Africa: From Mandela to Mbeki*. Bloomington, IN: Indiana University Press.

Louw-Vaudran, Liesl. 2015. 'Another President's Son Caught with his Hand in the Cookie Jar?' Institute for Security Studies (ISS). https://issafrica.org/iss-today/another-presidents-son-caught-with-his-hand-in-the-cookie-jar.

Mahoney, James. 2010. *Colonialism and postcolonial development: Spanish America in comparative perspective*. Cambridge University Press.

Mahoney, James, and Kathleen Thelen, eds. 2015. *Advances in comparative-historical analysis*. Cambridge University Press.

Malejacq, Romain. 2016. 'Warlords, Intervention, and State Consolidation: A Typology of Political Orders in Weak and Failed States.' *Security Studies* 25, no. 1 (February): 85–110.

Mandela, Nelson. 1994. *Long Walk to Freedom*. Boston: Little, Brown.

Marais, Hein. 2011. *South Africa Pushed to the Limit: The Political Economy of Change*. London: Zed Books.

Marshall, Monty G. 2017. 'Major Episodes of Political Violence (MEPV) and Conflict Regions, 1946-2016.' Center for Systemic Peace. http://www.systemicpeace.org/inscr/MEPVcodebook2016.pdf

Marshall, M. 2018. 'Major Episodes of Political Violence, 1946–2018.' https://www.systemicpeace.org/warlist/warlist.htm. Accessed 2 September 2020.

Marshall, M., T. Gurr, and K. Jaggers. 2019. "Polity iv project, political regime characteristics and transitions, 1800–2017." Database. Vienna, VA: Center for Systemic Peace. https://www.systemicpeace.org/polity/polity4x.htm. Accessed September 2, 2020.

Marx, Anthony. 1998. *Making Race and Nation: A Comparison of South Africa, the United States, and Brazil*. New York: Cambridge University Press.

Mbeki, Moeletsi. 2009. *Architects of Poverty*. Johannesburg: Picador Africa

McMillan, Margaret, Dani Rodrik, and Íñigo Verduzco-Gallo. 2014. 'Globalization, Structural Change, and Productivity Growth, with an Update on Africa.' *World Development* 63: 11–32.

Melling, Joseph. 1991. 'Industrial Capitalism and the Welfare of the State: The Role of Employers in the Comparative Development of the Welfare State. A Review of Recent Research.' *Sociology* 25, no. 2 (May): 219–39.

Menocal, Alina Rocha. 2015. 'Inclusive Political Settlements: Evidence, Gaps, and Challenges of Institutional Transformation.' University of Birmingham: Developmental Leadership Program.

Ministry of Education, Youth and Sports. 2014. 'Education Statistics and Indicators 2013/2014.' Phnom Penh: Educational Management Information System (EMIS) Office, Department of Planning.

MoEYS. 2016. 'Mid-Term Review Report in 2016 of the Education Strategic Plan 2014–2018 and Projection to 2020.' Phnom Penh: Ministry of Education, Youth, and Sport.

MoEYS. 2017. 'Education Congress—The Education, Youth and Sport Performance in the Academic Year 2015–2016 and Goals for the Academic Year 2016–2017.' Phnom Penh: Ministry of Education, Youth, and Sport.

Moore, Barrington. 1966. *Social Origins of Dictatorship and Democracy*. London: Penguin.

Moore, Mick. 2012. 'What on Earth Is a Political Settlement?' Falmer: Institute of Development Studies (IDS) Governance and Development Blog, University of Sussex.

Morriss, Peter. 2002. *Power: A Philosophical Analysis*, 2nd ed. Manchester: Manchester University Press.

Nattrass, Nicoli and Jeremy Seekings. 2010. 'The economy and poverty in twentieth century South Africa.' CSSR Working Paper No. 276. Cape Town: Centre for Social Science Research (CSSR), University of Cape Town.

Nazneen, Sohela, Sam Hickey, and Eleni Sifaki, eds. 2019. *Negotiating Gender Equity in the Global South: The Politics of Domestic Violence Policy*. London and New York: Routledge.

Net, Neath and Huon Chantrea. 2012. 'Country situation analysis: Health financing and human resources for health.' *Cambodia Development Resource Institute (CDRI) Annual Development Review 2011–2012*, 87–98. Phnom Penh: CDRI.

NIS (National Institute of Statistics). 2011. 'Statistical Yearbook of Cambodia 2011.' Phnom Penh: Ministry of Planning.

North, Douglass C. 1981. *Structure and Change in Economic History*. New York: W. W. Norton.

North, Douglass C. 1990. *Institutions, Institutional Change and Economic Performance*. Cambridge: Cambridge University Press.

North, Douglass C., John Joseph Wallis, Steven B. Webb, and Barry R. Weingast. 2007. 'Limited Access Orders in the Developing World: A New Approach to the Problems of Development.' Washington, DC: The World Bank, Independent Evaluation Group, Country Relations Division.

North, Douglass C., John Joseph Wallis, Steven B. Webb, and Barry R. Weingast. 2013. 'Limited Access Orders: An Introduction to the Conceptual Framework.' In *The Shadow of Violence: Politics, Economics, and the Problems of Development*, edited by Douglass C. North, John Joseph Wallis, Steven B. Webb, and Barry R. Weingast, 1–23. New York: Cambridge University Press.

North, Douglass C., John Joseph Wallis, and Barry R. Weingast. 2006. 'A Conceptual Framework for Interpreting Recorded Human History.' Working Paper No. 12795. Cambridge, MA: National Bureau of Economic Research.

North, Douglass C., John Joseph Wallis, and Barry R. Weingast. 2009. *Violence and Social Orders: A Conceptual Framework for Interpreting Recorded Human History*. Cambridge: Cambridge University Press.

O'Donnell, Guillermo. 1993. 'On the State, Democratization and Some Conceptual Problems.' Working Paper No. 192. Notre Dame, IN: Kellogg Institute.

O'Meara, Dan. 1983. *Volkskapitalisme*. Cambridge: Cambridge University Press.

O'Rourke, Catherine. 2017. 'Gendering Political Settlements: Challenges and Opportunities.' *Journal of International Development* 29, no. 5 (July): 594–612.

OECD. 2011. *From Power Struggles to Sustainable Peace: Understanding Political Settlements*. Conflict and Fragility Series. Paris: OECD Publishing.

Oleinik, Anton. 2016. *The Invisible Hand of Power: An Economic Theory of Gatekeeping*. New York: Routledge.

Olson, Mancur. 1993. 'Dictatorship, Democracy, and Development.' *The American Political Science Review* 87, no. 3 (September): 567–76.

Oman, Charles and Arndt, Christiane. 2006. 'Governance Indicators for Development.' No 33, OECD Development Centre Policy Insights, OECD Publishing. https://EconPapers.repec.org/RePEc:oec:devaac:33-en.

Opoku, Darko Kwabena. 2010. *The Politics of Government–Business Relations in Ghana, 1982–2008*. Basingstoke: Palgrave Macmillan.

Ortiz-Ospina, Esteban and Max Roser. 2017. "Financing Healthcare". Published online at *OurWorldInData.org*. Retrieved from: 'https://ourworldindata.org/financing-healthcare' [Online Resource]

Osei, Roberto Darko, Charles Ackah, George Domfe, and Michael Danquah. 2018. 'Political settlements and structural change: Why growth has not been transformational in Ghana.' In *Deals and Development: The Political Dynamics of Growth Episodes*, edited by Lant Pritchett, Kunal Sen, and Eric Werker, 159–82. Oxford: Oxford University Press.

Ostrom, Elinor. 1990. *Governing the Commons: The Evolution of Institutions for Collective Action*. Cambridge, UK: Cambridge University Press.

Ostom, Elinor. 2000. 'Collective Action and the Evolution of Social Norms.' *Journal of Economic Perspectives* 14, no. 3 (Summer): 137–158.

Otchere-Darko, Asare 'Gabby'. 2011. "'The Deal": Housing Agreement between Government of Ghana and STX Korea.' http://danquahinstitute.org/docs/TheDeal.pdf.

Pak, Kimchoeun. 2011. 'A Dominant Party in a Weak State: How the Ruling Party in Cambodia Has Managed to Stay Dominant.' PhD thesis. Canberra: The Australian National University.

Pak, Kimchoeun, Horng Vuthy, Eng Netra, Ann Sovatha, Kim Sedara, Jenny Knowles, and David Craig. 2007. 'Accountability and Neo-patrimonialism in Cambodia: A Critical Literature Review.' Phnom Penh: Cambodia Development Resource Institute.

Parks, Thomas, and William Cole. 2010. 'Political Settlements: Implications for International Development Policy and Practice.' The Asia Foundation Occasional Paper No. 2, July 2010. The Asia Foundation. https://www.asiafoundation.org/

Pateman, Carole. 1988. 'The fraternal social contract.' In *Civil Society and the State*, edited by John Keane, 101–27. London: Verso.

Pettersson, Thérèse, and Magnus Öberg. 2020. 'Organized Violence, 1989–2019.' *Journal of Peace Research* 57, no. 4 (July): 597–613.

Piketty, Thomas. 2020. *Capital and Ideology*. Cambridge, MA: Harvard University Press.

Pincus, Steve. 2009. *1688: The First Modern Revolution*. New Haven, CT: Yale University Press.

Policy Department. 2013. 'EU Development Cooperation in Fragile States: Challenges and Opportunities.' Strasbourg: Directorate General for External Policies of the Union, Directorate B.

Powell, Jonathan. M., and Clayton L. Thyne. 2011. 'Global Instances of Coups from 1950 to 2010: A New Dataset.' *Journal of Peace Research* 48, no. 2 (March): 249–59.

Pritchett, Lant. 2013. *The Rebirth of Education: Schooling Ain't Learning*. Washington, DC: Centre for Global Development Books.

Pritchett, Lant, Kunal Sen, and Eric Werker, eds. 2018. *Deals and Development: The Political Dynamics of Growth Episodes*. Oxford: Oxford University Press.

Pritchett, Lant, Kunal Sen, and Eric Werker. 2018. 'Deals and Development: An Introduction to the Conceptual Framework.' In Deals and Development: The Political Dynamics of Growth Episodes, edited by Lant Pritchett, Kunal Sen, and Eric Werker, 1–38. Oxford, UK: Oxford University Press.

Putzel, James, and Jonathan Di John. 2012. 'Meeting the Challenges of Crisis States.' Crisis States Research Centre Report. London: Crisis States Research Centre.

Queralt, Didac. 2019. 'War, International Finance, and Fiscal Capacity in the Long Run.' *International Organization* 73, no. 4 (Fall): 713–53. doi:10.1017/S002081831 9000250.

Republic of Ghana. 2013. 'The Budget Statement and Economic Policy of the Government of Ghana for the 2014 Financial Year.' Accra: Ministry of Finance and Economic Planning.

Reyntjens, Filip. 2013. *Political Governance in Post-Genocide Rwanda*. New York: Cambridge University Press.

Riker, William H. 1962. *The Theory of Political Coalitions*. New Haven, CT: Yale University Press.

Rocha Menocal, A. 2020. 'Why Does Inclusion Matter?: Assessing the Links between Inclusive Processes and Inclusive Outcomes.' OECD Development Co-operation Working Paper No. 71. Paris: OECD Publishing. https://doi.org/10.1787/22285d0e-en.

Rodrik, Dani. 2007. *One Economics, Many Recipes: Globalization, Institutions, and Economic Growth*. Princeton, NJ: Princeton University Press.

Roessler, Philip. 2011. 'The Enemy within: Personal Rule, Coups, and Civil War in Africa.' *World Politics* 63, no. 2 (April): 300–46.

Roessler, Philip. 2017. *Ethnic Politics and State Power in Africa: The Logic of the Coup–Civil War Trap*. Cambridge: Cambridge University Press.

Roser, Max. 2013. 'Economic Growth.' Published online at *OurWorldInData.org*. *Retrieved from*: *https://ourworldindata.org/economic-growth [Online Resource]*

Roser, Max and Hannah Ritchie 2013. 'Maternal Mortality.' Published online at *OurWorldInData.org*. Retrieved from: https://ourworldindata.org/maternal-mortality [Online Resource]

Roser, Max and Esteban Ortiz-Ospina 2013. 'Primary and Secondary Education.' Published online at *OurWorldInData.org*. Retrieved from: https://ourworldindata.org/primary-and-secondary-education [Online Resource]

Roser, Max and Esteban Ortiz-Ospina 2016. 'Financing Education.' Published online at *OurWorldInData.org*. Retrieved from: https://ourworldindata.org/financing-education [Online Resource]

Rousseau, Jean, Jacques. 1961. *The Social Contract: Discourses*, trans. G. D. H. Cole. London: J. M. Dent & Sons Ltd.

Schelling, Thomas. 2006. *Micromotives and Macrobehavior*. New York and London: W.W. Norton.

Schenoni, Luis L. 2021. 'Bringing War Back in: Victory and State Formation in Latin America.' *American Journal of Political Science* 65, no 2 (April): 405–421. doi.org/10.1111/ajps.12552

Schulz, Nicolai. 2014. 'Anti-Corruption Agencies: Why Do Some Succeed and Most Fail? A Quantitative Political Settlement Analysis.' Masters thesis. London: London School of Economics.

Schulz, Nicolai, and Tim Kelsall. 2021a. 'Political Settlements (PolSett) Dataset Codebook.' Manchester: Effective States and Inclusive Development Research Centre, The University of Manchester.

Schulz, Nicolai, and Tim Kelsall. 2021b. 'The Political Settlements (PolSett) Dataset. An Introduction with Illustrative Examples.' ESID Working Paper No. 165. Manchester: Effective States and Inclusive Development Research Centre, The University of Manchester. https://www.effective-states.org/wp-content/uploads/esid_wp_165_schulz_kelsall.pdf

Schulz, Nicolai, and Tim Kelsall. 2021c. 'The Political Settlements (PolSett) Dataset.' Manchester: Effective States and Inclusive Development Research Centre, The University of Manchester. Available via https://www.effective-states.org/political-settlements/ or https://bit.ly/3EyarlI

Seekings, Jeremy. 2000. *The UDF: A History of the United Democratic Front (UDF) in South Africa, 1983–1991*. Oxford: James Currey Publishers.

Seekings, Jeremy, and Nicoli Nattrass. 2005. *Race, Class, and Inequality in South Africa*. New Haven, CT: Yale University Press.

Seekings, Jeremy, and Nicoli Nattrass. 2015. *Policy, Politics and Poverty in South Africa*. Basingstoke: Palgrave Macmillan.

Sen, Amartya. 1999. *Development as Freedom*. Oxford: Oxford University Press.

Sen, Kunal. 2019. 'Political Settlements and Immiserizing Growth Episodes.' In *Immiserizing Growth: When Growth Fails the Poor*, edited by Paul Shaffer, Ravi Kanbur, and Richard Sandbrook, 85–105. Oxford: Oxford University Press.

Sen, Kunal, and Matthew Tyce. 2018. 'The Politics of Structural (De)Transformation: The Unravelling of Malaysia and Thailand's Dualistic Deals Strategies.' In *Deals and Development: The Political Dynamics of Growth Episodes*, edited by Lant Pritchett, Kunal Sen and Eric Werker, 285–338. Oxford, UK, Oxford University Press.

Skocpol, Theda. 1992. *Protecting Soldiers and Mothers: The Politics of Social Provision in the United States, 1870s–1920s*. Cambridge, MA: Harvard University Press.

Slater, Dan. 2010. *Ordering Power: Contentious Politics and Authoritarian Leviathans in Southeast Asia*. New York: Cambridge University Press.

Slocomb, Margaret. 2010. *An Economic History of Cambodia in the Twentieth Century*. Singapore: National University of Singapore (NUS) Press.

Sloper, D. 1999. 'Higher education in Cambodia: An overview and key issues'. In *Higher Education in Cambodia: The Social and Educational Context for Reconstruction*, edited by D. Sloper, 1–24. Bangkok: UNESCO Principal Regional Office for Asia and the Pacific.

Soifer, Hillel David. 2015. *State Building in Latin America*. New York: Cambridge University Press.

Sokhean, Ben. 2017. 'Government Proposes $6bn Budget for 2018.' The Phnom Penh Post, 30 October.

Sparks, Allister. 1996. *Tomorrow Is Another Country*. Chicago, IL: University of Chicago Press.

Steele, Abbey. A. 2017. *Democracy and Displacement in Colombia's Civil War*. Ithaca, NY: Cornell University Press.

Stiglitz, Joseph. 1987. 'The Causes and Consequences of the Dependence of Quality on Price.' *Journal of Economic Literature* 25, no. 1 (March): 1–48.

Supporting Economic Transformation (SET). 2020. 'Fostering an Inclusive Digital Transformation in Cambodia.' London: Overseas Development Institute. https://set.odi.org/wp-content/uploads/2020/07/Fostering-an-Inclusive-Digitalisation-Transformation-in-Cambodia-July-2020.pdf.

Tadros, Mariz, and Jeremy Allouche. 2017. 'Political Settlements as a Violent Process: Deconstructing the Relationship between Political Settlements and Intrinsic, Instrumental and Resultant Forms of Violence.' *Conflict, Security and Development* 17, no. 3 (June): 187–204.

Tandon, Prateek, and Tsuyoshi Fukao. 2015. *Educating the Next Generation: Improving Teacher Quality in Cambodia*. Washington, DC: International Bank for Reconstruction and Development (IBRD)/The World Bank

Thinking and Working Politically Community of Practice. 2013. 'The Case for Thinking and Working Politically: The Implications of "Doing Development Differently".' Retrieved from http://publications.dlprog.org/TWP.pdf.

Tilly, Charles. 1975. 'Reflections on the history of European state-making.' In *The Formation of National States in Western Europe*, edited by Charles Tilly, 3–83. Princeton, NJ: Princeton University Press.

Tilly, Charles. 1992. *Coercion, Capital, and European States, AD 990–1992*. Oxford: Blackwell.

Tilly, Charles. 1998. *Durable inequality*. University of California Press.

Tyce, Matthew. 2020. 'Unrealistic Expectations, Frustrated Progress and an Uncertain Future? The Political Economy of Oil in Kenya.' The Extractive Industries and Society 7, no. 2 (April): 729–37.

Un, Kheang. 2005. 'Patronage Politics and Hybrid Democracy: Political Change in Cambodia, 1993–2003.' *Asian Perspective* 29, no. 2: 203–30.

UNDP. 2011. 'Human Development Report 2011: Sustainability and Equity—A Better Future for All.' New York: United Nations. http://hdr.undp.org/en/content/human-development-report-2011.

UNDP. 2014. 'UNDP in Cambodia: Mellennium Development Goals.' New York: United Nations. http://www.kh.undp.org/content/cambodia/en/home/mdgoverview.html%3E.

UNESCO. 2010. 'UNESCO National Education Support Strategy, Cambodia 2010–2013.' Phnom Penh Office: UNESCO.

Van de Poel, Ellen, Gabriela Flores, Por Ir, Owen O'Donnell, and Eddy van Doorslaer. 2014. 'Can Vouchers Deliver? An Evaluation of Subsidies for Maternal Health Care in Cambodia.' *Bulletin of the World Health Organisation* 92, no. 5: 331–9.

Van De Walle, Nicolas. 2016. "Democracy fatigue and the ghost of modernization theory." In *Aid and Authoritarianism in Africa: Development Without Democracy*, edited by Tobias Hagmann and Filip Reyntjens, 161–178. London: Zed Books.

Vrieze, P., and Kuch, N. 2012. 'Carving up Cambodia: One Concession at a Time.' *Cambodia Daily Weekend*, 10–11 March.

Waldmeir, Patti. 1997. *Anatomy of a Miracle: The End of Apartheid and the Birth of the New South Africa*. New York: W. W. Norton.

Waldner, David. 1999. *State Building and Late Development*. Ithaca, NY: Cornell University Press.

Wales, Joseph, Arran Magee, and Susan Nicolai. 2016. 'How Does Political Context Shape Education Reforms and their Success? Lessons from the Development Progress Project.' Dimensions Paper No. 06. London: Overseas Development Institute.

Walton, Michael. 2010. 'Capitalism, the State, and the Underlying Drivers of Human Development.' Human Development Reports Research Paper. New York: United Nations Development Programme.

Welsh, David. 2010. *The Rise and Fall of Apartheid*. Charlottesville, VA: University of Virginia Press.

Whaites, Alan. 2008. 'States in Development: Understanding State-building.' DFID Working Paper. London: DFID.

Whitfield, Lindsay. 2010. 'Developing Technological Capabilities in Agro-industry: Ghana's Experience with Fresh Pineapple Exports in Comparative Perspective.' Working Paper 2010:28. Copenhagen: Danish Institute for International Studies.

Whitfield, Lindsay. 2011. 'Competitive Clientelism, Easy Financing and Weak Capitalists: The Contemporary Political Settlement in Ghana.' Working Paper 2011:27. Copenhagen: Danish Institute for International Studies.

Whitfield, Lindsay, and Ole Therkilsden. 2011. 'What Drives States to Support the Development of Productive Sectors? Strategies Ruling Elites Pursue for Political Survival and their Policy Implications.' Working Paper 2011:15. Copenhagen: Danish Institute for International Studies.

Whitfield, Lindsay, Ole Therkilsden, Lars Buur, and Ann Mette Kjaer. 2015. *The Politics of African Industrial Policy*. Cambridge: Cambridge University Press.

WHO. 2012. 'Official Development Assistance (ODA) for Health to Guinea.' https://www.who.int/gho/governance_aid_effectiveness/countries/gin.pdf?ua=1.

WHO. 2021. Global Health Expenditure database: http://apps.who.int/nha/database/Select/Indicators/en

Wiggins, Steve and Henri Leturque. 2011. 'Ghana's Sustained Agricultural Growth: Putting Underused Resources to Work.' London: Overseas Development Institute.

Williams, Timothy P. 2019. 'The downsides of dominance: Education quality reforms and Rwanda's political settlement.' In *The Politics of Education in Developing Countries: From Schooling to Learning*, edited by Sam Hickey and Naomi Hossain, 105–31. Oxford: Oxford University Press.

Wimmer, Andreas. 2002. *Nationalist Exclusion and Ethnic Conflict: Shadows of Modernity*. Cambridge: Cambridge University Press.

Wimmer, Andreas. 2018. *Nation Building: Why Some Countries Come Together While Others Fall Apart*. Princeton, NJ: Princeton University Press.

World Bank. 2011. 'World Development Report 2011: Conflict, Security and Development.' Washington, DC: The World Bank.

World Bank. 2014. 'Are Patients in Good Hands?' Unpublished manuscript. World Bank Human Development Unit, East Asia and Pacific Region.

World Bank. 2014b. 'World Development Indicators 2014.' Washington, DC: The World Bank.

World Bank. 2016. 'Enterprise Survey: Guinea 2016 Country Profile.' Washington, DC: The World Bank.

World Bank. 2019. 'Project Information Document (PID).' Guinea Education Project for Results in Early Childhood and Basic Education (P167478), Report No: PIDA26579. Washington, DC: World Bank.

World Bank. 2020. World Development Indicators. https://data.worldbank.org/. Accessed 2 September 2020.

World Bank. 2021a. World Development Indicators. http://data.worldbank.org/data-catalog/world-development-indicators

World Bank. 2021b. World Bank EdStats https://datatopics.worldbank.org/education/

World Bank. 2018. 'Country Partnership Framework for The Republic of Guinea for the Period Fy2018–Fy23.' Report No. 125899-GN. Washington, DC: World Bank.

Yanguas, Pablo. 2017. 'Varieties of State-building in Africa: Elites, Ideas and the Politics of Public Sector Reform.' ESID Working Paper No 89. Manchester: Effective States and Inclusive Development Research Centre, The University of Manchester. http://dx.doi.org/10.2139/ssrn.3031801.

Yanguas, Pablo, and Diana Mitlin. 2016. 'The Politics of Policy Domains: Understanding Mobilization and Change in Development Policy.' A draft paper prepared for ESID Synthesis Workshop, Rockefeller Centre, Bellagio, July 2016. Mimeo.

You, Jong-Sung. 2013. 'Transition from a Limited Access Order to an Open Access Order: The Case of South Korea.' *In the Shadow of Violence*, edited by Douglass C. North, John Joseph Wallis, Steven B. Webb and Barry R. Weingast, 293–327. Cambridge: Cambridge University Press.

Zysman, John. 1994. 'How Institutions Create Historically Rooted Trajectories of Growth.' *Industrial and Corporate Change* 3, no. 1: 243–83.

Index